Developing Capacity for Innovation in Complex Systems

Based on a theoretical analysis and supported by both explorative qualitative and quantitative research, this book examines the many reasons why an initiative becomes an innovation and why some organizations are better at innovation than others.

Developing Capacity for Innovation in Complex Systems offers insights into the history of the idea of innovation, as well as knowledge around different discourses on innovation. The purpose of this book is to help organisations further their aspirations and work with innovation. It is based on three premises: (1) that capacity can be developed, (2) that it is worthwhile trying to do so, and (3) there are however no guarantees for success. Providing a comprehensive view of innovation and discussing the theoretical challenges, the book contributes towards a holistic theory for capacity building for innovation. The book conveys frameworks, methodologies, and tools that are used in terms of innovation, and it explains positive strategies for innovation that are being developed. Complexity theory is presented and attributed to the construct of innovation to further the understanding of the intricacies and fallacies of innovation work.

This book will be of direct interest to scholars and subject matter experts in the field of innovation management. Business leaders and reflective practitioners will find the content relevant and accessible.

Christer Vindeløv-Lidzélius is the current principal and CEO of Kaospilot. He holds an MBA from Heriot-Watt University and a PhD from Tilburg University, and is an educated Kaospilot. His expertise lies in the intersection of strategy, leadership, and innovation. He has for the last 20+ years pursued a managerial and entrepreneurial career.

Routledge Studies in Innovation, Organizations and Technology

Frugal Innovation
A Global Research Companion
Edited by Adela J. McMurray and Gerrit A. de Waal

Digital Work and the Platform Economy
Understanding Tasks, Skills and Capabilities in the New Era
Edited by Seppo Poutanen, Anne Kovalainen, and Petri Rouvinen

The Future of Work in Asia and Beyond
A Technological Revolution or Evolution?
Edited by Alan R. Nankervis, Julia Connell and John Burgess

Society and Technology
Opportunities and Challenges
Edited by Ewa Lechman and Magdalena Popowska

Contextual Innovation Management
Adapting Innovation Processes to Different Situations
Patrick van der Duin and Roland Ortt

Research, Innovation and Entrepreneurship in Saudi Arabia
Vision 2030
Edited by Muhammad Khurram Khan and Muhammad Babar Khan

Developing Digital Governance
South Korea as a Global Digital Government Leader
Choong-sik Chung

Digital Business Models
Perspectives on Monetisation
Adam Jabłoński and Marek Jabłoński

Developing Capacity for Innovation in Complex Systems
Strategy, Organisation and Leadership
Christer Vindeløv-Lidzélius

For more information about this series, please visit: www.routledge.com/Routledge-Studies-in-Innovation-Organizations-and-Technology/book-series/RIOT

Developing Capacity for Innovation in Complex Systems

Strategy, Organisation and Leadership

Christer Vindeløv-Lidzélius

LONDON AND NEW YORK

First published 2021
by Routledge
2 Park Square, Milton Park, Abingdon, Oxon OX14 4RN

and by Routledge
52 Vanderbilt Avenue, New York, NY 10017

Routledge is an imprint of the Taylor & Francis Group, an informa business

© 2021 Christer Vindeløv-Lidzélius

The right of Christer Vindeløv-Lidzélius to be identified as author of this work has been asserted by him in accordance with sections 77 and 78 of the Copyright, Designs and Patents Act 1988.

All rights reserved. No part of this book may be reprinted or reproduced or utilised in any form or by any electronic, mechanical, or other means, now known or hereafter invented, including photocopying and recording, or in any information storage or retrieval system, without permission in writing from the publishers.

Trademark notice: Product or corporate names may be trademarks or registered trademarks, and are used only for identification and explanation without intent to infringe.

British Library Cataloguing-in-Publication Data
A catalogue record for this book is available from the British Library

Library of Congress Cataloging-in-Publication Data
Names: Vindeløv-Lidzélius, Christer, author.
Title: Developing capacity for innovation in complex systems : strategy, organisation and leadership / Christer Vindeløv-Lidzélius.
Description: First Edition. | New York : Routledge, 2020. | Series: Routledge studies in innovation, organizations and technology | Includes bibliographical references and index.
Identifiers: LCCN 2020018945 (print) | LCCN 2020018946 (ebook)
Subjects: LCSH: Organizational change. | Strategic planning. | Technological innovations—Management.
Classification: LCC HD58.8 .V556 2020 (print) | LCC HD58.8 (ebook) | DDC 658.4/063—dc23
LC record available at https://lccn.loc.gov/2020018945
LC ebook record available at https://lccn.loc.gov/2020018946

ISBN: 978-0-367-33654-7 (hbk)
ISBN: 978-0-429-32106-1 (ebk)

Typeset in Bembo
by codeMantra

 Printed in the United Kingdom by Henry Ling Limited

Contents

List of illustrations	ix
Preface	xi

**1 The innovation imperative – why we need
a holistic approach**   1

Introduction 1
Theoretical challenges 2
Capacity building for innovation – to what end? 5
Contents 7

2 The meaning of innovation   10

Introduction 10
A retrospective view of the idea of innovation 11
How to categorise innovation 19
Product, process, and service innovation 22
Measuring innovation 26
Innovation defined 28
Summary 34

3 Creativity and ideas   36

Introduction 36
Creativity 37
Creativity theories relevant to innovation 40
Ideas and ideation 42
Evaluation and selection of ideas 43
The messy front-end 45
Management and nurturing creativity and ideas 47
Summary 48

vi *Contents*

4 The making of innovation 50

Introduction 50
Sources of innovation 51
Models of innovation 54
Innovation processes 62
Innovation management 63
Summary 64

5 The spread and uptake of innovation 66

Introduction 66
Diffusion theory 67
Bounded rationality 69
Theory of reasoned action 70
Consumer behaviour theories 71
The role of branding and marketing 72
Absorptive capacity 73
Summary 74

6 Organisational learning 76

Introduction 76
Goals and measurement 77
Loops of learning 79
Knowledge creation, transfer, retention, and management 81
The learning organisation 82
Barriers to OL 84
Innovation as learning, learning as innovation 85
Summary 87

7 The drivers of innovation 88

Introduction 88
Why do we need innovation? 89
Technology 90
Competition 91
Globalisation 92
New business models 94
Self-actualisation 96
The concept of change 97
Summary 101

8 From chaos to complex adaptive systems – innovation as a complex adaptive system 102

Introduction 102

Chaos theory 104
Systems 105
Complexity theory 106
Complex systems 107
Complex adaptive systems 111
Innovation as a complex adaptive system 113
Summary 119

9 Innovation – between chaos and order   121
Introduction 121
Systems thinking and innovation 123
CRPs and innovation 125
Cynefin and innovation 128
Chaordic and innovation 130
Towards a theoretical foundation of innovation in, as,
   and of complex systems 132
Summary 134

10 Capacity building   135
Introduction 135
What is innovation capacity building? 136
Two challenges and opportunities with innovation capacity building 137
The 6P model 138
Measuring capacity building 141
Summary 141

11 Strategy   143
Introduction 143
Innovation strategy 144
Crafting an innovation strategy 145
Mergers and acquisitions 147
Partnerships 148
Internal development 149
Summary 150

12 Leadership   152
Introduction 152
The role and responsibility of leadership 153
Skills and style 155
Methodologies and tools 156
Leading innovation in complex systems 159
Summary 161

viii *Contents*

13 Organisation   162
Introduction 162
Creating space for innovation 164
Organisational culture 166
Moonshot factories 170
Summary 173

**14 The innovation imperative – towards a holistic
approach for developing innovation capacity**   174
Introduction 174
The kernel of innovation 175
Beyond the organisation – a systems view 178
An integrative approach 179
The lifeworld of innovation 180
Future areas of research 182
Conclusion 182

Appendix 1: Summary of Methodology   186
Appendix 2: Summary of Research   189
References   192
Index   215

Illustrations

Figures

2.1	Taxonomy of innovation	20
3.1	Freely after British Council	44
3.2	The FEI Process	46
4.1	The coupling of R&D and Marketing model	57
6.1	The intention-desirable learning matrix	78
10.1	The 6P model	139
12.1	The responsibility of a leader model	154

Tables

2.1	OECD typology of innovation, 2005, adapted from Oslo manual: guidelines for collecting and interpreting innovation data, 3rd edition	25
4.1	Five levels of innovation by Altshuller (Vincent, 2001)	55
4.2	Typology of innovation models, based on Rothwell (1992, 1994)	60
8.1	Complex adaptive systems and innovation characteristics	114
8.2	Complex adaptive systems and innovation properties	115
12.1	The four-level empowerment grid model, Bens (2006)	156
A.1	Overview of the research design and methodology	188
A.2	Overview of the research process	190

Preface

Introduction

Innovation is now a central theme in everything from governmental policies to company strategies and praxes, linked to themes such as competitiveness, wealth creation, and organisational vitality. However, innovation is an elusive phenomenon and a challenging concept for organisational success.

Today, as organisations, businesses, and countries are experiencing changes and challenges related to globalisation, migration, climate change, and technology – as well as customer and employee preferences and so forth – we more often than not turn to innovation for an answer. As such, becoming better at innovation is a key challenge for all organisations and looking at how we can develop the capacity for innovation can help us achieve this aim.

Purpose

The purpose of this book is to help organisations further their aspirations and work with innovation.

This book is about developing capacity for innovation in complex systems. It is based on two premises: (1) that capacity can be developed, and (2) that it is worthwhile trying to do so. Since the orientation around complexity suggests that there is no bullet-proof recipe for innovation and, even less, for success in innovation attempts, one could easily conclude that there is so much uncertainty (and also cost) that it is questionable whether the attempt is worth it. It is a fair argument, and, in the book, we will look at different ways to approach innovation. However, innovation is not so much a question of "yes or no," but rather more a question of "how," as regards to what the innovation is to result in for organisations.

Main arguments

This book suggests that innovation efforts are often ill-defined, poorly organised, and scattered, which results in undesirable outcomes. Although this is not the case all the time, research shows that there is plenty of room for improvement. As such, this book argues for the need for a holistic approach (as opposed to a partial approach).

xii *Preface*

As well, developing capacity for innovation is essentially an indirect approach, as innovation is more a description of a process or the result of a process (i.e. it is aimed at, and/or generates something considered to be new and valuable). Based on the research (Vindeløv-Lidzélius, 2018), the three areas which seem most potent and actionable in terms of improving the capacity for innovation are within the domains of strategy, organisation, and leadership.

Background

This monograph builds upon the PhD thesis "Innovation in complex systems: An exploration in strategy, leadership and organization" (Vindeløv-Lidzélius, 2018). After it was approved, a conversation was initiated by some of the committee members, suggesting that the topic held value for a broader audience. The main suggestions revolved around the aspects of sorting out terminology, unearthing facets of the concept, and bringing a complexity and social constructionist view to the table. A further conversation with the publisher of this monograph suggested taking the findings from the research one step further – to be more explicit and to some extent directive – so as to help managers, innovators, practitioners, and academics alike.

Challenges

Working with such a broad and widely discussed theme, one cannot avoid leaving out important findings and discussions. That does not suggest that what we have left out here is irrelevant or wrong. Rather, it is more a consequence of time, space, and limitations on behalf of the author.

Another important challenge is the nature of innovation itself and the challenges of providing findings – that is, knowledge, models, or methods – that are actionable and can be assumed to deliver results. Unfortunately, the research shows that success is often a consequence of the particulars of a given situation; indeed, sometimes these are conditions that are outside the control of the organisation. That does not, however, rule out that one can learn and make progress by learning from the example of others.

Research

This monograph is based on a PhD thesis, which in turn draws upon an extensive research into the literature and a combination of quantitative and qualitative methodologies. The main case study was on the Research and Development Department (PDI) of Telefónica Digital in Barcelona, and later, on Alpha (the moon-shot factory of Telefónica). In the appendix, the research process and methodology used is discussed in more detail.

It should also be noted that many of the considerations and insights have accumulated over author's own past 20+ years of experience in the field of innovation, leadership, and strategy.

1 The innovation imperative – why we need a holistic approach

Introduction

This monograph is about developing capacity for innovation in complex systems. It essentially addresses this through the constructs of strategy, organisation, and leadership. It is argued that capacity building efforts are often ineffective because they are underdeveloped, uncoordinated, and insufficiently purposeful. By adopting a holistic approach, organisations better position themselves for overcoming the uncertainty inherent to innovation approaches. While a holistic innovation approach is not enough to ensure capacity, it is a necessary start.

That innovation is a timely topic goes without saying. These days, one can hardly find a description of a company, an annual report, or a strategy document that lacks an explicit statement of the need for innovation, let alone one in which the need for innovation is flatout denied. In the world of business, we find a total commitment to innovation and a stated aspiration to continuously take it further. The typical justification is that companies that do not innovate – that is, companies that do not offer new products and services to their clients – will, sooner or later, become obsolete and give the upper hand to their competitors. Although this logic may not be entirely new in business, the need for innovation in society as a whole and even in our personal lives is now becoming more widespread and recognised.

Innovation is a multifaceted term that has gained much prominence in our time. Much of perceived organisational survival and success in the marketplace is attributed to the capacity to innovate. While much research has been devoted to the subject of innovation, it remains difficult for organisations to actually innovate. Equally so, capacity building is a term that has gained prominence over the last decade(s). Capacity points towards the notion of having what it takes to realise "something"; building capacity signifies that capacity can be created. Although it is often associated with competence, ability, and capability, exactly what constitutes capacity building remains vague and contextually dependent. Still, there are certain themes, setups, skills, and practices that are more widely accepted as important for building capacity, such as motivation, responsibility, coordination, and knowledge-sharing. This will be explored further in the coming chapters.

2 Why we need a holistic approach

Complexity, complex systems, complex adaptive systems, and systems thinking have also over the last decades found their way into organisational literature and terminology. Although many of these theories and methodologies have their roots and evidence in the natural world, they are also promising explanations for social and societal phenomena. In simplistic terms, complexity offers explanations as to why the best efforts do not always result in success and why certain efforts suddenly move from insignificance to prominence. Innovation efforts are subject to the complexity of the external world as well as to internal complexity. In this monograph, a complexity orientation is offered as a way to think about innovation and as a way for building capacity more effectively.

Even though much of the literature focuses on and promotes the idea of coordinated, purposeful action when it comes to innovation and innovation capacity building, there are still some inter-related, theoretical challenges that need to be addressed. First, we need to better understand what innovation is, or at least the different ways it is understood, as well as the different facets of the concept of innovation. Second, we need to address capacity building on a more encompassing level than, for instance, simply up-skilling staff or developing new initiatives. In this regard, we will discuss strategy, organisation, and leadership.

This monograph offers some new contributions to the discourse around innovation and the development of capacity for innovation in complex systems. First, it outlines a theoretical foundation for innovation in complex systems, helping us understand the nature of innovation in a new way. Second, it offers a theoretical foundation for developing capacity for innovation in complex systems. This foundation is then supplemented with a framework for identifying and understanding key challenges with capacity building. Third, it presents a holistic approach for developing capacity for innovation in complex systems. It brings together leadership, strategy, and organisation into a starting point – a kernel – which is helpful as an analytical framework and as a "method" for innovation capacity building in complexity.

This book intends to offer depth and breadth around the subject of innovation, allowing the reader – be it a practitioner, a manager, a student, or a policy maker – an opportunity to reflect and hopefully learn something new. It is not an easy "how-to" or "tips and tricks" book, but rather something more demanding.

Theoretical challenges

Innovation is an extensively debated topic that spurs vast amounts of research, thinking, and practice. As an academic and popular topic, it was only fairly recently that it gained the prominence it have today. Today, innovation is a priority for virtually all organisations of a certain size. Indeed, one can argue that it is a defining subject for all organisations – even if there is no awareness within the organisation itself about innovation as a subject. However, given the importance of the topic, it is surprising that there still exist large gaps in the efforts made by organisations. For example, there can be a lack of innovation strategies, clarity on innovation models and processes, and so forth. Regardless of the amount of work that has already gone into "figuring it out," there is still a long way to go for both academics as well as practitioners.

When it comes to innovation, and particularly capacity building for innovation, there are several types of challenges. The main challenges can be summarised as follows:

1 The meaning of innovation
2 Creativity and ideas
3 The making of innovations
4 The spread and uptake of innovations
5 Organisational learning

These broader challenges all contain a number of other challenges, and they also all overlap and interact to some extent. For instance, simply working on the making of innovations – as something that happens after an idea has seen the light of day – is to some extent limited as the original idea affects how we convert it successfully to a product, service, or process. It is also dependent on our notion of what constitutes an idea and other theoretical concepts. The challenges are interwoven. Although all of these challenges have been discussed in different ways in innovation literature, they are summarised and brought together below so as to give a fuller picture of the challenges at hand.

The meaning of innovation

How innovation is understood is in itself a challenge. Often we attribute the concept of innovation to the Austrian economist Joseph Schumpeter and his work in the 1930s, but as Fagerberg et al. (2006) point out, the idea is perhaps as old as mankind itself. The Schumpeterian techno-economical view of innovation as a new creation that generates economic value (1939 and 1942) has since been broadened. For example, Drucker (1985) points to social innovation as a significant value-creating process. The concept of innovation is discussed more in depth in Chapter 2, in which we look at its historical roots and towards a more contemporary view of innovation as a complex, contextually dependent, and socially embedded process. (Naturally, however, this topic is addressed throughout the book.)

Creativity and ideas

How we get ideas, what creativity is, and how creativity is developed is a vital area for innovation. According to Van de Ven et al. (1989), ideas for innovation originate from combining old ideas in a new way, from a schema that tests the current order, or from a unique approach that is perceived as

4   *Why we need a holistic approach*

new by the people involved. But defining an idea is also a question in itself. Whitehead (1961) states that an idea is a "force that can create movement and transformation or maintain the status quo." Pointing to where ideas come from, Saatcioglu (2002: 1) takes different approach and states that "an idea is a cognitive impulse enabled by social experience." Creativity can then be seen as the act of generating (or recognising) ideas. There are different strands in investigating creativity, such as the role of intrinsic and extrinsic motivation (Amabile, 1983), multiple intelligences (Gardner, 1983), and humanistic psychology (Maslow, 1974; Rogers, 1995).

The making of innovations

Most scholars see innovation as something beyond creativity. An innovation can be seen in a simplified way as the successful implementation of a (new) idea. But how that idea becomes an innovation is to a large extent an enigma. Several models have been suggested, and how we understand innovation processes has changed over time (Rothwell, 1992, 1994; Chesbrough, 2003). While the early models were linear and are viewed today as too simplistic, they were also easy to grasp on an overall level. The more complex, contemporary models – with their richer descriptions – come at the expense of understanding, communication, and transferability. Understanding how to make innovation happen from an organisational and process perspective must also take into account how we categorise (Afuah and Bahram, 1995; Edquist, 2001) and measure it (Rogers, 1995; Godin, 2002).

The spread and uptake of innovations

Successful implementation means that customers and users recognise and realise the value of the new products, services, experiences, or processes that are offered. How the uptake and spread of innovation happens can be analysed and explained through several different frameworks. Bounded Rationality (Simon, 1991), Diffusion Theory (Rogers, 1995), Extension Theory (Röling, 1988), the Theory of Reasoned Action (Parminter and Wilson, 2003), and Consumer Behaviour Theory (Kaine, 2004) all offer important contributions to the theoretical framework around how innovations are adopted and spread. Whereas one can probably discuss how much these theories really influence how organisations go about developing innovations in practice, they do hold a number of relevant considerations for organisations that go beyond just branding, marketing, and sales.

Organisational learning

An underlying question is how organisations become better at innovation. Learning is one way to describe this process. Organisational learning can be explained as the process of adopting, generating, retaining, and transferring knowledge and know-how within the organisation. But how organisations "learn" is not a very straightforward topic. Organisational change is not always the same as learning, nor is it always the consequence of learning. Knowledge is one unit to consider but knowledge comes in both explicit and implicit forms (Nonaka and Takeuchi, 1995). How to measure learning is also a challenging task and requires a mix of different methodologies (Dalkir, 2011). A learning organisation (Senge, 1990) is one way to describe how an organisation facilitates the learning of its members and transforms itself repeatedly.

Although this division of the theoretical challenges is a simplification, it illustrates the challenge of developing a unifying theory. Any discussion and explanation of innovation depends on one's perspective. If one looks at innovation from the perspective of value in the marketplace, it is actually quite difficult to draw a clear line back in time to an originating idea, research phase, or decision-making process. Sometimes there are several ideas, tinkering, and experimentation that go on that are not exactly aimed at innovation as we normally understand it, and vice versa. Retrospect and approximations make it easier to understand and communicate how innovations develop, but that do not necessarily create clear correlations from which one can deduce a success innovation formula. However, the absence of a success formula is not the same as the absence of knowledge and know-how. Whether or not a successful formula exists, it is more a question of localisation, assumptions, and perspectives.

Given the identified challenges, this monograph provides a relational and complexity approach to capacity building, encompassing the inherent uncertainties related to innovation and capacity building. This book then provides a step towards a holistic theory for building capacity in complex systems.

Capacity building for innovation – to what end?

Cohen and Levinthal (1989) defined the concept of absorptive capacity as a firm's "ability to recognise the value of new information, assimilate it, and apply it to commercial ends." Michie and Sheehan (1999) extend this absorptive capacity concept beyond R&D to the organisational setting and suggest that participatory practices are "positively correlated with the probability of innovating." Absorptive capacity can be seen innovation capacity, but in this book innovation capacity is presented as something that goes beyond "new information." It is closely related to Tidd et al. (2005), who state that innovation capacity is the ability of enterprises to identify trends and new technologies, as well as to acquire and exploit this knowledge and information – even though our definition of innovation capacity in this book goes beyond the position proposed by Tidd, Bessant, and Pavitt, as well as it takes into account existing resources and actual opportunities.

Innovation is seen as imperative for organisational success. As such it follows quite naturally that if innovation is something to aspire towards, an organisation's ability to innovate is a key focus area. However, as mentioned

6 Why we need a holistic approach

in the previous section, that ability is not static: it is contextually dependent, requires nurturing, and demands commitment and effort. Capacity building can be seen as an approach and a set of activities on behalf of the organisation that strengthens and expands the scope, range, efficiency, and impact of the organisation. This can be addressed internally as well as externally.

When considering capacity building for innovation, there are four typical positions an organisation can be in. The organisation:

- Knows what innovations are to be achieved, and knows how to do it
- Knows what innovations are to be achieved, but it does not know how to do it
- Does not know what innovations are to be achieved, but it knows how to do it
- Does not know what innovations are to be achieved, or know how to do it

The first position seems quite straightforward and can be seen as a textbook example of how things should be. However, very often things change along the way and what was clear can quickly become more obscure. This position is usually the most preferred, even though this position may not necessarily promote experimentation, since in this context, the considerations revolve more around providing the necessary resources and support needed to bring an innovation to life.

The second position is also relatively understandable, as it also provides a direction even though the steps for getting there are not clear. Here, a focus on testing and experimenting seems reasonable. A classic answer would be to increase expenditure in R&D, or perhaps obtaining the necessary know-how outside the organisation.

The third position is actually not as inconceivable as it might first appear. Often, organisations have certain designs, routines, and procedures that, regardless of what innovation are to be pursued, would have to be adhered to. This type of formalisation is obviously a challenge as these setups were designed to solve certain problems, and, although they were effective at the moment, over time they may become less effective as the nature of the innovation may require something quite different.

The last position is very often where we find organisations today; at least, it is often portrayed as the situation for many organisations. This may be true for the individual organisation as well as on a broader level for all organisations, factoring in time and change. However, it is not a singular truth. In fact, many problems in the world, and the proposal of several solutions, still exist. For example, food, clothing, environment, communication, and the pursuit of opportunity and happiness are matters that will likely not disappear any time soon. Existing organisations have experienced – at least when they started – that they could deliver value to customers and users and as such provided a rationale for their existence. Over time though, this ability may have decreased, their users and customers may have changed their preferences, or changes may have been made to legislation or access to resources that negatively impact the organisation's ability to succeed. Still, the absence of a clear "what" and "how" does not mean there is nothing to do. This situation simply requires a different strategy, leadership, and organisation.

Many large organisations would argue that they are in all four positions at the same time. And this is probably true given their size, as well as number of activities and markets they are engaged in. Finally, one can also view these four positions as a process (not necessarily in the order displayed above) that moves from uncertainty to greater certainty.

Developing capacity then can be seen in the light of certainty and uncertainty. The main question is: how can one build capacity towards something that is essentially uncertain? There are a number of possible answers, stretching from up-skilling and improving organisational culture to different forms of collaborations and other outreach initiatives. But there is also a link between innovation capacity, innovation performance, and innovation stimuli, as suggested by Prajogo and Ahmed (2006) and Jiménez-Jiménez and Sanz-Valle (2008). Both (ibid.) point out that innovation capacity is needed because there is no proven direct link between innovation stimulus and innovation performance. The question again comes into play: how can organisations obtain the stimuli, understand them, and then do the "right things" – given their own strengths and weaknesses – to deliver on the potential for innovation performance?

In this book, three overall factors are suggested that drive innovation and the development of capacity for innovation: strategy, leadership, and organisation. We will explore each in more detail.

Contents

To paint a picture of how we will explore these topics, a summary of the content of this monograph is provided below:

Chapter 2 discusses the concept of innovation. Building on the theoretical challenges portrayed in this chapter, a more in-depth presentation of how to categorise and measure innovation is offered. Defining innovation is a daunting task, which has been shown through the many different views and angles that have been used over the years. The chapter starts off with a historical view of the idea of innovation, which underpins the notion how the understanding and value of a word and a concept can change over the years.

Chapter 3 introduces creativity and ideas. Both creativity and ideas are seen as integral to innovation and the innovation process. This chapter explores what creativity and ideas are, and a number of theories on the subject of creativity understood as relevant for innovation. Considerations around selecting and evaluating ideas are also included in this chapter, as well as the notion of the "front-end of innovation." The chapter concludes by discussing how creativity is supported and managed.

8 *Why we need a holistic approach*

Chapter 4 looks at the making of innovation. Whereas ideas and creativity are more fluid and can point in many different directions, turning those into innovation requires a number of conditions. Of these conditions, one asserts that there are different sources of innovation, and in this chapter these sources are outlined and explained. There are several models of innovation, and these have undergone changes over the decades. Models of innovation, innovation processes, and innovation management are discussed in this chapter.

Chapter 5 discusses how different forms of innovations are actually spread and then taken up in the marketplace. Six theories and approaches are introduced and explored: diffusion theory, bounded rationality, the theory of reasoned action, consumer behaviour theories, the role of branding and marketing, and absorptive capacity. All of these theories and approaches are different from each other. As well, branding and marketing do not constitute just one theory. Moreover, absorptive capacity is by its nature different as it is not primarily a decision-making model, but rather refers to the capacity to apply new information for business purposes.

Chapter 6 take on the subject of organisational learning. In this book, learning is seen as an integral and vital part of the innovation process, being somewhat underrepresented in the discourse of innovation. In this chapter, we explore the topics of knowledge management and organisational learning, knowledge creation, knowledge transfer and retention, loops of learning, the learning organisation and management, barriers to organisational learning, and innovation as learning (and vice versa). Although learning is integral to all aspects of the innovation journey, we treat it separately for pedagogical reasons.

Chapter 7 discusses the drivers of innovation. In this chapter, we further our understanding of innovation and look at the reasons why we need innovation. Change is introduced, since innovation is a form of change and the notion of change is in itself a driver for innovation. Competition and globalisation, together with new business models and new technology, are introduced as factors for driving innovation. Legislation and changing customer preferences are not addressed directly in this book, but the section on globalisation and new business models take this into account, albeit indirectly.

Chapter 8 focuses on complexity. It describes the development of a new science from chaos theory to complex adaptive systems. Innovation as a process is considered to be a complex adaptive system. Thus, what is being considered in this monograph is in fact a complex adaptive system (innovation) *within* complex (adaptive) systems. This linguistic and terminological challenge is to a large extent limited to this chapter to make it easier for the reader to follow the central arguments. However, it is important to understand that innovation in fact correlates with many – if not all – of the characteristics of a complex adaptive system. This will be discussed in more detail in this chapter.

Chapter 9 examines five different approaches to complexity, their backgrounds, how they differ, and how they overlap. Even if some of these approaches suggest different worldviews, many similarities also exist which make them quite compatible in terms of application. Systems thinking, complex adaptive systems, complex responsive processes, Cynefin, and Chaordic are the five approaches presented here. At the end of the chapter, innovation and complex systems are discussed towards the idea of a theoretical foundation for innovation in complex systems.

Chapter 10 develops the discussion on capacity building as an essential aspect of organisational and business success. As such, it can be seen as a consequence of strategy and a managerial responsibility. In this chapter, we will look more closely at capacity building for innovation. We discuss some challenges and opportunities with respect to innovation capacity building before suggesting a 6P model for organisational capacity building. Finally, we explore how to measure innovation capacity building.

Chapter 11 looks at capacity building for innovation from a strategic perspective. Organisations have the opportunity to pursue different strategies, even if they are limited in their power to do so. This chapter begins by taking into account complexity before focusing on how strategies are developed. Subsequently, a number of strategies are presented and discussed. In particular, we look at three overall orientations: merger and acquisitions; partnerships and internal development; and, to some extent, implementation and dissemination.

Chapter 12 focuses on leadership and innovation. This chapter, like the two previous chapters, starts off with a section on complexity to situate the discussions and arguments. The concept of innovation management is introduced and reviewed. People, teams, and collaboration are one of the most important topics, only overshadowed by customers in terms of literature on innovation. Its placement in this book (i.e. in a later section) should not be seen as diminishing its importance; rather, it is simply a consequence of the unfolding of the argument of the book. We discuss innovation leadership tools in its own section. The chapter ends with a discussion about the central leadership responsibilities: direction, empowerment, and motivation.

Chapter 13 examines the organisation in relation to capacity building. The previous chapter was about different forms of organisation, but they are here seen more as strategic choices, and in this chapter we look more closely at some key aspects of organising for innovation. After discussing complexity and organisation, organisational culture is addressed since it is so fundamental for innovation. Innovation processes are discussed in their own right, in the same way as creativity and ideation. How we create space for innovation is explored in the final section of the chapter, pointing to what can be done to ensure fertile ground for innovation.

Chapter 14 concludes the monograph. It is not a summary or a conclusion as such, but more of a reflective, aggregated view on how to go about achieving a holistic approach for developing capacity for innovation. Applying the metaphor of the kernel (Rumelt, 2011) to innovation provides a conceptual framing around innovation. Additional views are also offered: the view of innovation as beyond an organisation, as well as an integrative approach. The chapter ends with a reflection around the lifeworld of innovation and suggests areas for future research.

2   The meaning of innovation

Introduction

In this chapter, we dive deep into the meaning of innovation as our notions of innovation have changed over time. Many (e.g. Darsø, 2003) consider Austrian economist Joseph Schumpeter, the father of innovation, and his work in the 1930s. However, innovation is not a new phenomenon and is arguably as old as mankind itself (Fagerberg et al., 2006).

Innovation can be defined as any new creation that generates economic value. Schumpeter's (1939, 1942) perspective was driven by an economic background; as such, the value he spoke of was economic. Today, it makes sense to take a broader perspective. Drucker (1985) points to social innovation as a significant value-creating process, where innovation is based on social needs rather than technology. An innovation is thus essentially something "new" and "valuable."

As innovation is considered an economic driver, it is of increasing importance and interest to policymakers; that is, they are increasingly concerned with how innovation can be fostered. At an organisational level, innovation is also key to staying competitive and generating growth. As such, current interest in innovation seems to be endless. It is a key subject in the study and application of many related fields, including technology, engineering, sociology, economics, business, and entrepreneurship. Indeed, it permeates all parts of society.

According to Berkhout et al. (2006), the most important changes in the world are now taking place in the so-called "innovation economy," where in addition to capital, labour, and knowledge, creativity is the fourth principal factor of production. Florida (2002) argues that creativity has become the principal driving force behind economic growth. This calls for a more nuanced and contemporary understanding of both creativity and innovation.

There are several dimensions involved in trying to understand innovation. Innovations can be both the output and the input of a process and are sometimes distinguished by the degree of change they demand or bring about: incremental or radical, emergent or revolutionary. Learning how to categorise and measure innovation offers insights but also theoretical and practical challenges. Innovation is often considered the output of a process, but increasingly it is also viewed as a process unto itself. This process follows several stages, beginning with the identification of a need or the beginning of an idea, followed by the development of that need into something useful, and finally the diffusion of the product of that innovation process into society.

This chapter offers a retrospective discussion about the history of the word "innovation" to help us understand the changes in meaning it has undergone and also shed light on its more contemporary definitions. We then present different categories of innovation, so as to broaden and deepen our understanding. This is followed by a discussion about measuring innovation. The chapter then ends with a thorough discussion about defining innovation, so as to lay a solid foundation for the arguments in the following chapters.

A retrospective view of the idea of innovation

> Our future progress and prosperity depend upon our ability to equal, if not surpass, other nations in the enlargement and advance of science, industry and commerce. To invention we must turn as one of the most powerful aids to the accomplishment of such a result.
>
> (McKinley, 2010[1])

One can easily imagine political and business leaders alike uttering the above statement today. However, it was said by William McKinley, the 25th President (1897–1901) of the US.

It is often assumed that the term "innovation" is fairly new, but its origins actually stretch deep into history. What *has* changed dramatically since its inception has been its meaning and usage. Today, innovation[2] – understood as (1) a new idea, device, or method, or (2) the act or process of introducing new ideas, devices, or methods – is primarily considered something good. Of course, one can speak of "failed," "poor," or "bad" innovations, but the term essentially connotes something desirable. This was not always the case. For instance, Edmund Burke characterised the French revolution as a "revolt of innovation":

> It is a revolt of innovation, and thereby the very elements of Society have been confounded and dissipated.
>
> (Quoted in O'Gorman, 2004: 153)

Only during the last century has the term become more widely used and our usage of it associated with something positive. Generally, this usage is assumed to have started with the work of Schumpeter (Schumpeter, 1939) on business cycles, but as we will see later in this chapter, this is a misconception (Godin, 2011, 2014a). According to Jill Lepore (2014), the word started being used outside expert circles in the 1990s and gained omnipresence only after 9/11. She points out that between 2011 and 2014, *Time, Times Magazine,*

12 *The meaning of innovation*

The New Yorker, Forbes, and even *Better Homes and Gardens* published special "innovation" issues – the modern equivalents of what, a century ago, were known as "sketches of men of progress."

The following sections go through the conceptual understanding of the word "innovation" (from a European/Western-centric perspective and classical division of history), from Classic Antiquity up to the Fourth Industrial Revolution. When used to describe certain periods of time, the word "revolution" essentially denotes "abrupt and radical change" (Mokyr, 2003; Roe Smith et al., 2003; Schwab, 2017). What follows is a high-level overview, since after roughly the late 1940s, studies and theories about innovation started to become more numerous and extensive, as well as far more nuanced. Several theories and studies about innovation are discussed in other sections in this book.

Innovation and classical antiquity

Classical antiquity is a historical period often considered to have begun with the poems of Homer around 700 BC and ending with the fall of the Roman Empire around 500–600 AD. Benoît Godin (2011) traces innovation as a concept back to this period. He further states that novelty was fairly regular and established at the time, in fields such as science and the arts. Innovation, however, was a different matter: it was a pejorative concept, a consequence of the figurative usage of the Greek word καινοτομια (Godin, 2011).

The word καινοτομια (*kainotomia*) means "making new cuttings" or "cutting fresh into" something. It is derived from the word καινος (*kainos*), meaning "new." It was only through the philosophers and their political works on the permanence and transformation of constitutions and the conventional orders that innovation gained the denotation of "introducing change into the established order" (Godin, 2011).[3]

We owe the root of the word to the Latin language. According to the *Etymology Dictionary,* innovation originates from the Latin *innovationem,* which is an agent noun of *innovare.* The same source also states that *innovare* dates back to 1540 and stems from the Latin *innovatus,* the past participle of *innovare,* meaning "to renew or change," from *in* ("into") and *novus* ("new"). The meaning "to make changes in something established" dates back to the 1590s.

We can see that innovation has transformed from Roman times to today, as we primarily view the idea as a technical or economical concept. Innovation can thus be considered an action or process that makes something new again, and not necessarily solely the introduction of something uniquely new. Among the works of Roman philosophers and writers, there aren't many occurrences of *innovare* or *innovatione* (meaning "renewing," or "a return to the past"). But words like *renovare* (in the sense of "renewing"), as well as *novitas* ("novelty") and *novare* ("in the act of innovating"), are more common (Godin, 2011).

Although the connection between the use of the word "innovation" in the Greek and Roman eras is unclear, their usage has had a significant impact. To the ancient Greek philosophers, innovation meant (1) introducing novelty of any kind, and (2) political or constitutional change. Similar usages of the ideas concerning innovation were common among Roman writers as well. The influence of Western political thought on our use of "innovation" was significant (Godin, 2011), and during the Renaissance, Roman ideas were widely embraced, leading to the adoption of the word throughout Europe (Skinner, 1978).

Innovation and the Middle Ages

The Middle Ages (or Medieval period) started after the fall of the Western Roman Empire in the fifth century and lasted until around the fifteenth century. No universally agreed-upon ending date exists; depending on one's perspective, the end point could be the Ottoman capture of Constantinople in 1453, the Protestant Reformation of 1517, or Columbus's first journey to the Americas.

Even though the Western Roman Empire had collapsed, strong constructs from the Roman world survived through the Eastern Byzantine Empire. Of course, writings and interactions between the West and other cultures and people over the centuries also helped Western ideas to survive and spread, but Byzantium is unique through its shared history with the Roman Empire.

A conventional view about Byzantium is that it was a conformist and conservative society, impervious to innovation. This view prevails today, and suggests that innovation did not really happen or that it was not considered positive (Spanos, 2010). Spanos challenges that perspective and argues that the real question to ask is not whether the notion of innovation existed at that time, but rather if it is possible to study whether the Byzantine idea of innovation aligns with ours.

The *Oxford Dictionary of Byzantium* defines *kainotomia as* "innovation," with respect to negative political and social changes. According to Spanos (2010, 2014), the Byzantines primarily used two words to indicate innovation: *kainotomia* and *neoterismos* (νεωτερισμός). The verb *neoterizein* is different in its meaning to *kainotomein*: whereas *kainotomein* means *making* new things, *neoterizein* means *doing* new things (Νεωτερίζει· καιναπράτ- τει).

Despite the negative connotations, diverse sources demonstrate that the Byzantines were not antagonistic to innovation as a principle, and that this idea could likely be a flaw in modern scholarship rather than a "truth" (Spanos, 2010, 2014).

Innovation and early modern Europe

This time period includes the Reformation, which started with Martin Luther and the publication of his famous 95 theses on October 31, 1517, and

14 *The meaning of innovation*

the Age of Enlightenment. The Reformation was intended to reform the Catholic Church and was rooted in a criticism of its system of indulgences. It sparked the way for a number of new traditions, including Lutheranism, Calvinism, Anglicanism, and Anabaptism. The Enlightenment, or the Age of Reason, dominated the European worldview in the eighteenth century. This period saw numerous new ideas in the areas of theology, government, and science. The central point was rationality, which went hand-in-hand with the scientific method and reductionism. The scientific revolution (ca 1520–1750), together with the first industrial revolution, laid the basis for an outburst of inventions (Roe Smith et al., 2003).

Despite the presence of inventors, inventions, and advancements in a wide range of areas (not least science and technology), the concept of innovation still did not resemble how we view it today. Men of the seventeenth century understood innovation as political (Godin, 2010b, 2012a, 2014a) and as such followed a tradition of thought that originated during the Reformation: "Science is method while innovation is politics" (Godin, 2014a: 6). Innovation, as an essentially political concept, was not a positive idea *per se*. For instance, in his book *The Prince* (1532), the Italian diplomat and political theorist Niccolò Machiavelli states: "The innovator makes enemies of all those who prospered under the old order, and only lukewarm support is forthcoming from those who would prosper under the new." He understood the innovator to be someone who changes the current political order, an activity not for ordinary men to engage in. Even for philosophers like Francis Bacon, who could see novelty everywhere, innovation was forbidden (Godin, 2014b). Godin suggests that both religion (2006) and politics (2011) have a special place in explaining the long pejorative meaning of innovation. History has certainly shown that new ideas can threaten authority, as we can see, for instance, in the treatment of Bruno and Galileo.

Innovation, the first industrial revolution, and the French revolution

The Industrial Revolution originated in Great Britain and is normally considered to have started around 1760. The period evolved into the Second Industrial Revolution sometime in the mid-1800s. This entire period marked a transition to new manufacturing processes, commonly understood as a shift from hand production methods to mechanical ones. In addition, this period saw new types of processes in areas such as iron production and chemical engineering, as well as growing use of steam power and more efficient use of waterpower. During this time, we also find the first examples of factories.

According to Roe Smith et al. (2003), the key aspect of the First Industrial Revolution was technology. Access to and acquisition of knowledge, be it through discovery of existing knowledge or the invention of new things, was easier and paved the way for feedback loops that allowed individuals to build on the findings of others. Still, knowledge discovery in this era was basically pragmatic, informal, and empirical (ibid.). During the First Industrial

Revolution, most technological developments had little or no real scientific basis (Mokyr, 2003). Thus, in the First Industrial Revolution we find an iron industry without metallurgy, a power industry without thermodynamics, and a chemical industry without chemistry. Things were known to work, but why they did so was rarely understood.

After the French Revolution, innovation began to take on a different meaning. Rather than being understood as a change in customs, it now came to be understood as novelty of any kind (Godin, 2011). In the nineteenth century, the depiction of innovation changes from that of a vice into that of a virtue (Godin, 2014a). Innovation goes from being a word to a concept (Godin, 2013a). Writers of this period begin to talk about innovation in terms of progress, and they move from religion as the primary focus to many other fields, including science. However, the concept of innovation during this period remains quite far from our present-day view. Godin (2014a, 2014b) argues that innovation in nineteenth-century science signified the application of the scientific method, and its understanding varied between different sciences. For example, in medicine, innovation essentially meant the development of new scientific instruments, whereas in education it concerned new practices and was still viewed as fundamentally negative.

Innovation and the Second Industrial Revolution

The Second Industrial Revolution is normally considered to have taken place between 1870[4] and 1914 and was characterised by rapid industrialisation. It was a period of expansion in the railroad (which had helped trigger the First Industrial Revolution), as well as in the technologies of the telegraph and later the telephone. Together, these developments allowed for unprecedented movement of people and ideas. The Second Industrial Revolution saw the beginning of electrification and the development of the combustion engine. Water and gas supplies, as well as sewage systems, became more widespread, enabled by advances in manufacturing and production. During this period, mass production arose (Schwab, 2017) and modern organisational methods for operating large-scale business were developed (Khurana, 2007). Furthermore, it was a time of accelerated inventive activity, largely driven by the rise of corporate research laboratories and measured by the surge of patents issued (Roe Smith et al., 2003).

According to Mokyr (2003), although the Second Industrial Revolution was in many ways a continuation of the First, it diverged in a number of key aspects: (1) it affected real wages and living standards, which changed dramatically between the beginning and end of the period, (2) it loosened the technological centre and leadership from Great Britain, giving it a more distributed locus, and (3) it changed the relationship between the knowledge of nature and technological practices. As such, it changed the way technological change itself happened. This paved the way for future industrial revolutions.

16 *The meaning of innovation*

According to Godin (2013a), innovation had until the Renaissance been a descriptive concept with different meanings. From the Renaissance to the eighteenth century, it became a linguistic concept to be used, without an exact definition, against enemies. During the nineteenth century, the concept begins to shift to something positive, as innovation starts to be seen as "instrumental" to progress or utility. This idea of innovation paved the way for political, social, and – later – economic goals (ibid.). In the systematic discussions of innovation found in the writings of social scientists, we can see that during this period, innovation came to be theorised as creativity (Godin, 2011). The French sociologist Gabriel Tarde, who began to publish his ideas and theories in the 1890s, is considered by Godin (2012c) to be the first theorist on innovation. Tarde made a distinction between theoretical invention (scientific discoveries) and practical invention (industrial inventions) at the turn of the century, much as anthropologists of the early twentieth century distinguish discovery from invention (Godin, 2014a).

Innovation and the Third Industrial Revolution

The Third Industrial Revolution started in the 1960s (Schwab, 2017) and is sometimes called the computer or digital revolution. (The period between the Second and Third Industrial Revolutions should not be seen as empty. Rather, different scholars and thought leaders use different names for different periods, and at times use different categorisation of periods of time altogether.) It covers the development of semiconductors and mainframe computing in the 1960s, personal computing in the 1970s and the 1980s, and the Internet in 1990s. It should be noted that there are many definitions and understandings of the Third Industrial Revolution. Rifkin's (2012) description, for example, overlaps quite a bit with what I refer to here as the Fourth Industrial Revolution. For the purpose of this book, it nevertheless makes sense to distinguish between the Third and Fourth Industrial Revolutions, due to the societal and economic implications (see below) of new technologies – such as the computer, the cellular phone, and the Internet – that were made possible by digital logic circuits.

Takeuchi and Nonaka (1995) emphasise that the Third Industrial Revolution also marked what is often referred to as the Information Age (Castells, 1997) and, later, the Knowledge Economy (Drucker, 1969). In the Information Age, mass production became mass customisation. Where previously labour had served machines, now technology served workers (Humbert, 2007).

In the period that started around World War I, there was an explosion of innovation. Maurice Holland (Godin, 2009) developed his research cycle (in which he portrayed the development of modern industries as a series of sequential steps from basic research to commercialisation of technological inventions) in the 1920s, and he was followed by the seminal icon of Schumpeter. Schumpeter (1939) saw technological innovation as a motor for business cycles and innovation as a source of economic change (1942). He distinguishes between invention and innovation, arguing that invention is "an act of intellectual creativity" that is "without importance to economic analysis" (1939: 85), whereas innovation is an economic decision – for example, a firm applying or adopting an invention. Interestingly, technological innovation for Schumpeter was also the new combination of means of production (i.e. a change in the factors of production) (ibid.: 87).

Although Schumpeter brought the concept of innovation into economic theory, according to Godin (2008), he provided few, if any, analyses of the process of innovation itself. He introduced the idea of the entrepreneur into the innovation process, but he did not study how it came about. Godin (2008) goes on to argue that it is to W. Rupert Maclaurin that we owe the first systematic studies on technological innovation. Maclaurin brought the linear model into science and innovation studies in the 1940s and 1950s (Godin, 2008), building on and developing Schumpeter's ideas. He saw technological innovation as a process composed of several steps.

Another influential but neglected contributor was the sociologist William F. Ogburn, who pioneered the idea that technological innovation has three dimensions: origins, diffusion, and effects (Godin, 2010a). And finally, another important strand in the development of the idea of innovation came from RK. Merton (1938, 1945) and his contributions to the sociology of science. Among other contributions, Merton suggested that the themes and dynamics of scientific activity are affected by social and economic considerations. Although this idea seems obvious to us today, at the time it was new.

After World War II, studies about innovation and our understanding of it increased. Today's dominant interpretation of innovation – as the "use of technological invention, as opposed to invention itself" (Godin, 2010a: 41) – gradually emerged. After the 1950s, innovation became an instrumental category as governments increasingly believed technology to be a source of economic progress (Godin, 2011). By the 1960s and 1970s, the number of relevant publications had exploded (Rogers, 1983). Since then, numerous journals, professional associations, and university departments focused on innovation have been created (Fagerberg and Verspagen, 2009).

Innovation and the Fourth Industrial Revolution

Regardless of the appropriateness of the description, we can definitely speak of a Fourth Industrial Revolution. For the purpose of this book, we can assume that present-day conditions have an effect on how we perceive innovation – among them, not least the measures companies and organisations use to meet challenges and opportunities.

Schwab (2017) sees the Fourth Industrial Revolution as beginning at the turn of the twenty-first century, and building upon the digital revolution. He suggests that it is coming about through a far more omnipresent and mobile

18 *The meaning of innovation*

Internet, smaller and cheaper sensors, artificial intelligence, and machine learning. He goes on to include other inventions in areas such as gene sequencing, nano-technology, renewables, and quantum computing. What differentiates this revolution from previous ones is the fusion of different technologies and their interaction throughout domains such as the digital, biological, and physical.

Brynjolfsson and McAfee (2016) have coined another term to refer to this current period: the Second Machine Age. They see the world at an inflection point where the effects of digital technologies will manifest through automation and the unparalleled making of objects.

Many specific technologies constitute part of this context, including advanced robotics, 3D printing, the Internet of Things (IoT), and blockchains (a distributed ledger; that is, a secure protocol where a network of computers collectively verifies a transaction before it is approved and recorded). But we also see the Fourth Industrial Revolution impacting different business models and consumer/producer interactions. For example, both the sharing economy and the platform economy open up for more effective usage of assets and for different relationships to exist between people and assets. The Fourth Industrial Revolution also asks fundamental, philosophical questions about modern life like, for example, the value of ownership. Goodwin (2015) wrote: "Uber, the world's largest taxi company, owns no vehicles. Facebook, the world's most popular media owner, creates no content. Alibaba, the most valuable retailer, has no inventory. And Airbnb, the world's largest accommodation provider, owns no real estate."

In terms of understanding innovation, it is still too early to distinguish any significant changes from the previous period. There are, however, a few areas in which we can envision new developments, whether that involves new trends or simply increased trends. Among these are social innovation (Mulgan, 2007) and social entrepreneurship (Bornstein, 2004), which Godin (2012c) believes appeared after the French Revolution, and which he argues had existed long before the idea of technological innovation. In short, the focus has been shifted from technological and commercial success to that of societal and social value creation.

In Conclusion

The above is not a comprehensive summary of important findings and trends on the subject of innovation. For instance, the theories around disruption (Christensen and Bower, 1995; Christensen, 1997; Christensen and Raynor, 2013) and dominant design (Utterback and Abernathy, 1975; Utterback, 1996) are widely recognised. It is also worth mentioning open innovation and platforms (e.g. Chesbrough, 2003, 2005, 2006), which essentially involve opening up and promoting the idea of connectivity, sharing, and sourcing from a distributed value chain as this relates to the considerations around capacity building later on.

The meaning of innovation   19

As a final note, in a digitised world, the cross-pollination of ideas is eased by their accessibility, which also speeds the diffusion and adoption of new ideas and innovations. Speed becomes a more volatile factor in terms of establishing and maintaining prominence in the marketplace.

How to categorise innovation

In trying to understand innovation and what brings it about, we need to divide innovation into categories (Edquist, 2001). Some accepted differentiations are niches: modular, architectural, incremental, or radical (Afuah and Bahram, 1995). However, an overabundance of definitions for innovation types has resulted in vagueness in the way the terms "innovation" and "innovativeness" are operationalised and utilised in the new product development literature (Garcia and Calantone, 2001). The ambiguity of classification makes it impossible to compare various studies and has hindered the development of knowledge in these fields (Coccia, 2006). Furthermore, in the economic literature on technical change we find different names to indicate the same type of technical change.

A clear taxonomy will help us distinguish what relates to what. When thinking about innovation, we normally think about outputs or outcomes (i.e. products). But outcomes/outputs – that is, what an organisation produces and offers – can also be intangible in the form of services. Innovation can also refer to the processes that bring products into being. Organisations usually bring about innovations, but sometimes individuals do so as well. Sometimes the innovation is genuinely new, sometimes it is more of a combination of existing components. To a large extent, what separates innovations from each other is the question of what is being produced and how that is done.

Edquist (2001) offers a taxonomy of innovation that divides innovation into *process* and *product*. Process is then divided into organisational and technological, and product is divided into goods and services. In this model, only products and technological processes are of a material or physical kind, whereas organisational processes and services are intangible. However, a product (e.g. a robot or car) can in the second round of development be part of a production/innovation process if the end product or service is not a robot or a car. For example, the development of a new type of car could impact the innovation process of taxi companies.

However, another way to portray the same taxonomy could be like the following (Figure 2.1):

What separates this model from Edquist's is the notion of ends versus means. Here, innovations in processes lead to more attractive products[5] or services. Innovation itself holds little value.

Depending on how one understands services and products, one can also harness the consequences of Pine and Gilmore's (1999) description of the "Experience Economy" and its consequences for innovation. They view experiences as different from services, in that experience happens whenever a

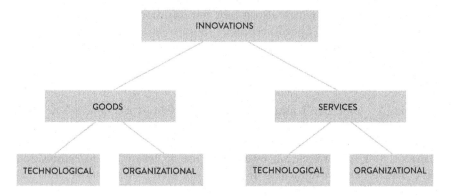

Figure 2.1 Taxonomy of innovation.
Source: Author.

company intentionally uses services as the stage and products as the props to engage an individual (ibid.).[6] This will be explored further in the "Service innovation methods" section.

Product and service innovation

The major separation between products and services is of course that products are physical while services are not. However, the effects of the services are often tangible: for instance, operations that are performed at hospitals or the services provided by banks (e.g. a repaired fracture or cash in the hand). At times, we define a service as the value that is produced and consumed simultaneously (although in reality, this implies a co-creation of value since the provider is dependent upon the receiver and vice versa). There are also forms of combined service operations in which products play a key part. A limousine service, for example, depends heavily on the existence of an actual vehicle. Thanks to the introduction, spread, and growth of technological, often Internet-based platforms, new forms of relationships and services are being developed and deployed at an increasing speed.

Product innovation methods

Among the established methodologies that exist to describe product innovation, the three most well-known are Phase review, stage gate, and product and cycle time excellence (PACE).

In Phase review, the product development cycle is divided into phases in which each is finalised and reviewed before moving into the next. A challenge with the model is that each phase exists independently from subsequent phases, and as such there is a low level of coordination, which can generate errors and undesired trade-offs.

The stage gate method is similar to Phase review but uses a synchronised product design process. It is based and executed according to a scheduled life cycle from the creation of a concept to the market launch (Cooper, 2008, 2013). Each stage is signed-off after proper evaluation and a (re-)design of the next phase.

PACE is concerned chiefly with developing product development strategies (McGrath, 1996). It ensures a link and fit between the business and product strategies. Here, the view of the customer is used throughout the whole product design process.

Service innovation methods

Although one could deploy the same type of innovation methods to service innovations, the methods described above were primarily developed with product (e.g. software) development in mind. Given that services are fundamentally different from products, an increasing amount of thought has gone into the innovation of services. Often these innovations arise from a combination of anthropological and ethnographical methods, as well as creative exercise. But the notion of service and the importance of the classical understanding of service are changing. Experiences as a focal point for business and innovation are growing in importance. Pine and Gilmore (1999), for instance, have argued that the developed world is moving from a service-based to an experience-based economy (Morgan et al., 2009). Such experiences are valued because they are unique, memorable, and engaged the individual in a personal way.

Experience design (XD) is the practice of designing products, processes, services, events, Omni channel journeys, and environments that focus on the quality of the user experience and culturally relevant solutions. It is a process for co-creation based on the idea of promoting specific emotions in the customer or user. One can identify three major shifts (Morgan et al., 2009) that change this relationship:

- A shift of emphasis from the rational to the emotional aspects of consumer decision-making
- A transition from satisfying needs to fulfilling aspirations, desires, and dreams
- A change in the role of the customer to an active participant rather than a passive consumer

These three shifts really point to a new way of thinking and practice when developing relationships with customers and users, and even employees. Empathy is key.

It can be argued whether XD is a method for service design or the same as service design, or if it is a unique category in itself. Generally speaking, it is normally treated as a subset of service design.

22 *The meaning of innovation*

Process innovation methods

Process innovation is not so much about what an organisation does, as it is about how the organisation does it (Davenport, 1992). Here, process is viewed as a set of "planned" or connected activities designed to convert inputs into defined outputs, and innovation is about finding a better way (or method) to produce the desired output. As such, it concerns all the activities that lead to customer value, be that less stock, better purchases, fewer errors, or faster production. Well-established methodologies include total quality management (TQM), just-in-time (JIT), LEAN, supply chain management, and enterprise resource planning (ERP).

TQM is about introducing systems that avoid the occurrence of defects. It seeks continuous improvement from all members of the organisation and is credited with introducing standards such as ISO9000.

JIT is a method designed to increase production rates and prevent excess stockpiles by ensuring the right material at the right time in the right quantity.

LEAN, or lean manufacturing, seeks to reduce waste across the organisation's operations. Examples of waste are overproduction and waiting time: it essentially involves anything that reduces value. In many ways, it is an integrated system since it encourages TQM, integrated supply chain, and others.

Supply chain management emphasises the flow of materials and information across the entire value chain, from supplier to customer. Value is created by more integration with customers and suppliers.

ERP is a system normally rooted in a software solution that integrates all organisational information into one system. The system supports other approaches – see above – and aims to reduce bottlenecks and waste, and increase coordination and planning.

Product, process, and service innovation

Even though they have been discussed independently, product, process, and service innovations are often highly interdependent. Product innovation is often what receives headlines when innovation is being portrayed, but as Utterback (1996) has pointed out, process innovation for organisations becomes increasingly important relative to product development once the dominant design of a product has been established. This is because as the dominant design takes form, the amount of process innovation also gradually decreases. The configuration of the process becomes more correct, and fewer opportunities to innovate appear as the life cycle of the product nears its end. Utterback (ibid.) sees this development going through three phases: the fluid phase, the transitional phase, and the specific phase. It is in the transitional phase where process innovation gains the upper hand over product innovation. In order to obtain competitive advantage over time, process innovation cannot be neglected.

In today's technological environment, digitisation is penetrating every corner of our society. An increasing number of services are now offered over

The meaning of innovation 23

the net. This change doesn't merely signify that we have exchanged an individual for an app or a digital service; rather, entirely new services and interactions have been introduced that would not have been possible otherwise. In that respect, "innovations" in the form of apps and other artefacts have become the carrier and enabler of further innovation. Easily accessible, powerful digital tools are now in the hands of many people, allowing individuals to more easily and more cheaply develop innovations by themselves.

Radical and incremental innovation

We can also distinguish between forms of innovation in terms of scope and magnitude: whether they are incremental or radical (Freeman et al., 1982). Radical innovations indicate major changes that impact the efficiency or revenue of an organisation (McLoughlin, 1999). They can be so massive that they actually destroy existing market preferences, creating new standards and expectations, and thus transforming the industry itself[7] (Utterback, 1996; Christensen, 1997). Utterback (1996) provides the following definition of a discontinuous or radical innovation: "change that sweeps away much of a firm's existing investment in technical skills and knowledge, designs, production technique, plant and equipment."

Incremental innovation refers to smaller changes and alterations to products, services, and processes. It can be seen as a way to decrease the risk of failure, and is normally easier to manage and less costly. Obviously, incremental innovation does not offer the same opportunity for large returns on investment as radical innovation, but it also involves less risk. Companies often pursue a dual strategy, working on a set of radical innovations in tandem with incremental changes.

Other categorisations

Innovation has often been categorised as either radical, incremental, architectural, modular, or niche, based on the effects it has on the competence, other products, and investment decisions of the innovating entity (Afuah and Bahram, 1993).

It may seem easy and effective to categorise innovation as radical or incremental, but this approach may be over-simplistic, resulting in a lack of understanding. To combat this, Abernathy and Clark (1985) came up with a grouping model consisting of four categories relating to the impact of the innovation on the innovating firms' capabilities and knowledge of its technology and market. The model's four categories are regular, niche creation, revolutionary, and architectural. As the impact on firms' capabilities and knowledge of its technology and market increase, eventually it can be categorised as architectural.

Tushman and Anderson (1986) categorised innovations according to whether they are "competence destroying" or "competence enhancing,"

24 *The meaning of innovation*

depending on the effect of the innovation on the knowledge base of the innovating entity.

It is useful to keep the intended entity (e.g. user or market) in mind when categorising innovation. The taxonomy created by Booz, Allen, and Hamilton (1982) is a widely used framework that categorises new products along two dimensions that mirror their level of newness to (1) the developing firm and (2) the marketplace that consumes or uses them. But innovation does not only affect the company and/or its customers – it also affects its suppliers. To deal with this, Afuah and Bahram (1995) have suggested a model they call "the hypercube of innovation," which stresses the value-adding supply chain that provides key components to complementary innovators.

Another way of categorising innovation is through the lens of product newness. According to Olson et al. (1995), product newness is a reflection of firm and marketplace experience. Their product innovation view suggests a four-level categorisation: products new to the world, line extensions, products new to the organisation but not the market, and product modifications.

The Management of Technologies uses the following taxonomies to classify product innovation [this list – here summarised – is taken from Garcia and Caltone (2002) as outlined in Coccia (2006)]:

- Eight categories – reformulated, new parts, remerchandising, new improvements, new products, new users, new market, new customers (Johnson and Jones, 1957).
- Five categories – systematic, major, minor, incremental, unrecorded (Freeman, 1994).
- Tetra categorisation – incremental, modular, architectural, radical (Henderson and Clark, 1990); niche creation, architectural, regular, revolutionary (Abernathy and Clark, 1985); incremental, evolutionary market, evolutionary technical, radical (Moriarty and Kosnik, 1990); incremental, market breakthrough, technological breakthrough, radical (Chandy and Tellis, 2000); incremental, architectural, fusion, breakthrough (Tidd, 1995; Tidd et al., 2001).
- Triadic categorisation – low, moderate, high innovativeness (Kleinschmidt and Cooper, 1991); incremental, new generation, radically new (Wheelwright and Clark, 1992).
- Dichotomous categorisation – discontinuous, continuous (Robertson, 1967; Anderson and Tushman, 1990); instrumental, ultimate (Grossman, 1970); variations, reorientation (Norman, 1971); true, adoption (Maidique and Zirger, 1984); original, reformulated (Yoon and Lilien, 1985); innovations, reinnovations (Rothwell and Gardiner, 1988); radical, routine (Meyers and Tucker, 1989); evolutionary, revolutionary (Utterback, 1996); sustaining, disruptive (Christensen, 1997); really new, incremental (Schmidt and Calantone, 1998; Song and Montoya-Weisse, 1998); breakthrough, incremental (Rice et al., 1998); radical, incremental (Freeman, 1994; Balachandra and Friar, 1997).

Table 2.1 OECD typology of innovation, 2005, adapted from Oslo manual: guidelines for collecting and interpreting innovation data, 3rd edition

Type of innovation	Description
Product innovation	A good or service that is new or significantly improved. This includes significant improvements in technical specifications, components and materials, software in the product, user friendliness, or other functional characteristics
Process innovation	A new or significantly improved production or delivery method. This includes significant changes in techniques, equipment, and/or software
Marketing innovation	A new marketing method involving significant changes in product design or packaging, product placement, product promotion or pricing.
Organisational innovation	A new organisational method in business practices, workplace organisation or external relations.

Garcia and Calantone (2001) use macro-level versus micro-level and marketing versus technology perspectives, and also apply Boolean logic to identify three labels for innovations: radical, really new, and incremental.

In addition to the above listed taxonomies, the OECD uses a widely spread typology of innovation (Table 2.1):

As we can see there are certain overlaps with previous classification schemes, but in this case marketing is an added dimension.

In addition to the ones already listed here, even more popularised categorisations of innovation exist. For brevity's sake, I will only include one more, perhaps the most well-known: Doblin's ten types of innovation (Keeley et al., 2013). It is worth inclusion here because, unlike the other schemes described in this section, this one is a pedagogical model, demonstrating the different areas where innovation takes place when we are using the firm as the unit of analysis. As such, it helps us look beyond mere technological, product-related advancements. The ten types of innovation are profit model, network, structure, process, product performance, product system, service, channel, brand, and customer engagement.

Disruption

In recent years, the concept of disruption has gained much attention and popularity. The word itself means "a break or interruption in the normal course or continuation of some activity, process, etc."[8] and was coined in its current sense by Clayton Christensen in an article called "Disruptive Technologies: Catching the Wave," written with Joseph L. Bower in the *Harvard Business Review* in 1995. Christensen's book *The Innovator's Dilemma* (1997) became an instant success and has been followed up by several publications, such as *The Innovator's Solution* (Christensen and Raynor, 2013). In short, Christensen argues that companies that act in a rational

26   *The meaning of innovation*

way to remain on top are vulnerable to smaller, faster, and more inventive companies that manage to discover new ways to serve customers in a less expensive way. In short, one can fail by doing the right thing, in the wrong situations.[9]

Christensen defines disruptive innovation as the process by which "technologically straightforward" services and products target the bottom end of an established market, then move their way up the chain until, eventually, they overtake the existing market leaders (Christensen, 1997).

Some years later, Larry Downes and Paul F. Nunes conceptualised "Big Bang Disruption" (2013), which suggests that new solutions such as smartphones enable innovations that provide customers better solutions at lower costs. In another article (2014), they analyse the much-discussed acquisition of WhatsApp for $19 billion as a necessary response by established companies to the challenges and opportunities of the marketplace.

Christensen's theories have had a huge influence – see, for instance, Accenture's technology vision from 2014 ("From Digital Disruption to Digital Disrupter").[10] But there have also been critical voices, among others Jill Lepore (2014), who questions his background material. She argues that the theory cannot be used to predict, but only functions as a label after something has already been established as fact. She states, "Transfixed by change, it's blind to continuity. It makes a very poor prophet."

Measuring innovation

Today, one can hardly avoid being exposed to lists about innovation and innovativeness. These may be on a country level, such as the *World Economic Report on Global Competitiveness*,[11] *Bloomberg*'s "World's Most Innovative Economies,"[12] or the *Global Innovation Index*[13] (published by Cornell University, INSEAD, and the World Intellectual Property Organisation). Or they may be on a company level, for instance, *Forbes*' "The World's Most Innovative Companies,"[14] *Fast Company*'s "The World's Most Innovative Companies,"[15] or *The Boston Consulting Group's*[16] "On The Most Innovative Companies." They might even concern specific products and individuals, such as *Wired*'s "The World's Most Innovate Objects,"[17] or *Fast Company*'s "The Most Creative People in Business."[18]

Still, the more relevant question may not be the actual lists themselves, but rather how the lists are compiled. The purpose of this book is not to make a full comparative analysis of how such lists differ in terms of methodology, but a few general comments can be made. They are:

Look at different indicators   These areas could be patents, high-tech intensity, productivity, researcher concentration, quality of scientific research institutions, university-industry collaboration in research and development, company spending on research and development, and so on. The *Global Innovation Index*, for example, uses 79 indicators to rank 140 countries.

Use different methodologies For example, *Forbes* uses "the wisdom of the crowd" to generate their World's Most Innovative Companies list, relying on investors' ability to identify firms they expect to be innovative now and in the future.[19] In contrast, the Boston Consulting Group conducts a survey of thousands of senior-level executives in order to produce their report. Some more speculative lists essentially only rely on an author/journalist/individual's appreciation of what or who is innovative.

Have different perceived stature Where the more established rankings and lists, by respected entities such as the World Economic Forum, are more widely recognised and used for different purposes (e.g. policy development or advertisement), the less recognised can be of more value to the individual company or person (or perhaps simply to the one making the list).

But why do we measure? One reason could be entities like the EU. The EU states that research and innovation are crucial for bringing about a return to competitiveness for Europe and that the European Commission is committed to building a "stable economy for the future based on smart sustainable growth."[20] This is what the EU's growth and jobs strategy aims to do (i.e. Europe 2020).[21] The European Commission's "Indicator of Innovation Output"[22] "measures the extent to which ideas from innovative sectors are able to reach the market, providing better jobs and making Europe more competitive." The assumption is that composite indicators can be used to measure the impact of research and innovation policies. The proposed indicator is based on four components chosen for their policy relevance:

• Technological innovation as measured by patents
• Employment in knowledge-intensive activities as a percentage of total employment
• Competitiveness of knowledge-intensive goods and services. This is based on both the contribution of the trade balance of high-tech and medium-tech products to the total trade balance, and knowledge-intensive services as a share of the total services exports
• Employment in fast-growing firms of innovative sectors

These four components also represent some of the challenges that arise from any attempt to measure innovation: that is, what exactly is to be measured and what taxonomy is to be used?

Godin (2002) traces back governmental interest in innovation to the 1960s: the first worldwide survey on innovation was conducted in the late 1950s in Great Britain, and in 1962, Everett Rogers (1983) created classifications to measure levels and degrees of innovation and innovativeness. However, the OECD countries only started to conduct innovation surveys systematically from the 1980s. In 1993, 12 European countries conducted the first-ever co-ordinated survey of innovation activities.[23] It was based on the Oslo manual

28 *The meaning of innovation*

(*OECD Proposed Guideline for Collecting and Interpreting Technological Data*), which had been adopted by the OECD in 1992[24] (and is now in its third edition[25]).

The whole point of this methodical work was to develop output indicators. It would measure innovation by measuring the products, processes, and services that arose from innovation activities, but as Godin (2002) shows, it strayed from this objective to focus on activities. To this day, this division creates uncertainty in the value of the measurements. National governments and the OECD ended up measuring innovation by the way they measure R&D – in terms of input factors and activities (ibid.). But, since innovation also can and should be understood as the degree to which it has impact, a comprehensive system would have to account for both input and output.

Godin (2002) points to three factors that explain the current practice of innovation as an activity rather than as an output:

- The reliance on the linear model by policy makers (i.e. focusing on what comes out of basic research, not its effect)
- The control exercised by governments over measurement instruments (e.g. expenditures for activities – not using data or databases developed elsewhere)
- That innovation is a fuzzy concept (i.e. defined either as an activity/ process or as a product, being new to the firm or the world, etc.).

Innovation is, as we have seen, a multifaceted word, a concept that has permeated our language and our world to the extent that it is now a category in itself. Innovation has even become an end in itself (Godin, 2011). But the value of innovation also relies on it being something that can be understood, argued over, and compared. Put differently, one can argue that innovation is what can be understood or measured.

Innovation defined

It has been shown throughout this chapter that defining innovation is not a simple task. According to Schein (1998), the definition of innovation is itself a major problem. He goes on to say that it is "itself a property of culture."

When going through the literature on the topic of innovation, one striking aspect is the variety of meanings, interpretations, and definitions that unfold. On the one hand, the richness of descriptions speaks to the "living" and "evolving" value of the concept; on the other, since it is so hard to find an agreed-upon definition, the concept could be said to have lost its real value.

A brief historical overview

As discussed earlier in this chapter, the concept of innovation is of Greek origin from the fifth century – *kainotomina*. It derives from *kainos* ("new") and originally means "cutting fresh into." To Greek philosophers, it meant two things: introducing novelty (of any kind) or introducing political or constitutional change (Godin, 2012a). Innovation comes from the Latin *innovationem*, the noun of action deriving from *innovare*. The *Etymology Dictionary*[26] describes *innovare* as dating back to 1540 and stemming from the Latin verb *innovates*, meaning "to renew or change."

During the Middle Ages and after, innovation continued to mean novelty; it was not until the twentieth century that it started to obtain the meaning that we understand today (Godin, 2011). Godin (2008) suggests a genealogical history of innovation through the three concepts of "imitation," "invention," and "innovation." But the story of innovation is also the story of an idea that, far from the negative connotations associated with its origins, has been redeemed to the extent that, starting with Schumpeter's study of business cycles (1939) and continuing into today, it is almost an exclusively positive term. Today innovation is virtually regarded as a panacea in politics, business, and everyday life. Of course, there are voices of dissent – for instance, Jill Lepore (2014), who claims that "The idea of innovation is the idea of progress stripped of the aspirations of the Enlightenment, scrubbed clean of the horrors of the twentieth century, and relieved of its critics." But it is questionable if critics like her are criticising the actual concept, or rather the undying devotion to it, which shies away from some of its social consequences.

Innovation and its synonyms

Innovation is used interchangeably in literature and in everyday language with a number of other concepts and words. It is helpful to explore these in order to make distinctions and understand the different meanings and nuance in the literature. The following words tend to recur when scanning and analysing definitions and explanations of innovation:

- Invention
- Creativity
- Novelty
- Commercialisation
- Success
- Change

Many other words have also been used interchangeably with innovation over time. Some of the more common words to be found in texts from the twentieth century and onwards are as follows:

- New
- Newness
- Fashion
- Imitation

30   *The meaning of innovation*

- Reformation
- Original
- Alternation
- Revolution
- Altering
- Introduce
- Endeavour
- Enterprise
- Disruption
- Transform

By no means is this an exhaustive list, but already two things stand out: (1) all these words are primarily positive, but (2) at the same time, although they all exist in the same arena, they are also distinct. Given our purpose here, there is a need to find a common ground around what we mean when we speak about innovation.

Innovation and change

Griffin et al. (1993) state that innovation is to be characterised as a subset of the broader umbrella of organisational change. Here, we find a breadcrumb that trails to earlier meanings of innovation. The authors go on to say that although organisational change can include innovation, much organisational change is not really innovation at all. They also note that innovation may not always be about creating something new, but also the adaption of pre-existing products and services.

Creativity, newness, and innovation

Boden (1991) defines creativity as the ability to come up with ideas or artefacts that are new, surprising, and valuable. Following this, Griffin et al. (1993) define organisational creativity as the creation of valuable, useful new products, services, ideas, procedures, or processes through the cooperation of individuals working in a complex social system. They see organisational creativity as a subset of the broader domain of innovation.

Schumpeter (1934) defined innovation as consisting of any one of the following phenomena:

- The introduction of a new good
- The introduction of a new method of production
- The opening of a new market
- The conquest of a new source of supply of raw materials or half-manufactured goods
- The implementation of a new form of organisation

This is a fairly broad definition of innovation, essentially covering improvements in process and production. Although his definition doesn't refer to the adoption, impact, or success of what is being introduced, these were probably implicit in Schumpeter's thinking.

By this point, it is quite evident that the idea of innovation was already being transformed: far from its original meaning of "change," innovation was now to be understood as creativity (i.e. the deliberate work of man's imagination) (Godin, 2011). But what does creativity do? It emphasises originality: inventing something new or doing something differently. Schumpeter's definition goes even further and assumes that innovation holds value – at least to the organisation. Today, social scientists place explicit emphasis on utility or usefulness. Innovation is theorised in terms of introducing or adopting some novelty into practice.

What about the ideas of "new" or "newness"? Schein points out that defining what is "new" is problematic, which leads to problems defining innovation (Schein, 1998). He goes on to say that we must ultimately define innovation through the perceptions of both members within an organisation and the "outsiders" who interact with the product of that innovation. These "outsiders" are in a position to perceive the changes in question. If both groups – insiders and informed outsiders – think that something really is new, then it is likely an innovation. In this way, Schein sees innovation "as itself a property of culture" (1998).

Invention and innovation

The division between invention and innovation has been recognised by many scholars (Van de Ven et al., 2008). Schumpeter himself stated: "Innovation is possible without anything we should identify as invention and invention does not necessarily induce innovation." The distinction is one of economics: invention is an act of intellectual creativity and "is without importance to economic analysis" (Schumpeter, 1939: 84–85), whereas "innovation is an economic decision." According to Senge (1990), an invention is said to exist when it is proven to work in a laboratory, but only when it can be replicated reliably on a meaningful scale at a practical cost can it be considered an innovation. As Van de Ven et al. (2008: 9) state: "Whereas invention is the creation of a new idea, innovation is more encompassing and includes the process of developing and implementing a new idea." The *Collins Dictionary* puts it even more succinctly when comparing the two: "Invention means to create or devise something new," and "innovation means introduction of something new."

R&D and innovation

R&D is often associated with innovation, but they do not refer to the same thing. OECD's "Frascati Manual" (2015: 28) states:

- R&D comprises creative and systematic work undertaken in order to increase the stock of knowledge – including knowledge of humankind, culture, and society – and to devise new applications of available knowledge

32 *The meaning of innovation*

- A set of common features identifies R&D activities that aim to achieve either specific or general objectives, even if these are carried out by different performers. For an activity to be an R&D, it must satisfy five core criteria. The activity must be as follows:

  - Novel
  - Creative
  - Uncertain
  - Systematic
  - Transferable and/or reproducible

Different definitions – an overview post-World War II

Various different definitions of innovation stem from the idea of newness and the concept of a successful (and, most often, commercial) introduction. Something is an innovation when:

- An invention is introduced commercially as a new or improved product or process (Maclaurin, 1953)
- An idea, practice, or object is perceived as new by an individual or another unit of adoption (Rogers, 1983)
- A new technology or combination of technologies has been introduced commercially to meet a user or market need (Utterback and Abernathy, 1975)
- An act endows resources with a new capacity to create wealth (Drucker, 1985)
- People who engage in transactions with others over time within an institutional context develop and implement new ideas (Van de Ven, 1986)
- Individuals turn opportunity into new ideas and put those into widely used practice (Tidd et al., 2005)
- Organisations engage in a multi-stage process in order to transform ideas into new/improved products, services, or processes, in order to advance, compete, and differentiate themselves successfully in their marketplace (Baregheh et al., 2009)
- A viable offer is made that is new to a specific context and time, creating user and provider value (Kumar, 2013)

The above are just a sampling of definitions. In a survey of the literature on innovation, Edison et al. (2013) found over 40 definitions. They found the following to be the most complete:

> Innovation is: production or adoption, assimilation, and exploitation of a value-added novelty in economic and social spheres; renewal and enlargement of products, services, and markets; development of new

The meaning of innovation   33

methods of production; and establishment of new management systems. It is both a process and an outcome.

Although this may be a comprehensive definition it is not an easy one to remember.

Two more formal definitions of innovation are worth mentioning: the OECD (2005) definition and how it distinguishes product and technological innovation, and that of the United Kingdom Department of Trade and Industry (2007):

> A technological product innovation is the implementation/commercialization of a product with improved performance characteristics such as to deliver objectively new or improved services to the consumer. A technological process innovation is the implementation/adoption of new or significantly improved production or delivery methods. It may involve changes in equipment, human resources, working methods or a combination of these.
>
> (OECD, 2005)

> Innovation is the successful exploitation of new ideas.[27]
> (United Kingdom Department of Trade and Industry, 2007)

Again, the difference is striking. The OECD definition seems comprehensive but it does not take into account all categories of innovations discussed, for example, by Schumpeter (e.g. the opening of a new market, the conquest of a new source of supply of raw materials or semi-manufactured goods, or the reorganisation of an industry).

The United Kingdom Department of Trade and Industry definition is very short and easy to remember, yet also open to numerous interpretations.

The word or concept of innovation has been defined, therefore, in many different ways. Broadly speaking, these definitions fall into two categories, or a combination of these two: outcomes (i.e. the idea, product, service, or practice) and processes (i.e. the way something comes about, from idea to utilisation).

An illustration of the challenge with definitions

Freeman and Engel (2007) state that "innovation refers to a process that begins with a novel idea and concludes with market introduction." Here, innovation is seen as a process that starts when an idea is formulated and stops when it has been brought into the market. This definition suggests that invention by itself is not innovation.

What this definition lacks are the processes and events that precede a formulated idea and the actual success of the idea (e.g. product, etc.) in the marketplace. Furthermore, the term "market" tends to imply commercialisation, but today we often speak about other forms of innovation (e.g. social innovation) that do not necessarily have a commercial orientation.

Finally, this definition does not outline how "process" should be understood. Is it linear or more complex? Does process refer to *what* is happening (i.e. the steps, events, etc.) or more *how* certain things happen (i.e. fast, slow, etc.)?

Thus, the beauty of a short and concise definition may quickly be eroded by confusion and uncertainty.

In conclusion

Thus, innovation is not just invention, creativity, novelty, commercialisation, success, or change – it can encompass each of these aspects as well as all of them together.

The attempt to get to a workable definition leaves us with a few different points:

- Does innovation refer to a product or to an activity?
- Is it new to the world (or a given market) or to the firm?

I suggest the following working definition of innovation: *innovation is the process of bringing something different and valuable successfully into being.* This may be a bit loose, but it does address the point of newness and utility without compromising the many different ways in which this can be done.

Summary

This chapter has been dedicated to understanding innovation as both a word and a concept. The meaning of innovation can be addressed in many different ways. Here, we have offered a historical view of how the idea of innovation has changed over time. These days, it is a word that has penetrated all aspects of societal life. It is predominantly seen as a positive word, something to aspire to. There are different categories of innovation that can help us achieve clarity about what it is we are aiming for. These categories then indicate different ways to go about innovation. Measuring innovation is not a trivial aspect, but it is questionable how well this is being done today. Finally, although defining innovation is not so difficult, achieving consensus on the definition is. In this book we suggest (for the moment, as we have not yet taken the consequence of complexity theory into this definition) that innovation be defined in the following way: *the process of bringing something different and valuable successfully into being.*

In the next chapter, we will take a more thorough look at creativity and ideas as these are two qualities that are integral to the work of innovation.

Notes

1 Note. The actual page for the quote is not accessible from the Google Book library.
2 Merriam-Webster Online Dictionary.
3 Plato's *Republic* and *Laws*, Aristotle's *Politics*, and Polybius's *Histories* are examples of these political works.
4 There are several suggestions on when the First Industrial Revolution ended and the Second started and ended. Here, approximate years are offered.
5 From this point on, I will refrain from using the term 'goods,' but will instead use the more common expression 'product' – and use 'service' as a different category.
6 Even if it could be argued that we should have included in this section a sub-heading of "Experience innovation methods," it would not serve our purpose, since the design is for products, services, and events with a focus on the user experience.
7 See below for a more thorough discussion of the concept of disruption.
8 https://www.merriam-webster.com/dictionary/disruption
9 http://www.nytimes.com/2012/11/04/business/a-capitalists-dilemma-whoever-becomes-president.html?pagewanted=all&module=Search&mabReward=relbias%3Aw&_r=0
10 https://www.accenture.com/us-en/insight-from-digitally-disrupted-digital-disrupter
11 http://www3.weforum.org/docs/gcr/2015-2016/Global_Competitiveness_Report_2015-2016.pdf
12 https://www.bloomberg.com/news/articles/2017-01-17/sweden-gains-south-korea-reigns-as-world-s-most-innovative-economies
13 http://www.wipo.int/econ_stat/en/economics/gii/
14 https://www.forbes.com/innovative-companies/list/
15 https://www.fastcompany.com/most-innovative-companies/2017
16 https://www.bcgperspectives.com/content/interactive/innovation_growth_most_innovative_companies_interactive_guide/
17 https://www.wired.com/2016/12/2016-innovative-objects/
18 https://www.fastcompany.com/most-creative-people/2016
19 Read more here: https://www.forbes.com/sites/innovatorsdna/2015/08/19/how-we-rank-the-worlds-most-innovative-companies-2015/#5aa0fbc55f8c
20 https://ec.europa.eu/jrc/en/research-topic/measuring-research-innovation
21 http://ec.europa.eu/eu2020/pdf/COMPLET%20EN%20BARROSO%20%20%20007%20-%20Europe%202020%20-%20EN%20version.pdf
22 http://ec.europa.eu/research/innovation-union/index_en.cfm?pg=output
23 http://cordis.europa.eu/news/rcn/10048_en.html
24 http://www.oecd.org/officialdocuments/publicdisplaydocumentpdf/?cote=OCDE/GD(92)26&docLanguage=En
25 http://www.oecd.org/science/inno/oslomanualguidelinesforcollectingandinterpretinginnovationdata3rdedition.htm
26 http://www.etymonline.com/index.php?term=innovate
27 https://webarchive.nationalarchives.gov.uk/+/http://www.dti.gov.uk/innovation/innovation-dti/page11863.html

3 Creativity and ideas

Introduction

Creativity, the ability to create. To bring something out of seemingly nothing. What could be more God-like of our human qualities? Like Prometheus, who stole the fire and gave it to man, we have long been obsessed with finding out what can make us more creative. Creativity, creative people, creative processes, creativity management, and similar concepts all speak to the notion of creativity as vital to the individual, as well as organisational and societal life.

This chapter deals with creativity and ideas. It defines creativity and ideas in a way that is meaningful to innovation. Creativity permeates much of our everyday discourse and is often portrayed in media and organisational life as something attractive and desirable. For organisations competing in the Information Age, it is widely considered a distinctive and decisive factor for organisational vitality and success. Creativity is closely connected to the notion of ideas, but is not synonymous: whereas creativity is more of an ability, something required to generate ideas, not all ideas are considered creative. Indeed, most of our ideas are not seen by others as very creative.

There are some fundamental differences in how creativity is viewed. Some people view creativity as something only a few special people have, whereas others see it as something fundamentally innate to all human beings. Some believe something creativity can be improved, while others see it as a fixed quantity, the application of which makes the difference. Creativity can be viewed as something that is more or less triggered, a consequence of surroundings and input. Or it can be seen as independent of its context.

Logically, if creativity and ideas are desirable, it is in the interest of organisations to become skilled in managing and supporting creative processes and the generation of ideas, and there is a growing perspective that organisations can do so. It follows that more experience and knowledge, as well as better models, techniques, and focus, are important for managing creativity and the creative process.

Creativity is a key aspect of innovation. Depending on how one understands creativity, it is either absolutely vital for understanding and ensuring innovation, a possible source of innovation, or simply what underlies all possible sources and actions in terms of innovation. Innovation is not just a key focus area for business, it is a necessity. In the words of Leonard and Strauss (1997), it is a question of "innovating or falling behind: the comparative imperative for virtually all businesses today is that simple." But, as Amabile (1998) questions, "If the business climate is to innovate or die, why do so many companies seem to be choosing the latter option?" This is indeed an interesting paradox, but perhaps it is not only about making a choice; rather, it is also about the ability to innovate and understand the consequences of different courses of action.

This book suggests that organisations can support their own creative processes and outputs, even though, like innovation, these cannot be guaranteed as they are dependent on context. Following this section, we will discuss in more detail what creativity is before describing the theories of creativity that are relevant for innovation and innovation processes. After, we take on the subject of ideas and ideation – since it is one thing to generate or develop ideas, and another to evaluate and select them – before delving into the "front-end of innovation." The chapter concludes by discussing how creativity is supported and managed.

Creativity

Is there anything these days that is sought after by organisations and individuals alike? In addition to success and satisfaction in general, creativity would probably rank high. For example, industry giants like Google and Lego look for people that can think in new and different ways. In our everyday life, we often attribute creativity as something that is associated with art and culture. It is something that refutes categories or the effort of being pinned down. Although creativity is indeed hard to grasp and prescribe, we can still say something about it and work with it. But in order to do so, we need a better understanding of what it is.

There are various definitions of creativity. The Merriam-Webster online dictionary defines creativity as "the ability to make new things or think of new ideas."[1] Tamm (1987) says creativity is like "(by) thinking creating,"[2] meaning to bring something out of nothing. Boden (1991) argues that if we are to take the dictionary definition of creativity seriously (to bring something into being or form out of nothing), creativity seems to be not only unintelligible, but also impossible. She states that creativity is the ability to come up with ideas or artefacts that are new, surprising, and valuable. Csíkszentmihályi (1997) sees creativity as a process by which a symbolic domain in the culture is changed. Griffin et al. (1993) define organisational creativity as the creation of a valuable, useful new product, service, idea, procedure, or process by individuals working together in a complex social system.

Research on creativity has been carried out most frequently in the natural sciences, to a lesser extent in the arts and humanities, and to only a very slight extent in professional domains like management (Simon, 1986).

38 *Creativity and ideas*

Theories of creativity have focused on a variety of aspects. The dominant factors are usually identified as "the four Ps" – process, product, person, and place (Rhodes, 1961). Richard Ogle (2008) points to a series of important advances that have occurred over the last decades in the philosophy of the mind and the empirical brain/mind science that together open up a new way of understanding breakthrough creativity: the recognition that the mind extends beyond the brain, a renewed interest in the mind's imaginative faculties and the analogical qualities that underlie them, and the emergence of a new science of networks. In a summary of scientific research into creativity, Michael Mumford suggested: "Over the course of the last decade, however, we seem to have reached a general agreement that creativity involves the production of novel, useful products" (2003: 110).

Although Simon (1986) does not follow the distinction others make between innovation and creativity, most scholars do not consider them the same. Griffin et al. (1993) frame the definition of organisational creativity as a subset of the broader domain of innovation, where innovation is characterised as a subset of the even broader construct of organisational change. Although organisational change can include innovation, much organisational change is not innovation. Creativity without innovation is certainly possible, whereas innovation without creativity seems improbable. Edward De Bono sees creativity as essential to humanity and says we owe our success as a species to it (1971). Creativity is concerned not only with bringing about new ideas and updating outdated ones, but also escaping from irrelevant ones. Continuity is the reason for the survival of most ideas, not a repeated assessment of their value.

The simplest way to unearth a definition of creativity is to observe when people apply the term to some human act. Acts are considered to be creative when they produce something that is novel and that is thought to be interesting or to have social value (Simon, 1986).

Psychologists have long believed that creativity results from the formation of a large number of associations in the mind, followed by the selection of associations that may be particularly interesting and useful (Amabile et al., 2002).

Drawing upon Wallas (1926), Tamm (1987) divides the creative process into four phases: (1) preparation, where an idea is formed; (2) incubation, where the idea matures; (3) unnamed phase where the creative problem finds its solution through a sudden insight (an "aha" moment), and (4) verification, where the creative product is presented and "assessed" by the public. She states that the four-phase description must be considered a simplification of a much more complicated process.

Simon (1986) asserts that expertise is a prerequisite for creativity. "Accidental" discoveries are exceedingly common in the history of science (take, for instance, Becquerels's discovery of radioactivity, or Fleming and penicillin). While other scientists could have made such discoveries, they could not have been made by just anyone. As Tamm (1987) says: "Thousands

Creativity and ideas 39

of people have seen an apple fall from a tree, but it required a mighty thinker – Newton – to discover the principle (law) of gravity from such an occurrence." In reference to Sutton (2002), creativity isn't about wild talent so much as it is about productivity. Creativity draws crucially on our ordinary abilities. Noticing, remembering, seeing, hearing, understanding language, and recognising analogies: all these basic skills are important (Boden, 1991).

Human creativity is something of a mystery, to say nothing of a paradox. One new idea may be creative, while another is merely new (Boden, 1991). If by creativity we mean an idea or action that is new and valuable, then we cannot simply accept one person's own account as the criterion for its existence. Therefore, creativity does not happen internally, but in the interaction between a person's thoughts and a sociocultural context. It is a systemic rather than an individual phenomenon (Csíkszentmihályi, 1997). Griffin et al. (1993) state that individual creativity is a function of antecedent conditions, cognitive styles and abilities, personality, motivational factors, and knowledge. These individual factors are influenced by and influence in turn social and contextual factors. But as Boden (1991) observes, there might be more to creativity than expertise and commitment; inborn factors may also play a role.

In terms of understanding whether or not something is creative, March's (1976) notion of choice in organisations is helpful. He argues that we find it natural to base an interpretation of human choice behaviour on a presumption of the pre-existence of a human purpose. This reflects a strong tendency to believe that a useful interpretation of human behaviour involves defining a set of objectives that (1) are prior attributes of the system, and (2) make the observed behaviour in some sense intelligent vis-à-vis those objectives.

According to Simon (1986), the creative processes are problem-solving. Schön (1986) says that problems are not given: human beings construct them in their attempts to make sense of complex and troubling situations.

Effective problem-solving rests on knowledge, including the kind of knowledge that permits the expert to grasp situations intuitively and rapidly (Simon, 1986). But intuition is no mysterious talent. It is the direct by-product of training and experience that has been stored as knowledge.

There is another unspoken truth about creativity: it isn't so much about original creation as it is about using old ideas in new ways, places, and combinations (Sutton, 2002). Richard Ogle (2008) argues that creative breakthroughs come about when individuals and groups access new idea-spaces and exploit the principles that govern them. According to Johansson (2004), placing oneself at the intersection of different areas, disciplines, or cultures can lead to the combination of existing concepts into a large number of extraordinary ideas. This points back to a suggestion made by Leonard and Strauss (1997) on how to avoid dying because, rightly harnessed, the energy released by the intersection of different thought process propels innovation.

According to Boden (1991), creativity happens in three main ways: it occurs by making unfamiliar combinations of familiar ideas, exploring conceptual

40 *Creativity and ideas*

spaces, and transforming conceptual spaces in people's minds. Conceptual spaces should be understood as structured styles of thought. They are normally derived from one's own culture, but are also sometimes borrowed from others. As such, they are already present, so to speak, and are not created by one individual mind.

These spaces – manifested in forms as various as myths, business models, scientific paradigms, social conventions, practices, institutions, and even computer chips – are rich with embedded intelligence that we have progressively offloaded into our physical, social, and cultural environment for the sake of simplifying the burden on our own minds of rendering the world intelligible. Sometimes the space of ideas thinks for us (Ogle, 2008: 2).

Creativity theories relevant to innovation

As we saw in the previous section, there are several ways to understand creativity. Bringing creativity into the workplace and into an innovation process requires an understanding and some level of proficiency over the application of these theories and models. It is important to remember that even if much surrounding ideas and creativity seems like a mystery, decades of research have gone into this area. So even if creativity cannot be prescribed, there are a number of theories that can help us improve. In their book *Creativity as A Bridge Between Education and Industry Fostering New Innovations* (2014), Tanner and Reisman outline a number of theories relevant to innovation.

In terms of the specific creative processes used by creative people, George Wallas' four-stage process[3] – from his book *The Art of Thought*, published in 1926 – is one of the first complete models of the creative process. It involves the following:

1 **Preparation**: where preparatory work on a problem occurs, involving focusing the individual's mind on the problem and exploring the problem's dimensions
2 **Incubation**: where the problem is internalised into the unconscious mind and nothing seems externally to be happening
3 **Illumination**: where the creative idea bursts through from its preconscious processing into conscious awareness
4 **Verification**: where the idea is consciously verified in terms of appropriateness, elaborated upon, and then applied

One can ascertain that the idea behind this theory (or model) is that creativity and creative thinking is largely a subconscious process that cannot be steered or guaranteed, and that analytical thinking is not in opposition to creative thinking.

Another important theory concerns creative problem-solving (Ravenell, 2018), i.e. The Osborn-Parnes creative problem-solving procedure from

Creativity and ideas 41

1959. Creative problem-solving is the ability to view a problem from different angles and the attempt to solve it in a new way. Osborne, an advertising executive in the 1940s, proposed that getting more people in the room and having them follow a simple procedure would generate more – and better – ideas. Even though brainstorming is probably the most widespread method for enhancing creativity and generating ideas, not all scientists are convinced about its effectiveness (Mullen et al., 1991). Regardless of how effective it really is, brainstorming is still a key theory and approach for the practical application of creative problem-solving. The process is normally divided into three main steps, each including two parts:

1 Fact-finding

   a   Problem definition (Picking out problem)
   b   Preparation (Gathering and analysing data)

2 Idea finding

   a   Idea production (Generating ideas and possible leads)
   b   Idea development (Selecting, adding, and reprocessing ideas)

3 Solution finding

   a   Evaluation (Verifying tentative solutions)
   b   Adoption (Deciding on and implementing final solution)

All of these procedural steps require careful effort and, indeed, creativity. As well, the model calls for an understanding of the difference between divergent and convergent thinking and their applicability in the process.

Amabile (1983) brings forth a combination of diversity and motivation. She suggests that intrinsic motivation is superior in generating creativity than extrinsic motivation. Furthermore, she suggests that diverse teams are required. People should come from different parts of the organisation to nurture different perspectives, exploration, and discussion. These individuals should not only come from different departments, they should also have different areas of expertise, abilities, and perspectives. This diversity leads to new and divergent ideas.

Csíkszentmihályi (1997) looks beyond the individual to focus more on the interplay between people, the discipline, and the field. From this perspective, certain individuals (often managers or leadership) can permit or inhibit creative behaviour. The theory of "flow" is also very linked to the idea of creativity as it suggests that people are at their happiest when they are in the state of flow – i.e. being completely involved in an activity for its own sake. To reach a state of flow, there must be a balance between the skill of the actor and the challenge of the task.

Indeed, both Csíkszentmihályi and Amabile lean towards intrinsic motivation, which then becomes a slightly more challenging managerial task in terms of enhancing the level of creativity.

42 *Creativity and ideas*

Organisations do not just assume that they can bring anyone onboard and that, with good technique and structure, creativity will spontaneously flourish. They actively hire people they consider to already be creative. But what constitutes a creative person is also a question to ponder. Different theories about defining creative people have been suggested.

Abraham Maslow's famous *Hierarchy of Human Needs* (1943 and 1974) helps us understand how humans intrinsically partake in behavioural motivation. It is of interest in terms of managerial consideration on several levels. As an example, the theory suggests that if basic needs are not met (e.g. safety, belonging, etc.), more advanced stages into his "pyramid" will be irrelevant. The highest levels – esteem and self-actualisation – are the ones that we most easily associate with creativity and ideas. So if we are not seen, or recognised, we don't develop sufficient self-esteem and as such we would not trust our own ideas and capacity for creative thinking.

The Torrance Test of Creative Thinking (1966) is probably the most used creativity measurement in the world. It is a psychometric test that measures creativity along different scales[4]: Fluency (i.e. the total number of interpretable, meaningful, and relevant ideas generated in response to the stimulus) and Originality (i.e. the amount of detail in the responses).

Sternberg (1986) proposed his Triarchic Theory of Human Intelligence which argues that creativity is a balancing act between three forms of thinking: analytical, creative, and practical. Managers tend to be trained in analytical thinking and often deal with judging, criticising, analysing, comparing, and assessing. In contrast, the creative involves imagination, discovery, and invention, and the practical concerns everyday problem-solving.

Howard Gardner (1983) suggested the theory of multiple intelligences. He initially proposed that the following types of intelligence exist: linguistic, logical-mathematical, musical, spatial, bodily/kinesthetic, interpersonal, intrapersonal, and naturalistic. Later, he suggested that existential and moral intelligences might also be included as forms of intelligence. Even though Gardner's theory is primarily associated with learners and learning, it is relevant to creativity since being a better learner and exercising different forms of intelligence imply a higher chance of exhibiting creativity. It should also be noted that Gardner's theory has also received criticism for lacking empirical evidence, and being too ad hoc and simplistic. Regardless of the criticism, his theory, along with the others, has impacted the ways organisations and managers think about creativity, skill, and learning.

Ideas and ideation

What are ideas, really? This may seem like a somewhat irrelevant question, but it can be of value to consider what defines an idea. Ideas are concepts, a way to frame something, and they often suggest a potentiality and valuable difference.

The consideration of ideas stretches back in history and philosophy. Plato offered a view on ideas that seems quite different from how we normally consider the concept today: he suggested that ideas exist independently of people, and that ideas are what separate opinion from knowledge.

In terms of the classic, stereotypically linear innovation process, ideas are generally seen as the fruit of creativity and the start of the innovation process. In that context, ideas represent an unrealised potential value. But ideas are integrated far more broadly into the innovation process: they are not just as a precursor to the "real" innovation process, but are also vital solutions and ingredients throughout the entire process. Ideas are often the consequence of stimuli, internal or external. They are closely connected to problems, challenges, and opportunities, as ideas may arise as a consequence of these phenomena. In reverse, ideas can also generate problems, challenges, and opportunities. Whitehead (1961) suggests that an idea is "a force that can create movement and transformation or maintain the status quo." The description of an idea as a force suggests that it has power in itself, regardless of the power of the one who came up with it. Whitehead's assertion echoes the famous quote by Victor Hugo: "There's nothing more powerful than an idea whose time has come."

It is questionable if ideas happen in isolation or if the generation of ideas depends on stimuli. As social creatures, humans interact with their environments. Saatcioglu (2002: 1) proposed a definition that takes into account the relational involvement: "An idea is a cognitive impulse enabled by social experience." In terms of innovation, an idea is simply a thought or a suggestion that makes progress on either a problem, a challenge, or an opportunity. It can also simply be the perception of a situation.

Ideation is commonly seen as the creative process that brings forth ideas. It includes generating, developing, and communicating (new) ideas. Like creativity, ideation is not necessarily confined to early phases in (or before) the innovation process, but rather occurs throughout the innovation process. Ideation has been criticised as meaningless jargon, which may hold some truth to it since it is simply a different name for creative techniques and for what creative process generates. On the other hand, the term may help steer managerial activities and detach it from the broader term of creativity. In the end, it is a matter of preference.

Evaluation and selection of ideas

In terms of innovation, the creative process is aimed at generating more and better ideas. But how do we define "better"? How should this activity be handled by the organisation? Depending on which methodology is used, the creative process involves phases for narrowing down (i.e. assessing and selecting ideas) as well as phases in which one or several ideas are selected for further development in the innovation process. An example of such a model is the Double Diamond Model, proposed by the British Council. Similar to

44 *Creativity and ideas*

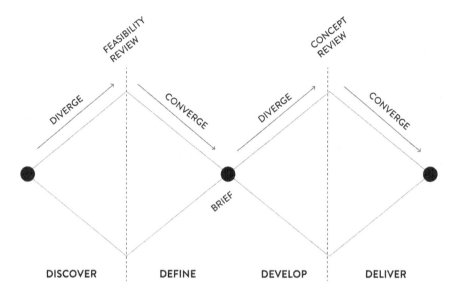

Figure 3.1 Freely after British Council.

Osborne's line of thinking, there are divergent and convergent phases in this model. Convergent phases are about selecting specific ideas to move forward with (Figure 3.1).

The selection of ideas is a critical phase. Koen et al. (2001: 51) assert that "… the critical activity is to choose which ideas to pursue in order to achieve the most business value." Moreover, selecting ideas is also about risk management. The ability to reduce risk during this phase lowers risk later on (Sherman et al. 2005: 401).

How ideas are selected varies significantly. How does one compare one idea with another? Financially speaking, we can make decisions based on return on investment, discounted cash flow, and so forth, but these considerations may be too far-fetched and complicated to apply at this stage. In addition, not all innovations necessarily involve financial considerations. On the other hand, financial considerations cannot be ignored since profitability is ultimately the bottom line for companies.

Developing a set of criteria seems logical as way to look at one idea in relation to another. This also provides transparency. A structural approach to assessing and selecting ideas makes sense on a motivational level among an organisation's employees as it provides a rationale for the selection of particular ideas.

The criteria can be quite varied from organisation to organisation but they frequently involve considerations regarding organisational strategies and objectives, culture, and organisational resources. The criteria tend to fall into two main categories: risk and reward. Büyüközkan and Feyzioglu (2004) suggest a model for new product idea evaluation, using the criteria of benefit and the criteria of risk.

The model offers an interesting perspective as it considers the tangible/intangible and systematic/unsystematic. Like other models, this one is highly subjective. As criteria are critical to the assessment of ideas and inform their choice, companies should explore which criteria actually fit the organisation in question and their particular situation. Questions around the impact of the idea on potential clients, market considerations, financial projections, and development and productions costs are only some of the criteria to consider.

The main difficulty is not deciding between a bad and a good idea, but rather between multiple good ideas in situations where applying the criteria is not decisive. Oftentimes, this is when the true quality of experience and judgement calls comes into play. It is not just the sheer quality of an idea, i.e. as would be considered by an expert group. Rather, it is about having the organisation accept it. The best idea is the idea that is acted upon. As some people may favour an idea that has not been chosen, and given that acceptance and support for implementation is critical, a key aspect is getting that decision-making process right – that is, it is transparent, fair, and rational. This is a key aspect of managerial responsibility and a decisive success factor of the "front-end of innovation" phase.

The messy front-end

The "front-end of innovation" is a term that has gained prominence in the last two decades. To some extent, the phrase overlaps with ideation, ideas, and creative processes, but it is also a term that encapsulates virtually everything that comes before the choice of which products and services a company will develop. That is, the term includes much of what happens before any ideation process occurs, as well as stimuli (e.g. information on trends, new discoveries). Koen (2007) suggests that the term includes the activities that take place before a Stage-Process and New Product Development. Most experts agree that the phase ends with the agreement about which idea(s) will be taken further.

Exactly what happens in this phase and what an effective front-end process look like is a bit obscure. Cooper (1998) proposed a four-phase description: the generation of an idea, initial screening, preliminary evaluation, and concept evaluation. Even though Cooper's description does not oppose other descriptions, others have broadened the scope in different ways. Khurana and Rosenthal (1998) bring to the table a need for product strategy, communication, and planning, and Tatikonda and Rosenthal (2000: 402) increase the focus on projects, suggesting a division of new product development into project planning and execution. Project terminology in general seems quite potent in terms of being applied to creativity and ideas by giving those concepts direction and format. Indeed, Darsø (2001) and her work on innovation proposed a pre-project labelling for this unformed and malleable phase. She (ibid.) distinguishes the "project" phase as one in which the goal is to search and diverge. In contrast, she sees the project phase is goal-oriented and convergent. The project phase is linear, limited in time, and driven by results and decisions. On the other hand, the "project" phase is non-linear, demands "chaos time," is process-driven, and requires an open decision room.

The "front-end of innovation" is not really fuzzy, nor is it just a standardised, linear, or confined phase. Below is a general model that encompasses the more widely recognised activities in this phase. In the model, learning allows for continuous improvement as well as for better management of original uncertainties as knowledge is created along the way. In general, this phase involves exploration, creativity, and validation (Figure 3.2).

One interesting aspect of this phase is not only what it contains (i.e. stages and areas), but also the way one works in this phase. Today, a lot of effort is given to researching the world and trying to nail down a challenge worth investigating. In the last decade, methods from the design community have started gaining more prominence in this phase. The root of many of these fashionable methods and techniques often stretches back to anthropological and ethnographical toolboxes. These are simply paired with creativity techniques and business verification logic.

This phase is vital: it deserves much attention, since it is in this phase that resource allocation for further development occurs. Getting this phase right does not guarantee success, but it is far more promising to start with ideas that have been tested and validated. The cost of changes and experiments in this phase is also lower than having to redo work later in the process.

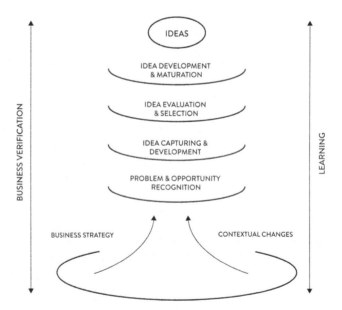

Figure 3.2 The FEI Process.
Source: Author.

Management and nurturing creativity and ideas

As organisations come to understand that creativity and ideas are vital for success, increasing focus is allocated towards this area. But since this phase and space is often difficult to define, it is an area that is difficult for leadership to manage. This is perhaps also the driver for the development of concepts like ideation and the front-end of innovation. By defining these concepts, explaining the space of creativity becomes easier and the idea and exercise of control and influence is maintained, giving comfort to managers.

Vandenbosch et al. (2006: 260) suggests that idea management is a way to support ideation and the front-end of innovation. Often, the main challenge is not the ideas themselves (or the lack of ideas) but rather the management and implementation of them.

According to Amabile (1998), managerial practices affect creativity. They fall into six general categories: challenge, freedom, resources, work-group features, supervisory encouragement, and organisational support.

In terms of managing creativity, however, management depends on influencing the accomplishments of others (Simon, 1986). As such, the peculiar characteristic of managerial creativity is that we must assess it not by the personal accomplishment of managers, but by the achievements of the organisations for which they are responsible (Simon, 1986). As Sutton (2002) points out, the only thing that is more important than optimism is the capacity to drop a bad idea.

However, not everyone is equally devoted to creativity. Ted Levitt (1963) argues that creativity as it is commonly defined – the ability to come up with brilliant or novel ideas – can actually be destructive to business. According to Levitt, putting innovation in the hands of

> creative types, is the worst thing a company can do. These people disdain much of what companies and organisations are all about – mundane realities of organisational life – and designed to do – by their very nature promote order and routine. They are as such inhospitable environments for innovation.

Nonaka and Takeuchi (1995), who examined several successful Japanese companies, saw creativity and knowledge creation as important to the success of organisations. Yet creativity does not necessarily flourish in organisational settings. Amabile (1998) points out that creativity is killed much more often that it is supported. The problem is not that managers smother creativity intentionally, but rather that business needs for coordination and control can inadvertently undermine the ability to put existing ideas together in new and useful ways.

Leonard and Strauss (1997) assert that the manager who is successful at fostering innovation has figured out how to get different approaches to grate

48 *Creativity and ideas*

against one another in a productive process they call "creative abrasion." Managing differences effectively is imperative because today's complex products demand the integration of the expertise of individuals who do not innately understand one another.

Amabile et al. (2002) state that time pressures have a hampering effect on creativity because creativity depends on immersion in the problem or challenge. Csíkszentmihályi named this mental state "flow" (see an earlier section in this chapter).

The best way to avoid undue time pressure is to articulate goals throughout all levels of the organisation that are realistic and carefully planned, avoiding the optimism bias that plagues much of corporate planning (ibid.).

Amabile (1998) notes that intrinsic motivation is the most potent lever a manager can use to boost creativity and their company's future success. While extrinsic motivators may not prevent creativity, in many situations it does not boost creativity either.

Levitt (1963) argues that ideation is relatively abundant; it is implementation that is scarcer. The proof of the value of ideas is through their implementation. Furthermore, Sutton (2002) states that finding a few ideas that work requires trying many that don't, and that filling a company with great ideas requires filling it with great people.

Some innovations spring from a flash of genius, but most result from a conscious, purposeful search for opportunities (Drucker, 1985). This process requires diligence, persistence, and commitment. According to Simon (1986), the traits in management and business that seem to characterise unusually creative companies are as follows:

- Sensitivity to opportunity and the ability to marshall fluid resources to initiate new programs of activity
- Attention to strategic planning; to understanding relevant future trends, opportunities, and developments; and to the setting of long-term goals
- An openness to adventure, even with the risk of failure

Summary

Ideas and creativity are a vital component of the innovation process. Even if by its very nature it is difficult to stipulate great ideas, growing understanding regarding *contextualised* ideas as the real focus (as opposed to a focus on the great ideas themselves) is gaining ground. A fit between opportunity, resources, and risk is necessary. But even though increasing focus is allocated to this precious stage of the innovation process, more research (and innovation) is still necessary. Ultimately, it is not only about ideas and creativity but what a company can do with those elements. That will be the focus of the next chapter.

Notes

1 http://www.merriam-webster.com/dictionary/creativity.
2 I have translated Maare Tamm's definition from Swedish, "skapande tänkande," published in *Psykologi* (1993), page 93.
3 Wallas four-stage process is sometimes presented as a five-stage process, then including intimation as stage three.
4 Examples taken from Wikipedia, https://en.wikipedia.org/wiki/Torrance_Tests_of_Creative_Thinking

4 The making of innovation

Introduction

Creating innovation, innovations, or innovative organisations is not a linear, straightforward endeavour. There are numerous challenges associated with managing innovation, but balancing profitability and the need for renewal seems to be the hardest part. Even if there is no "one size fits all" formula for innovation, new ideas often emerge when we cannot make existing systems or the categories we have available to us accommodate new developments (Darsø, 2003). Achieving innovation is difficult, because it takes place when different ideas, perceptions, and ways of processing and judging information collide (Leonard and Strauss, 1997). This requires collaboration between actors who see the world in very different ways, which leads to inevitable disagreement and arguments that often end up in conflicts rather than creative tensions.

Creativity is the complex product of a person's behaviour in a given situation (Griffin et al., 1993). The situation is characterised in terms of the contextual and social influences that either facilitate or inhibit creative accomplishment. The person is influenced by various antecedent conditions, and he or she brings to bear both cognitive abilities and non-cognitive traits or predispositions. As creativity can be a co-creational act, the level of complexity and challenges increase, but so do opportunities. Widening the scope to include innovation increases the complexity further.

Attempting to innovate can be seen as an application of the creative act towards value creation. In the same way that not all creative thinking leads to clear and concise ideas, not all clear and concise ideas lead to new products and services. Creativity and ideas seem to come from everywhere – from everyday interactions with potentially anything. When analysing what makes innovation possible, there are a number of factors throughout the innovation process that present themselves. Whereas some appear perhaps less crucial after closer inspection, some remain important over time. These could encompass specific people, technological breakthroughs, or changing market conditions. When examining what makes an innovation possible, we must pay attention to certain existing – and, specifically, changing – conditions. Drucker's seven

The making of innovation 51

sources of innovation offer a potent beginning for understanding the elements that should exist or change in order to allow for innovation to occur.

From this initiation, organisations have different ways of bringing innovation to life. Some have a very strict, conscious, single approach; others have a pluralistic approach; and still others seem quite unaware of how they actually make innovation happen. Over the last many decades, models for innovation have evolved. At least, our understanding of the complexity of generating innovations has evolved and we are now much more aware of the challenges with the very simplistic, but communicative, models of the past. Models in general are aimed at explaining how things happen, but they can also be formative and impact how an activity should occur. Our understanding of innovation models, then, also impacts what is actually possible in an organisation. Thus, the perceived and stated model may be either a hindrance or an aid for bringing innovations to life.

A newly introduced product or service is labelled a "successful innovation" only after it has been proven in the market. Certainly, market failures of products and services (or their improvements) are much more common than commercial successes, which is a significant drawback (Kusiak, 2007). As Simon (1986) remarked: "Chance, in the words of Pasteur, favours the prepared mind." It seems expertise and commitment are the major characteristics to look for when preparing the way for innovation.

Innovation management can be understood as how we deal with innovation. But management tends to be drawn towards control, predictability, and essentially a reductionist approach, and this also impacts how we look at innovation. Innovation management is a necessary aspect of innovation, but a balance is needed between what and how to manage in the sense of controlling and predicting, and what and how to manage in sense of letting go and allowing for uncertainty. Today, much of the literature on innovation management highlights three areas of management responsibility: organisation, competition, and value realisation.

This chapter is divided into the following sections: sources of innovation, models of innovation, innovation processes, and innovation management.

Sources of innovation

We can have a better chance of identifying what spurs and propels innovation depending on how we define it. Creativity can be viewed as something quite fundamental: the ability to create and foster ideas. But understanding innovation – given our previous discussion on defining the word – benefits from a more precise orientation of where innovation possibilities stem from.

Perhaps the most illustrative identification of innovation sources was presented by Peter F. Drucker in his book *Innovation and Entrepreneurship* (2006), in which he states: "Entrepreneurs innovate and innovation is the specific instrument of entrepreneurship" (ibid.: 44) and "systematic innovation therefore consists in the purposeful and organised search for change, and in the

52 The making of innovation

systematic analysis of the opportunities such change might offer for economic or social innovation" (ibid.: 49). Drucker thus sees innovation as a tool, a way to change something. It is about purposeful, focused change that will serve the organisation well.

What is highlighted here is the identification and analysis of opportunities. The criteria for choosing them should consider the scope for improvement with respect to customers, suppliers, and internal processes. Innovations must be focused on success in the marketplace.

Drucker's seven sources of innovation are (ibid.) as follows:

1 Unexpected success or failure

   Opportunities to innovate can arise from understanding the reasons for the unexpected success or failure of a product. Drucker offers the case of IBM, which wanted to sell accounting machines to banks but discovered that it was libraries that wanted to buy these machines. If a product fails, it can give companies new ideas that may help them to come up with something that the market wants.

2 The incongruity between what actually happens and what was supposed to happen

   Scope for innovating can be found if things are not happening. Examples could be when a failure to reduce costs opens the way for someone else to do so, or in growing industries where margins are falling. Drucker offers the case of the how container ships emerged by focusing on the ship's turnaround time rather than fuel efficiency.

3 The deficiencies in a process that are taken for granted

   If a process is inefficient or suffers from a big gap, there is scope to innovate. At times, a process that is widely used may have certain shortcomings. An innovator, by thinking differently, may come up with a new idea that removes this shortcoming. Drucker points to Pilkington's float glass manufacturing process as an example of something that paved the way for the development of glass with a smooth finish.

4 The changes in industry or market structure that catch everyone by surprise

   Serving the needs that arise from the emergence of new, fast-growing segments provides scope for innovation. According to Drucker, the success of the small, floppy-disk drive manufacturers had much to do with the emergence of new customer segments who wanted smaller and lighter disk drives.

5 Demographic changes

   Demographic changes result in new wants and new lifestyles that desire or demand new products. Demographic changes provide innovation opportunities that are the most rewarding and the least risky, as the trends are easier to predict. For example, Drucker points out that robotics was pioneered in Japan due to the anticipation of rising levels of education and the consequent shortage of blue-collared workers.

The making of innovation   53

6   Changes in perception
     New needs can be created by changing the common perception of people. As an example, by capitalising on general concern about health and fitness, a thriving industry has emerged for exercise and jogging equipment.
7   The changes brought about by new knowledge
     Innovative products can utilise new knowledge for its development. Usually, innovations of this sort combine many types of knowledge. As an example, Drucker proposes the development of the computer, as it was facilitated by a combination of binary arithmetic, calculating machines, punch cards, audion tubes, symbolic logic, and programming. He (ibid.) also points out that such innovations are also risky, because there is usually a gap between the emergence of new knowledge and its conversion into usable technology, and another gap before the product is launched in the market.

Drucker's seven sources of innovation were presented above in increasing order of difficulty. He asserted:

> Contrary to almost universal belief, new knowledge is not the most reliable or most predictable source of successful innovations. For all the visibility, glamour and importance of science-based innovation, it is actually the least reliable and least predictable one.

Apart from Drucker's seven sources of opportunity for innovative organisations, two other sources can be added:

Internal development   Although it might arguably fit under Drucker's third source, this can also be its own category. Internal inventions, improvements, or changes may not only reduce internal costs or increase output, they can also be sources of new products and services. An improvement in one place may be equally valuable in others.

Changes in legislation   This may arguably underlie several of Drucker's other categories, but it is in itself such a potential game-changer that it is worth highlighting. Take, for instance, the current focus on climate change, the environment, and sustainability. New standards and demands may open up for new entrants and approaches.
     Opportunities to innovate are provided by new customer segments which are just emerging, customer segments that existing competitors are neglecting or not serving well, new customer needs which are emerging, and new ways of producing and delivering products to customers. According to Drucker, "New opportunities rarely fit the way the industry has always approached the market, defined it, or organised to serve it. Innovators therefore have a good chance of being left alone for a long time."

54 *The making of innovation*

Models of innovation

When we speak about models of innovation, we normally associate them with explanations of *how* innovation happens. As such, they rest upon an idea of what innovation is (see Chapter 2). Some use the concept of a "model" to discuss the organisational format from which innovation originates. For example, Freeman and Engel (2007) discuss the corporate model and the entrepreneurship model. Most scholars, though [for instance, Rothwell (1992, 1994)], view and explain innovation models in more generic terms: for example, as how companies structure their innovation processes over time, as how scholars interpret the processes that happens, or sometimes as how scholars (and practitioners) think it should be done.

According to Godin (2006), the linear model of innovation is one of the first conceptual frameworks developed for understanding the relationship between science, technology, and economy. It did not arise from the mind of one individual, but was rather developed over time in three steps. The first of these connected applied research to basic research, the second brought experimental development, and the third supplemented this with production and diffusion. Sequential descriptions, such as invention to diffusion, were introduced by economists from the late 1940s to the early 1950s (Godin, 2013b).

While the majority of early studies on innovation are clearly Western, one could argue that the first main model of innovation was actually developed by the Soviet inventor and patent specialist Genrich Altshuller (1926–1998). Altshuller began to work on the model, later called TRIZ (in English, the "theory of the resolution of invention-related tasks"), in 1946, but his first article on the topic was not published until 1956. In his work, which involved assisting the initiation of invention proposals and the preparation of applications to the patent office, he recognised patterns among the proposals. He started researching in order to develop a set of generic rules that would explain the creation of new, inventive, patentable ideas.

After correlating thousands of patterns, he discovered that all industries used the same underlying inventive principles (Sheng and Kok-Soo, 2010). These principles could be generalised and applied regardless of industry. He found that a problem demands an inventive solution if there is an unsolved conflict in which improving one parameter negatively influences another. Based on this finding, Altshuller developed a contradiction matrix as an extension of the 40 conceptualised principles. In that matrix, the contradictory elements of a problem were catalogued according to a list of 39 factors that could impact the others. After completing the analysis of patents required to create TRIZ, Altshuller identified five different levels of innovation (see Table 4.1), together with the frequency with which they appear in the database of patent literature [e.g. by Vincent (2001) and Cortes Robles et al. (2009)].

Even though the five levels of innovation do not exactly constitute an innovation model (since they comprise more a classification of inventions and

Table 4.1 Five levels of innovation by Altshuller (Vincent, 2001)

Level	Description	Origin of knowledge	% of patient
1	Apparent solution: solution by/ methods well-known within specialty (slight changes in parameters)	A person	32
2	Small improvement inside a paradigm: improvement of an existing system without changes in functional principle	A firm, a company	45
3	Substantial invention inside technology: essential improvement of existing system, changes in functional principle	Inside an industrial domain	18
4	Invention outside paradigm: new generation of design using science not technology	All industrial domains	4
5	Discovery: major discovery and new science (essential changes in civilisations)	Set of knowledge	<1

TRIZ more resembles a problem-solving model), Altshuller's work helps us understand the background of the development of innovation models and their relationship to technology and science (Table 4.1).

One of the leading scholars on innovation process models is Roy Rothwell. The following models of innovation are largely influenced by his division of generations (Rothwell, 1992, 1994). It is important to note that a shift from one generational model to another does not mean that the previous one has disappeared or that progress has necessarily occurred. The models may be linked, used in parallel, and so on. The transition from one generation to another has more to do with changing attitudes.

First generation – the linear technology model

As stated previously, the linear model of innovation is an early model that developed over time. It is considered to be the first generation of theoretical models (Rothwell, 1994; Godin, 2006, 2013). In this model, innovation is *pushed* through different phases. Collins (2006) portrayed the process like a funnel, where an organisation pours a number of ideas into the top and at the other end innovations come out. Two alternatives of the same process are described by Godin (2006), as well as by Savioz and Sannemann (1999) for a single product. Godin (2006) describes a move from basic research, to applied research, to development and finally to production and diffusion. The model by Savioz and Sannemann (1999) also consists of four phases but

56 *The making of innovation*

are labelled: product idea, product development, production, and product introduction.

This model was widely used from the 1950s to the end of 1960s. During those years, companies sought scientific advances and built production capacity to achieve economic growth. One can say that the view of the customer (and the market) was simplistic: that is, what was being sold was also being bought. Still, the push model stresses scientific importance over subsequent phases, which means it incorporates market information very late in the process. Because of this, it is also a highly criticised model (Fagerberg et al., 2006). As early as the 1960s, the model had numerous opponents, primarily due to its linearity (Godin, 2006). However, this model has been by far the most influential one, due to its simplicity. Moreover, official statistics have gathered data according to its three components (basic research, applied research, and development).

Second Generation – the market pull model

The other linear model is the market pull model (Rothwell, 1994; Collins, 2006). Here, the market or the customer (i.e. the needs or wants of society or a certain group in the market) is the stimulus for innovation. This need is captured by an entrepreneur or company, who ideally have accurately understood the requirements and are able to provide a desirable solution. The model arose in the mid-1960s, when growth in consumption power and increased competition altered market conditions. Rothwell outlines the four phases as: market need, development, manufacturing, and sales.

Although both linear models (push and pull) received criticism due to the way they disregard feedback and loops among their different stages, the market pull model has additionally been said to undermine the innovation process because it asks its customers what they want (Ulwick, 2002). In other words, the customer does not know that they want the innovation until it is presented to them.

As an example of the push model, research into the origins of the gasoline-powered motorcar reveals that necessity did not inspire its inventors. The automobile was not developed in response to some grave international horse crisis or horse shortage. National leaders, influential thinkers, and editorial writers were not calling for the replacement of the horse, nor were ordinary citizens anxiously hoping that someone would soon fill a serious societal and personal need for motor transportation. In fact, during the first decade of its existence (1895–1905), the automobile was a toy, a plaything for those who could afford to buy one (Basalla, 1988: 198).

So, where both the push and pull models are linear, the theory behind them differs in a crucial way: in the push model, the market is seen as the receiver of an R&D pursuit (a supply view of innovation), but in the pull model, the market is the instigator for appropriate technology to be developed which is then "guaranteed" a waiting market.

Third generation – the coupling of R&D and marketing

According to Rothwell (1992), the period from the 1970s to the early 1980s was characterised by high inflation and demand saturation. Rationalisation, consolidation, and a focus on costs became central to corporate strategies. Technological innovation was understood as coming from the combination or blending of technological possibilities and market needs. Opportunities were essentially created by coupling R&D and marketing, since innovation was seldom the output from either forces of technology (push) or forces of market (pull). Although this model is also sequential, it contains a new feature: feedback loops (Rothwell, 1992). Kline and Rosenberg's Chain-Linked Model (1986) is an example of a coupling model where the innovation process is divided into interdependent stages with feedback loops that link back to previous stages. According to Berkhout et al. (2006), third-generation models can be seen as "open R&D models," emphasising product and process innovation (technical), and neglecting organisational and market innovations (non-technical). As such, a company's new technological capabilities, rather than solutions for institutional barriers and societal needs, tend to be the focus.

A very simplified version of a model representing the third generation could be portrayed in the following way (based on the Kline and Rosenberg's Chain-Linked Model) (Figure 4.1):

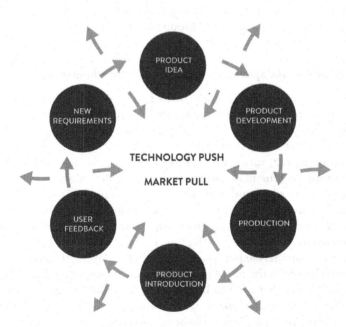

Figure 4.1 The coupling of R&D and Marketing model.
Source: Author.

58 *The making of innovation*

Fourth generation – the integrated model

Rothwell (1992, 1994) states that the fourth generation of innovation models marks the shift from viewing innovation as a predominately sequential process (where development moves from function to function) to viewing it as a parallel process. That is, the fourth-generation models include elements such as R&D, prototyping, and development taking place simultaneously.

As the economy recovered, lessons from Japanese manufacturers found their way to Western companies, emphasising collaboration with suppliers and customers as well as better integration internally. According to Berkhout et al. (2006), the history of the development of innovation models is often divided into three generations, but a fourth is needed to encapsulate current developments in open innovation networks. Fundamental changes in industry have generated a new commercial environment in which business processes cross traditional company boundaries and are brought together across industrial sectors, a notion that is shared by many authors on innovation.

Berkhout et al. (2006) proposes a model that replaces the traditional "chain concept" with a circle of change. This differs from Rothwell's suggestion, but it shares some of the same characteristics (e.g. that innovation is not a linear process and that there is a need for cooperation). Henry and Mayle (2002) refer to a model by Graves from 1987, describing new product development at Nissan. Here, emphasis is placed on bringing marketing, R&D, product development, product engineering, suppliers, and manufacturing closer together through, for instance, joint group meetings.

Fifth generation – the systems integration and networking model

According to Rothwell (1992), the fifth generation represents an idealised version of the integrated model whereby much stronger strategic integration drives innovation not only as a cross-functional process, but also as a multi-institutional networking process. As the 1990s unfolded, new technology found its way into business processes more rapidly and significantly, thereby automating them. Networking processes, the recognition of the need for strategic partnership, and tighter integration were ways to ensure not only flexibility but also the need for speed in development. But while fast and accelerated innovation processes were a way to increase competitiveness, they also increased development costs (Rothwell, 1994). Vertical relationships with customers and suppliers (e.g. those involved in the development of new products and/or sharing in the use of technical systems) took many different forms, including alliances. Yet most radical feature of the fifth-generation model is the increasing exposure to and reliance upon computers and electronic tools for innovation. An example that illustrates this is the systems integration and networking model by Trott (2005), which can be found in Du Preez et al. (2006). The model emphasises accumulation of knowledge over time, the integration between marketing and sales, finance, R&D and engineering and manufacturing, as well as external inputs towards the firm.

Table 4.2 summarises this comparison of innovation models [based on Rothwell (1992, 1994)]. Rothwell's argument about these models begins with a consideration of the general economy and market conditions, which then frames the corporate strategy, which in turn informs the innovation model.

While the above classification serves as a valuable framework for understanding the historical development of innovation models, it cannot claim complete, universal representation. To do so would require all organisations to be affected in the same way by market conditions, as well as that organisations by and large (1) have an innovation model and (2) that their model results from corporate strategy. It also seems like the classification applies more to large enterprises than to start-ups, where even though market conditions may define the playing field, some rules of the game may have to be re-written.

As Rothwell illustrates (1992), investments in innovation are increasingly linked to corporate strategy as well as to an increasing understanding of what drives innovation. The models themselves have undergone changes: some have variations (e.g. the addition of phases such as "sales" to the first-generation model) and others have different applications or ways of structuring [e.g. "Stage Gate Systems" (Davila et al., 2006), which introduces readiness criteria for moving between the different phases]. Changes to industry have also created a need to develop the innovation model (e.g. as discussed by von Hippel, 1986, 2005, 2007; Senge, 1994; Chesbrough, 2003; Poole and Van der Ven, 2004; Berkhout et al., 2006; Van de Ven et al., 2008; Christensen and Raynor, 2013). Gassmann (2006) references Porter and Stern when he asserts that external sources of knowledge and innovation have become increasingly relevant.

Furthermore, externalisation of innovation is not only adequate for incremental development activities, but also for sources of radical innovation. Chesbrough (2003) claims that open innovation is "the new imperative for creating and profiting from technology." Chesbrough (2003) suggests open innovation as a new model and expands upon it several times (e.g. 2005 and 2006). Du Preez et al. suggest it at as the sixth-generation innovation model (2006).[1] Hartmann and Trott (2009) argue that many may consider this paradigm to be little more than the repackaging of the last 40 years in innovation management literature. Furthermore, they argue that this model has gained traction due to its simplicity (as well as the fact that it retains the linear notion of science in the marketplace) and "the partial deception which was created by describing something which is undoubtedly true in itself (the limitations of closed innovation principles), but false in conveying the wrong impression that firms today still follow these principles."

Another model that has gained attention is the User Innovation model (von Hippel, 1986, 2005, 2007) or user-driven innovation. Normally it refers to the users of something an organisation has produced, as opposed to the

60   *The making of innovation*

Table 4.2 Typology of innovation models, based on Rothwell (1992, 1994)

?	Time period	Market Conditions	Corporate Strategy	Innovation Process
1G	1950s to mid-1960s	• Characterised by post-war recovery, the growth of new technology-based sectors, and the technology-led regeneration of existing sectors • Introduction and rapid diffusion of major new product ranges • Demand exceeds production capacity	• Corporate strategic emphasis on R&D and manufacturing build-up	Technology push: • Simple linear sequential process • Emphasis on R&D • The market is a receptacle for the fruits of R&D
2G	Mid-1960s to early 1970s	• Period of general prosperity	• Emphasis on corporate growth, both organic and acquired • Growing level of corporate diversification • Conglomerates formed through acquisition and merger • Capacity and demand more or less in balance • Growing strategic emphasis on marketing	Need-pull: • Simple linear sequential process • Emphasis on marketing. • The market is the source of ideas for directing R&D • R&D has a reactive role
3G	Mid-1970s to early 1980s	• Period of high inflation and demand saturation • Supply capacity exceeds demand	• Strategies of consolidation and rationalisation with emphasis on scale and experience curve benefits • Some de-diversification • Growing strategic concern with accountancy and financing issues (cost focus)	Coupling model: • Sequential, but with feedback loops • Push or pull or push/pull combinations • R&D and marketing more in balance • Emphasis on integration at the R&D/marketing interface

The making of innovation 61

?	Time period	Market Conditions	Corporate Strategy	Innovation Process
4G	Early 1980s to 1990	• Period of economic recovery	• Concentration on core businesses and core technologies • Growing awareness of the strategic importance of emerging generic technologies with increased strategic emphasis on technological accumulation (technology strategy) • Growing emphasis on manufacturing (manufacturing strategy) • Growth in strategic alliances, strategic acquisitions, and internationalisation in ownership and production • Global strategies	Integrated model: • Parallel development with integrated development teams • Strong upstream supplier linkages • Close coupling with leading edge customers • Emphasis on integration between R&D and manufacturing (design for marketability) • Horizontal collaboration (joint ventures, etc.)
5G	1990s–	• Major impact of new technologies • High rates of technological change • Intense competition	• Rapid product cycles with growing strategic emphasis on time-based strategies • Increased intra-firm and inter-firm integration (networking) • Integrated technology and manufacturing strategies • Emphasis on flexibility and product diversity and quality • Continued emphasis on technological accumulation • Environmental issues of growing strategic concern	Systems integration and networking model: • Fully integrated parallel development • Use of expert systems and simulation modelling in R&D • Strong linkages with leading edge customers ('customer focus' at the forefront of strategy) • Strategic integration with primary suppliers, including co-development of new products and linked cad systems • Horizontal linkages: joint ventures, collaborative research groupings, collaborative marketing arrangements, etc. • Emphasis on corporate flexibility and speed of development (time-based strategy) • Increased focus on quality and other non-price factors

62 *The making of innovation*

suppliers of that organisation. These "users" can be intermediate (e.g. user companies or organisations) or end-users and communities (e.g. individual consumers). Where it has its obvious advantages in ensuring a more valuable output, it can also help build the company (Magee, 2008). However, this model also suggests challenges to bringing forth radical innovation since customer may be inclined towards "me-too" solutions (Ulwick, 2002).

Innovation processes

Rothwell (1992) sees the innovation process as that by which innovation is commercialised. It follows that one can define models of innovation as models of an innovation process(es). The different innovation models presented so far in this manuscript have all been explanations, interpretations, or idealised illustrations of how innovation arises. Kusiak (2007), however, presents a generic innovation process, applicable to different types of capitalist organisations (Nambisan and Sawhney, 2007). Even though the model (i.e. the process) takes a starting point from the process of innovation intermediaries (invention-, innovation-, and venture capitalists), it can be seen as a potential framework for how executives go about innovation within (or without) their companies. Furthermore, it could be argued that Kusiak's generic innovation process (2007) is a way to present an innovation model across five basic activities, without paying much attention to the complexities involved. The five activities in Kusiak's generic innovation process model are search, evaluate, refine, develop, and connect.

This model resembles the Stage-Gate Model presented earlier in this chapter, and in its simplified presentation, it seems very linear. However, since the visual is not descriptive, it says very little about how each phase comes about. In the search phase, for example, ideas can arise from everything from brainstorming to customer feedback. Ideas are then evaluated for fitness, and, if selected, those ideas will be refined and developed according to corporate strategy and other requirements.

Often present is an underlying idea of controllability – that is, that managers should be able to control processes of innovation (Aasen and Johannessen, 2009) – that is rooted in the notion that many companies actually do survive and renew over time (Tidd et al., 2005). However, innovation processes are essentially complex and uncertain (Tidd, 2001). Van de Ven et al. (2008), referencing Dooley and Van de Ven (1999), describe how divergence and convergence are core processes underlying most theories of organisational change and development. They echo what March (1991) described as an exploration (of new opportunities) and exploitation (of old certainties). Austin and Darsøe's (2009) work around closure in the innovation process can be viewed as a deeper investigation of the moment in which cyclical behaviour shifts from one behaviour to another. Takeuchi and Nonaka (1986) point to three changes in the product development process: (1) a more adaptive management style due to less project linearity, (2) a new type of learning that harnesses accumulated knowledge from across the entire organisation and its boundaries, and (3) a new mission or a new view on the product development where it is not only a generator for future revenue but also a catalyst for organisational change. As Van de Ven et al. (2008: 66) state, "If an innovation is to have a chance to succeed, traditional notions of managerial control may need to be relaxed somewhat. It is not that such letting go will ensure success, merely that it may be a necessary condition."

There is no real formula for innovation (Darsø, 2003). However, a language is emerging that eases our understanding of early innovation processes in a way that helps further them. Schön (1986) and Morgan (1996) suggest that managers will benefit from using a greater diversity of models as metaphors or lenses through which they can obtain new knowledge and identify new opportunities. One example of this is the suggestion of comparing the innovation process with a journey (Van de Ven et al., 2008, Austin and Darsøe, 2009).[2] To some extent one can see similarities and draw inspiration from religion, folklore, and other related genres (consider, for example, Odysseus or Buddha). The idea of the journey may also draw on imaginary related to the archetypal "hero's journey" that is often portrayed in movies (Campbell, 1993). Many times, such a journey begins with a call (i.e. the task, the longing, the need). A group is then summoned that brings together a diverse number of skills, expertise, and experiences – and, along with that, the development of trust, respect, and commitment among team members. The team encounters problems that need to be overcome in order to reach the end. The process includes framing and reframing the problem, including challenging one's own knowledge and assumptions and learning along the way. This view of process as a journey of discovery and exchanging the old for the new through transformational learning can also be seen in associated areas [e.g. Otto Scharmer's Theory U (Scharmer, 2009)].

Innovation management

According to Aasen and Johannessen (2009), recent literature on innovation management brings into focus three particular areas of management responsibility: organisation, competition, and value realisation. Organisation involves the identification of organisational characteristics for promoting company innovativeness and innovation management. Competition involves competitive conditions (see, for instance, Grant, 2001 and Teece et al., 1997) as a way to understand decisions that are seen as strategically important, implying that managers can choose a strategic view towards innovation, depending on available resources and the competitive context. Value realisation refers to factors that have an impact on the outcome of innovation processes.

Whereas this entire book can be said to address these areas, this section takes a closer look at how innovative organisations are created. The idea of innovation management is important because it can be seen as a difference in the form, quality, or state over time of the management activities in an organisation,

64 *The making of innovation*

where change represents a novel or unprecedented departure from the past (Van de Ven, 1986; Van de Ven and Poole, 1995: 512; Hargrave and Van de Ven 2006). Birkinshaw et al. (2008) define innovation management as the invention and implementation of a management practice, process, structure, or technique that are new and that are intended to further an organisation's goals. Hamel (2006) states that innovation management changes how managers do what they do, and that in large organisations, the only way to change how managers work is to reinvent the processes that govern that work.

Aasen and Johannessen (2009) suggest that innovation management involves participatory actions intended to influence emerging patterns of themes, in support of the collective movement towards a desirable future. The view presented by Birkenshaw et al. suggests the introduction of novelty in an established organisation and subsequently a particular form of organisational change. Although there are similarities, Aasen and Johannessen present something different in nature. Here, innovation is "communicative interaction," leading to the experience of evolving patterns of themes.

Van de Ven et al. (2008) argue that managers at different hierarchical levels are involved in the management of innovation and that, despite the general view that managers have a uniform, common viewpoint, managing innovation does involve diversity and conflict.

There is a challenge in finding common ground around what exactly is being innovated, but Birkinshaw et al. (2008) suggest two levels of analysis: (1) the more abstract management of ideas (e.g. scientific management, TQM, and the learning organisation), and (2) the more operational level (e.g. management practices, processes, and techniques, as well as organisational structures). According to Aasen and Johannessen (2009), the obvious challenge is to create an environment of perpetual innovation, where everyone is committed to excellence, resulting in growth and sustained competitive advantage. Furthermore, the main challenge seems to be the ability to simultaneously manage the demands of profitability, which is necessary for immediate survival, and innovation, which is essential for long-term viability (Tidd et al., 2005; Aasen and Johannessen, 2009).

Kaplinksy (2011) describes the innovation cycle in a classic way (essentially in line with previous push models) but points out the importance of management (Tidd et al., 2005) as a crucial role throughout the development and application of knowledge, as well as in the phases of invention and innovation.

Summary

In this chapter we have discussed the making of innovation. In a simplified view, it can be seen as how creativity and ideas are brought to the dissemination phase. We also added to Drucker's sources of innovation "internal changes" and "legislative changes."

Models and processes describing how innovation arises are popular among both researchers and managers. As the understanding of the complexity of innovation has increased, so have the models and the descriptions of the processes. Today, organisations develop procedures and practices, even if they do not necessarily recognise them as models or processes. It is a clear managerial responsibility to continuously develop to ensure effectiveness in the innovation process. Innovation management as a topic, and also as a set of abilities within organisations, is an increasingly important aspect of organisational life.

In the next chapter we will look at how innovation truly becomes innovation – i.e. by the spread and uptake of ideas, methods, products, and services.

Notes

1 They also suggest that there is a seventh-generation model – the Extended Innovation Network – which combines Open Innovation and network models.
2 Many innovation experts and consultancies have used the analogy of a journey, such as John Kao (Jamming, Innovation Nation, etc.), David Sibbet and the Grove Consultants, and Kaospilot.

5   The spread and uptake of innovation

Introduction

Everyday conversations in organisations and media seem to put a premium on creativity and ideas – the front-end of innovation – and not so much on how these are introduced into the marketplace. On the other hand, researchers have for decades been interested in how the spread and uptake of innovations occur.

How innovations spread and are taken up by users and consumers is of utmost importance to research, organisations, and society at large. From a theoretical standpoint, it is arguable that one can actually talk about an innovation if that innovation has low traction, since that would indicate that the "innovation" has low value. In a sense, it can be seen as a failure of the innovation process. This suggests that one can evaluate the success of one innovation compared to another through its success in the marketplace. More sales, more use, and more changes could all be considered "clinical" end points of the implementation of the innovation process. It goes without saying that for an organisation, innovation that simply remains an R&D effort has little or low value if it does not produce some sort of perceived value – at the very least, for the organisation itself. Questions around effective dissemination and uptake of new ideas, findings, and innovations are also very much a societal issue as they can promote significant societal gains in terms of healthcare, education, sustainability, etc. In short, the more one can understand the process of adoption, the more probable that challenges with adoption can be tackled and subsequently lead to initial implementation.

An adoption process is normally viewed as a process where the consumer or user moves from one state to another, starting with a pre-adoption phase (Wisdom et al., 2014). Adoption normally starts with the recognition of a need, and moves to the search for solutions and initial decision-making, then to the attempt to adopt a solution, and ultimately to the actual decision to proceed with the implementation of the solution (Damanpour and Schneider, 2006).

The focus on diffusion and adoption started to gain momentum in the US between World War I and World War II in rural sociology. As agricultural technologies evolved, researchers investigated how farmers adopted new inventions such as techniques, equipment, and hybrid seeds (Valente and Rogers, 1995). Over the years, the interest and focus on diffusion and adoption has spread and been applied to many fields and contexts. Adoption is an individual process detailing the stages from first hearing about a product to finally adopting it. Diffusion signifies a group phenomenon, which suggests how an innovation spreads. The key to adoption is that the individual must view the innovation (i.e. the idea, behaviour, product, or service) as new and valuable. It is by this that diffusion is possible. This also emphasises the importance of branding and marketing.

The sequence from making an innovation public or available to its use and adoption is not necessarily linear. More often than not, organisations try to predict consumer and user preferences, and subsequently attempt to adhere to and/or influence them. As such, this process is not only a push effort, but more of a mix between push and pull.

Several theories and theoretical frameworks exist to study how innovations spread and are adopted. Tabak and Khoong (2012) synthesised a collection of 61 theoretical frameworks that are necessary for quality dissemination and implementation research. Wisdom et al. (2014) identified and reviewed 20 theoretical frameworks. In this chapter, diffusion theory, bounded rationality, theory of reasoned action (TRA), consumer behaviour theories, the role of branding and marketing, and absorptive capacity are introduced and examined as ways to understand the spread and uptake of innovation. There are other theories as well, such as Extension Theory, which comes from rural sociology (like diffusion theory) and has over time become more aligned with communication and social psychology (Röling, 1988). However, as it has been mostly used in the field of agriculture, we will not discuss it further here.

Note: while all of the below outlined theories have been exposed to critique for various reasons, it is not within the scope of this book to offer a full review of those criticisms, however valuable they may be.

Diffusion theory

In 1962, Everett Rogers promoted diffusion theory in his book *Diffusion on Innovations* (Rogers, 1995). It is one of the oldest social science theories, and it aims at explaining why, how, and how quickly ideas and technology spread. Adoption is the "end-state" of a new idea, behaviour, product, or service, which implies that the individual who has adopted an innovation is behaving differently now compared to before. According to Rogers (2003), there are four chief elements that affect the spread and adoption of an innovation:

- The innovation itself
- The communication channels
- Time
- The social system (i.e. the nature of society where the innovation is introduced)

Rogers (1995) explains that diffusion is not a singular, all-encompassing theory in itself but rather an umbrella term that consists of four main theories:

68 *The spread and uptake of innovation*

innovation-decision process theory, the individual innovativeness theory, the rate of adoption theory, and the theory of perceived attributes.

The innovation-decision process theory describes five stages that one undergoes when adopting an innovation: knowledge (becoming aware of the innovation and learning about it), persuasion (learning and becoming convinced about the merits of the innovation), decision (considering advantages and disadvantages and making a choice to either adopt or reject the concept of change), implementation (using the innovation to some extent and assessing its value), and confirmation (ratifying or not ratifying the decision to adopt the innovation).

The individual innovativeness theory suggests that adoption is a process and obtains traction by different groups of people over time. When promoting an innovation to a target group, appreciating the characteristics of the target group that will support or hinder adoption of the innovation is key. Some people adopt an innovation earlier than others, and researchers suggest that these groups have different characteristics:

Innovators (2.5%) enjoy being first and are not afraid of taking risks. This group requires little to nothing in terms of convincing, beyond the belief that the innovation is new and valuable.

Early Adopters (13.5%) are opinion leaders and welcome change. Since there is no real need to convince them about the need for change, it is more a question of providing them with information on how to change.

The Early Majority (34%) are never the ones to take the very first steps, but still adopt innovations before the majority. This group requires evidence in terms of usefulness and success stories.

The Late Majority (34%) are sceptical of change and follow only after successful use by the majority. This group requires evidence that many are already onboard and that the innovation has actually been valuable.

Laggards (16%) are resistant to change and are conservative and traditional by nature. This group requires perceived convincing material, such as statistics and the appeal to fear.

According to Rogers (1995), there are factors that may slow down or accelerate the diffusion process apart from the particulars at the individual level. Examples are as follows: how and by whom has the decision been made to adopt an innovation (e.g. by a central authority, collectively, or by individuals), which communication channels have been used to get the information (e.g. mass media or interpersonal), the nature of social system where the adopters act (e.g. their norms and values), and the promotion efforts by different change agents (e.g. by advertisers).

The rate of adoption theory is a theory that proposes that the adoption of the innovation follows an S-curve. It is slow in the beginning, but after some time, it accelerates until it starts to lose momentum and stabilises before it finally declines (Rogers, 1995).

The theory of perceived attributes proposes that the adoption of innovation relies upon five factors, which play a role to varying degrees in the innovation–decision process theory. These factors are as follows:

Relative Advantage the degree to which an innovation is seen as better than what it replaces

Compatibility the degree to which an innovation is coherent with the values, needs, and practices of the potential adopters

Complexity the degree to which the innovation is hard to comprehend and use

Triability the degree to which the innovation can be tried or tested with/without adopting it

Observability the degree to which the innovation delivers tangible results

More than 4,000 articles have been published across many disciplines on the topic of diffusion of innovations (Greenhalgh et al., 2005). What exactly triggers an adoption is hard to know and measure as the social processes are so complex. There are several well-documented limitations of the diffusion of innovation theory. Rogers (2003) himself described the criticism according to four groupings: pro-innovation bias, individual blame bias, recall problem, and issues of equality.

Bounded rationality

Bounded rationality is a theory that looks at the decision-making process as a whole, rather than dividing it into parts. It is valuable as it promotes an understanding of the intention behind decision-making processes, and it also highlights that decision-making processes occur based on imperfect information (Simon, 1991). The term "bounded rationality" was originally coined by Herbert Simon to describe his view that the classic idea that economic behaviour is fundamentally rational was wrong. In his view, this behaviour is neither fully rational nor totally non-rational. Simon asserted that today's complex world does not allow individuals to obtain or process the information needed to make fully rational decisions. So instead of trying to maximise decisions, the consumer should focus on "satisficing" decisions, where "satisficing" is a hybrid between "satisfy" and "suffice." In practice, this means that a practical decision-maker looks for satisfying courses of action rather

70 *The spread and uptake of innovation*

endlessly searching for the ideal solution. Instead, people make decisions that are good enough, representing outcomes that are reasonable or acceptable. The consumer considers only those factors that he is aware of, understands, and regards as relevant. For Simon, efficiency is the driving force, which can be viewed as the alternative that produces the largest outcome given the application of resources.

Thus, human decision-making requires a less grand view, representing these limitations. Simon called that view "bounded rationality" or "intended rational behaviour." He (ibid., 1991) defined bounded rationality as "the property of an agent that behaves in a manner that is nearly optimal with respect to its goals as its resources will allow."

Theory of reasoned action

The TRA describes the correlation between behaviours and attitudes when it comes to human action. It explains the drivers of individual behaviour and not how that individual makes decisions about adopting or rejecting an innovation. That is, it centres its analysis of the importance of pre-existing attitudes in the decision-making process. It is used mainly to predict how individuals, based on their behavioural intentions and attitudes, will behave. Ultimately, it suggests that an individual's attitude towards behaviour is linked to an assumption of how beneficial that particular behaviour is for them. The more valuable the behaviour is considered, the more positive the attitude.

According to this theory, specificity is key in the decision-making process. A consumer only acts when a specific result is expected. The consumer reserves the right to change his or her mind and to pursue an alternative course of action until the last moment. As such, a decision is only one, albeit important, step.

Martin Fishbein and Icek Ajzen developed this theory in 1967 to understand behaviour related to health, but they later suggested that it could be applicable in any context where there is a need to understand and even predict human behaviour (Fishbein and Ajzen, 1975).

An applied development of the TRA is the EKB model (Engel et al., 1978), which was developed in the late 1960s. It presents a five-step process that consumers engage in when making a purchase:

Problem recognition in which one identifies or generates consumer needs (i.e. a gap between an existing and an ideal situation)

Information search in which the consumer searches for information through his/her own memory and experiences as well as from external sources

Assessment of options in which the consumer examines other alternatives (influenced by beliefs, values, circumstances, intentions, etc.) in order to make the best decision

The spread and uptake of innovation 71

Choice in which a decision to purchase is made from the assessment of available options in the market. Changes in income, preferences, and other factors might affect the decision

Outcome in which the choice results in either satisfaction or dissonance, where satisfaction is a customer who is happy with their choice (i.e. the choice meets or exceeds expectations, values, etc.) and dissonance is a consumer who doubts the value of the choice, its relative value against other options, or is outright dissatisfied

Consumer behaviour theories

The theories that can be considered part of consumer behaviour theories vary significantly. For instance, some authors suggest that the theory of reason action and the Engel Kollat Blackwell Model of Consumer Behaviour are consumer behaviour models. This is arguably true given the broader orientation of consumer behaviour theories, but this would mean that Roger's diffusion theory would also be included. Because consumer behaviour theory is a very broad space, it is more helpful to categorise the theories in terms of spread and uptake of innovations.

Consumer behaviour theory (or theories) deals with how consumers (i.e. individuals, groups, and organisations) allocate their disposable resources when purchasing and using goods and services (i.e. these theories attempt to analyse and understand why, when, and how people make purchases). The theory is also concerned with the emotional, mental, and behavioural responses preceding and following these activities (Kardes et al., 2011). In short, consumer behaviour studies involve purchasing activities, use of consumption activities, and disposal activities (ibid.). The field emerged in the 1940s and 1950s within the marketing field, but it draws from and links to fields such as psychology, sociology, and economics. A basic assumption of the theory is that consumers try to maximise the utility or satisfaction from the expenditure of given amount of money. Because of this, it is a useful framework for understanding how an innovation can satisfy the wants of an adopter.

Since this book makes no distinction on the types of innovations being discussed (e.g. if they are aimed at business to business, business to consumer, or other alternatives), there are a few theories worth mentioning in this section, even though there will be some overlap with the next section branding and marketing.

One important theory that was mentioned in the chapter on ideas and creativity (Chapter 3) is the motivation-need theory (i.e. the hierarchy of needs) developed by Abraham Maslow. In this section, this theory supports the idea that innovations serve different needs, and that the way in which an innovation is portrayed and how it is appreciated will affect its adoption.

The Hawkins Stern Impulse Buying Theory (Stern, 1962) states that unexpected or sudden buying impulses fit together with more rational purchasing decisions. Impulse purchases are largely driven by external stimuli and have almost no relationship to conventional decision-making. Impulse buying is

72 The spread and uptake of innovation

"triggered when a shopper sees a product for the first time and visualises a need for it."

Other important aspects in consumer behaviour theories are (a) the area of risk (Dowling and Staelin, 1994) and (b) external influences (Torelli and Rodas, 2017).

The role of branding and marketing

According to the American Marketing Association, a brand is a "name, term, design, symbol, or any other feature that identifies one seller's good or service as distinct from those of other sellers."[1] Branding is the endowment of products and services with the power of a brand (Kotler and Keller, 2015). Marketing is defined by the American Marketing Association as "the activity, set of institutions, and processes for creating, communicating, delivering, and exchanging offerings that have value for customers, clients, partners, and society at large."[2]

According to Florea (2015), "despite being major components of the body of knowledge in marketing, the relationship between branding and diffusion of innovation is a blurred picture, without any clear view that sums up different perspectives of this relationship." But even if there is a lack of explicit and clear correlations, a link still exists. Most practitioners would argue that the role of branding and marketing is essential in terms of innovation spread and uptake, since they are integral to communicating the value of an innovation. It is virtually impossible to imagine any successful adoption and implementation of an innovation that does not involve branding and marketing activities, regardless of the purposefulness of those activities.

Branding can be seen as something that comes before marketing. It is an expression of a fundamental belief or truth – the essence or aspirations of an entity (e.g. an organisation, product, or service). Marketing is the way of bringing that value to the attention of customers and users in a way that is aligned with the brand.

As the market diffusion process describes how an innovation spreads through a market, branding and marketing are important in terms of understanding how to position and approach potential customers and users. It can be helpful for allocating resources and leveraging appropriate activities. For example, a somewhat simplistic take on the Rogers' model suggests that there is a critical point after the early majority adopts an innovation. The role of the marketer is to facilitate the adoption of a product or service by early adopters and the early majority in order to reach that critical point. When these groups have adopted the innovation, the momentum will support driving the innovation from introduction towards growth stages.

There are many different methodologies one can use when developing a tool, but among the most common are the development of:

- Brand definition
- Brand promise

The spread and uptake of innovation 73

- Brand positioning statement
- Brand identity

Marketing is a massive subject in terms of the spread and uptake of innovation. The most well-known and used methodology is the marketing mix and its 4 Ps:

- Product
- Price
- Place
- Promotion

Understanding purchasing and consumption behaviour is a key challenge for marketers. Consumer behaviour, in its broadest sense, is about understanding both how purchase decisions are made and how products or services are consumed or experienced. In terms of the spread and uptake of innovation, branding and marketing offer valuable ways of understanding and becoming more effective when it comes to the process of dissemination, adoption, and implementation.

Note: Innovation can occur within the areas of marketing and branding themselves (i.e. making these activities and propositions more effective). However, it is not within the scope of this book to address these topics.

Absorptive capacity

Absorptive capacity is a theory that differs somewhat from the others presented in this chapter in that it is perceived as an ability and is not primarily a decision-making model. Instead, it is about an organisation's capacity to obtain external information, comprehend its value, absorb it, and then apply the new information for business purposes. Cohen and Levinthal (1989, 1990) defined it as the firm's "ability to recognise the value of new information, assimilate it, and apply it to commercial ends."

Cohen and Levinthal view absorptive capacity as cumulative; that is, it is easier for a firm to invest consistently over time in its absorptive capacity rather than investing only once. As such, research and development (R&D) and the continuous investment in R&D are central to this model. Efforts made to develop absorptive capacity in one period make it easier to accumulate more capacity over time.

Zahra and George have shown that many other areas could be used for developing an organisation's absorptive capacity (2002). They reviewed the concept, expanding the original concept into "a set of organisational routines and processes by which firms acquire, assimilate, transform and exploit knowledge to produce a dynamic organisational capability."

They suggest two different absorptive capacities: potential absorptive capacity and realised absorptive capacity (ibid.). The potential absorptive capacity

74 *The spread and uptake of innovation*

consists of knowledge acquisition and assimilation capability, whereas realised absorptive capacity is made up of transformation capability and exploitation capability. The authors suggest a number of possible indicators that can be used to measure and evaluate each element of absorptive capacity:

Knowledge acquisition capability   The number of years ears of R&D experience and size of R&D expenditure

Assimilation capability   The number of cross-patent citations and number of citations from another firms' development

Transformation capability   The number of new product ideas and the number of new research projects initiated

Exploitation capability   The number of patents, new products, and the length of product development cycle (ibid.)

There have been some discussions on how widely one can utilise the theory of absorptive capacity before it becomes meaningless and about the value of distinguishing between potential and realised absorptive capacity. Similarly, some question whether transformation is a step that follows assimilation or if it is more likely an alternative to the first. Regardless, it is evident that absorptive capacity is a strong predictor of innovation adoption (Aboelmaged and Hashem, 2019) and is therefore important for an organisation's innovation capacity. Zou et al. (2018) conducted a meta-analysis on absorptive capacity, and they found:

- Absorptive capacity is a strong predictor of innovation and knowledge transfer, and hence financial performance
- The firm size to absorptive capacity relationship is positive for small firms but negative for larger firms
- The firm age to absorptive capacity relationship is negative for mature firms and not significant for young firms
- Social integration, knowledge infrastructure, management support, and relational capability all have a positive and significant impact on the relationship between absorptive capacity and innovation

The theory of absorptive capacity is studied not only on the level of the firm but also on the individual, group, and national levels. As a theory, it is strongly connected to the resource-based view of the firm (Barney, 1991) and dynamic capabilities (Teece et al., 1997) – indeed, it can be seen as a dynamic capability in itself.

Summary

This chapter has presented several theories on the topic of the spread and uptake of innovation. Diffusion theory, bounded rationality, the TRA, and consumer behaviour theories all offer different perspectives on the how innovations truly become innovations instead of simply remaining products and services. It is through their recognition and use that innovation is justified. Branding and marketing are key aspects as they point to an organisation's own efforts that can increase the likelihood of spread and uptake of innovations. Finally, absorptive capacity is different from the other theories as it more resembles an ability than a decision-making model. Insofar as it represents the capacity to turn new information into something of value, it can be seen an indicator of innovation adoption.

Learning is an increasingly important topic when it comes to innovation as it implies the ability to become better or different over time. In the next chapter we will discuss learning as a key aspect of innovation endeavours and the innovation process.

Notes

1 https://www.thebrandingjournal.com/2015/10/what-is-branding-definition/
2 https://www.ama.org/AboutAMA/Pages/Definition-of-Marketing.aspx

6   Organisational learning

Introduction

Learning is not as straightforward to encompass as one may think, even though we use the word regularly everyday speech, not to mention in schools. Learning is not restricted to human beings since animals and plants (and, today, even machines) are all capable of learning. As well, learning is not just about individuals: organisations and societies also learn, since learning is a useful way to cope with change and to increase well-being, organisational vitality, and societal gains.

There is widespread agreement that learning goes beyond mere memorisation and recall of knowledge. It involves such aspects as understanding, critical thinking, the ability to connect ideas and knowledge, and the capacity to transfer knowledge and skill from one context to another. Merriam-Webster defines learning as:

- The act or experience of the one that learns
- Knowledge or skill acquired by instruction or study
- Modification of a behavioural tendency by experience (such as exposure to conditioning)[1]

There are a few important considerations here. Learning is not something that someone does to another but rather an act performed on oneself (be that individuals, groups, or organisations). It is a response to the interpretation of stimuli and experiences. Learning changes something within the learner, and that change take place in terms of knowledge, behaviour (including skills), and attitude. Arguably, learning results in a relatively permanent, somewhat measurable change in behaviour. But there are a couple of questions here: Can behaviour change without actually learning something? And is it possible to learn something and yet not change behaviour?

In this book, we follow the definition by Ambrose et al., who define learning as "a process that leads to change, which occurs as a result of experience and increases the potential for improved performance and future learning"

(Ambrose et al., 2010). Furthermore, we will focus on human learning and will not differentiate between groups, organisations, and inter-organisations in terms of knowledge creation and learning.

There is a substantial body of work on the subject of organisational learning (OL). Chris Argyris and Donald Schön (1978) defined organisational learning as "the detection and correction of error," where an error is an incongruity of intentions and what really happens. On the same note of "bettering" or "enhancing," Fiol and Lyles see learning as "the process of improving actions through better knowledge and understanding" (1985). Huber (1991) emphasises that learning occurs in organisations if the range of the potential behaviour of the organisation is changed by processing information. In his review on OL literature, Dodgson (1993) suggests that it is a complex topic that requires a multi-disciplinary approach to obtain a fuller understanding. He (ibid.) views OL as "the way firms build, supplement, and organise knowledge and routines around their activities and within their cultures and adapt and develop organisational efficiency by improving the use of the broad skills of their workforces."

The idea of the learning organisation (LO) was coined by Peter Senge. In basic terms, it can be said that an LO continuously transforms itself and facilitates the learning of its members. Put differently, a "learning organisation is an organisation that is continually expanding its capacity to create its future by joining adaptive learning with generative learning, seeking out and mastering change" (Senge, 1990). Dodgson (1993) states that a LO "is a firm that purposefully constructs structures and strategies, to enhance and maximise Organisational Learning."

Connecting learning and innovation is important because we have seen in previous chapters that knowledge about innovation and obtaining new skills, as well as forming new procedures and approaches, is of utmost importance. But as an organisation, and also as individuals in the organisation, how we learn is also a matter for innovation as there may be advantageous reasons for organisations to ascertain how they learn best.

In this chapter, we will discuss OL in the light of innovation and also indirectly shed some light on the importance of viewing capacity building as a process that relies heavily upon learning. But, first, there will be some attention given to knowledge, knowledge management, and OL.

Goals and measurement

OL is not just something that happens in certain places, at given times, or at a specific pace. Instead, it is an organisation-wide phenomenon that occurs with different intensities and speed. It is essentially a condition that one can affect. According to Dodgson (1993), organisations learn in order to better their adaptability and efficiency in times of change, and Grantham and Nichols (1993) suggest that learning enables faster and more effective responses to a complex and dynamic milieu. Implicit in both of these views is that:

- Uncertainty demands learning
- The greater the uncertainties, the greater the need for learning

The goal of OL is to improve or retain effectiveness – that is, competitiveness, productivity, and innovativeness – in ambiguous and changing circumstances. However, learning is not only of interest to these overall objectives but to all levels.

Before discussing how to measure learning, let's turn our focus to the relationship between learning and intent, since learning is often assumed to be a desirable, planned activity.

Learning in organisations can happen by default (i.e. not intended) or according to a plan (i.e. intended), and can also be seen as desirable or non-desirable (Figure 6.1).

Clearly, the learning any organisation wants is one that is desirable, regardless of the intent. Non-intended, desirable learning can often be seen as local, self-directed learning when overcoming challenges in a new way or when trying to solve a matter. These learnings are unexpected. Unfortunately, organisations (or individuals in organisations) also learn non-desirable things as well. An intended and non-desirable learning could refer to a situation where what is learnt has a damaging impact: for example, the implementation of a new customer practice that is solely based on assumptions about the customer, and which turns out to be wrong. It is also true that organisations learn non-intended, non-desirable things. For example, employees may learn the behaviour of "talking behind others' backs" due to managerial practices that do not adequately address the needs of employees.

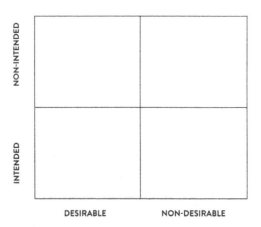

Figure 6.1 The intention-desirable learning matrix.
Source: Author.

Learning ultimately implies change on some level. After learning has occurred, something is different. Research in OL is interested in changes in the cognition, routines, and behaviours of an organisation and its individuals (Easterby-Smith et al., 2000). This also has some impact in terms of measurement, as it is questionable whether learning itself can be measured (as opposed to the effects of learning). There are different methods organisations and researchers adhere to when measuring learning.

One of the more common OL methods is called the learning curve. A learning curve displays the relationship between developments in productivity, quality, or efficiency (or other relevant output metric) in relation to experience (or a metric relevant to experience). Argote (2013) states that "large increases in productivity typically occur as organisations gain experience in production." It is no surprise that since OL rates vary, so do learning curves. Argote (ibid.) points out three factors impacting learning rates:

- Increased proficiency of individuals
- Improvements in an organisation's technology
- Improvements in the structures, routines, and methods of coordination

Most organisations do not measure as comprehensively as learning curves despite their obvious and quantitative advantages. Some organisations are simply unaware of this relatively simple framework. Others need more information about how to properly measure, and for still others, the nature of their work makes it difficult to develop measurable comparisons. For instance, a bespoke consulting company may make unique products and services with different specifications every time.

What organisations often do instead is to rely on self-assessment of different kinds (i.e. sense of learning). Sometimes, that self-assessment is combined or replaced with observations about changes in work practice that are often based on managerial, subordinate, or peer-to-peer reviews (i.e. relying solely on opinion). Or an organisation might consider learning in relation to changes in tangible outputs (similar to what the learning curve suggests). Oftentimes, however, there is little to no consideration of the output in relation to experience metrics (e.g. when a school make a new curriculum). Often, we measure what is easier, not what is necessarily important. The problem is that if learning is not properly assessed, we end up misinterpreting reasons for performance, making the wrong adjustments, or simply missing out on new opportunities.

Loops of learning

Organisations learn in different ways. Following previous statements on learning through experience, it is worth looking at Kolb's classic Experiential Learning Cycle. According to Kolb, "learning is the process whereby knowledge is created through the transformation of experience" (Kolb, 1984).

80 *Organisational learning*

Following this logic, learning is seen as a development process that has four stages. The individual (1) has a concrete experience, followed by (2) observation of and reflection on that experience, which leads to (3) the formation of abstract concepts (analysis) and generalisations (conclusions), which are then (4) used to test hypotheses in future situations, resulting in new experiences (McLeod, 2013).

In 1978, Chris Argyris and Donald Schön developed the idea of single-loop and double-loop learning, which focuses on the mismatch between intention and outcome. In response to a problem, one might look for a new way to remedy the situation. Another response might be to look at values and goals instead. The model helps us to understand that learning occurs on different levels in an organisation and that as an organisation, one can choose where to focus in any given situation.

- Single-loop learning refers to any situation where a mistake (or an error) has been noticed and then rectified by different means, but goals and policies and so on remain the same. Single-loop learning is also echoed by other writers and models such as Fiol and Lyles' "Lower-Level Learning" (1985), Senge's "Adaptive Learning" (1990), and Mason's "Non-Strategic Learning" (1993). Single-loop learning is not necessarily inferior to double-loop learning; it is simply different. Dodgson (1993), for example, argues that the activities performed enlarge the knowledge base or firm-specific competencies or routines.
- Double-loop learning is a more complicated process in which a mistake is amended by rethinking the initial goal, policies, and so forth. This type of learning does not rule out rectifying single errors. Again, other writes have used different names to refer to this type of learning, such as Fiol and Lyles' "Higher-Level Learning" (1985), Senge's "Generative Learning" (1990), or Mason's "Strategic Learning" (1993). Similarly, Dodgson (1993) states that apart from simply adding to organisation knowledge base or firm-specific competences, double-loop learning changes them.

Some authors have suggested a third loop, sometimes called Deutero-learning (for example, Visser, 2003, 2007) from Gregory Bateson, but here referred to as triple-loop learning.

- Triple-loop learning refers to the process whereby an organisation learns about how it learns and is able to change. It can feasibly be seen as a meta-loop of the single- or double-loop process, but it is here presented individually as it implies a different level of consciousness that not only aims at solving a given problem, but also improving the learning capacity of the organisation. It's about learning about and from single- and second-loop learning processes – and working on them.

Organisational learning 81

The first two loops as described above resemble the work of Watzlawick et al. (1974) on change. They suggest first- and second-order change, where first-order changes indicate changes that occur within the existing norms, and second-order changes refer to changes that occur when the norms of the system themselves are questioned and changed.

Knowledge creation, transfer, retention, and management

Dodgson (1993) states that OL happens when we generate an organisational knowledge base, firm-specific competencies, and routines. Knowledge bases are generated by acquiring, storing, interpreting, and manipulating information both from within and without the organisation. Mason (1993) suggests that strategic applications of information systems for knowledge acquisition can take two forms: assimilating knowledge from outside and creating new knowledge. This points to a managerial responsibility and focus towards knowledge, and it is becoming an increasingly important, organisational-wide task as the world is becoming increasingly more knowledge-based. Sustainable strategic advantages are gained more from an organisation's knowledge assets than from the more traditional types of economic resources (Drucker, 1993). This is echoed by Campos and de Pablos (2004) when they state that it is the "ever increasing importance of knowledge-based resources in today's competitive environment" that "calls for a shift of our thinking concerning organisational learning and innovation."

It is widely acknowledged that there are three main processes that push and, to some extent, condition OL: knowledge creation, knowledge retention, and knowledge transfer. This "raises questions about how organisations create, develop, deploy, renew and store knowledge, in sum, how organisations manage their knowledge" (Campos and de Pablos, 2004).

As experience is considered vital for learning, knowledge is of vital interest in terms of learning and innovation. Knowledge creation connects to creativity and its relationship to experience (Argote, 2011). A model for knowledge creation is the SECI model originally developed by Professor Ikujiro Nonaka in 1990, which presents four types of knowledge conversations:

- Tacit-to-tacit (socialisation)
- Tacit-to-explicit (externalisation)
- Explicit-to-explicit (combination)
- Explicit-to-tacit (internalisation)

After internalisation, the circular process continues at a new "level," hence the metaphor of a "spiral" of knowledge creation (Nonaka and Takeuchi, 1995).

Knowledge transfer can be considered part of the knowledge creation process if one assumes that knowledge creation is essentially a replication of

82 *Organisational learning*

existing knowledge by the "not-knowing" individual. However, it is more often than not considered something different. Nevis et al. (1995) point out that learning increases "information sharing," which can be seen as a form of knowledge transfer, but normally knowledge transfer is conceptualised as the way experience is disseminated and implants itself within the organisation. Knowledge transfer can be about both, for which to ensure it actually happens. Factors that impact the effectiveness of knowledge transfer stretch from the nature of the knowledge itself, to the view and understanding of the knowledge (including its importance and usability) and its transferring system.

Knowledge retention refers to the knowledge that has found its way into the organisation and is now established in some way. Knowledge retention does not necessarily occur all the time, but is considered part of an organisation's memory. One can conceptualise memory as existing in certain individual or combinations of domains (that may be explicit or tacit):

- Existing only within a person
- Existing between several people
- Existing between all people
- Existing as codified in the knowledge management systems
- Existing in the public sphere

It is quite evident that there is more risk of losing knowledge when it is retained in individuals, since the knowledge disappears when they leave the organisation. High levels of turnover only increase that risk.

The consequence for management is then that merely creating knowledge may not be enough. Transferring and retaining knowledge are important tasks, just as trying to make tacit knowledge more explicit is crucial. To connect back to the original reference to Drucker and the observation that the world is becoming increasingly knowledge-based, one could also add that it is also becoming increasingly more knowledge-oriented.

The learning organisation

In 1990, Peter Senge published *The Fifth Discipline*, which popularised the idea of the "learning organisation." According to Senge, "a learning organisation is a group of people working together collectively to enhance their capacities to create results they really care about." Dodgson echoes this idea when he states that a LO "is a firm that purposefully constructs structures and strategies so as to enhance and maximise organisational learning." Whereas the concept of a LO was enormously popular among organisations and practitioners in the 1990s, it seems to have worn off somewhat by the end of the first decade of the 2000s, perhaps due to research like the one performed by Nevis et al. (1995) on learning systems that concluded: "all the firms they observed were learning systems."

This is of course intuitively correct: an organisation that does not learn has slim chances of surviving. However, the underlying premise of a "learning organisation" is not that organisations do not learn, but rather that (a) how it learns can be affected, (b) some learn better than others, and (c) becoming better at learning increases the chances of achieving one's goals in a competitive market. As such, it is a concept worth revisiting in terms of OL and innovation.

Peter Senge (1990) presents five disciplines that together encompass the art and practice of the LO:

- Personal mastery
- Mental models
- Shared vision
- Team learning
- Systems thinking

Systems thinking is the fifth discipline of OL. To some extent, Senge considers systems thinking to surpass the other four disciplines, but all are seen as essential components that work together.

In the same way that individual learning is important for the individual, organisation, and society, so it is for OL. Learning is a way for organisations to grow and become better at handling challenges, such as catering for, adapting to, and feasibly affecting changes. What separates a random cohort of people from an organisation is that a rationale exists for those individuals to be part of that organisation, and the organisation itself has a purpose and has developed ways for collaborating in pursuit of its objectives. A LO, then, puts the focus of learning in an effective, coordinated format.

With conscious effort, organisations will not reduce their learning abilities when people leave. Instead, organisations become more resilient when they establish routines, cultures, and so forth, that are transmitted to new members and are adopted by them through being socialised into the organisation's values and norms. Learning also increases information sharing, communication, understanding, and the quality of decisions made in organisations. Stata (1989) argues that learning takes time, but once the process has started, it feeds on itself and organisational members improve their work more rapidly.

The other side to this is about forgetting or eliminating unproductive behaviours: that is, learnings that are obsolete and wrong, or that stand in the way of new and more important learning. Hamel and Prahalad (1994) speak of the need to develop an unlearning organisation in tandem with the LO. In practice, however, unlearning is a somewhat dubious concept, since it is impossible to unlearn some things (e.g. reading). The intention of "unlearning" makes sense in terms of obtaining better knowledge and behaviours. Instead of "unlearning," we could propose calling it "on-learning" to indicate that new learning becomes the focal point by being laid on top of existing knowledge.

84   *Organisational learning*

OL is different from individual learning in the sense that the former has a political dimension. An LO is the consequence of a political decision, and the results largely depend on power struggles and mediations within the organisation. This becomes very obvious when we observe how an organisation goes about becoming, seeing, or acting as an LO. In that sense, it is a question of "us," and how we view "us," as opposed to individuals. An LO then can be seen as a consequence of balancing factors such as structure, strategy, environment, technology, and culture.

As theoretical and other scholarly treatments of OL emphasise intangible and long-term benefits (Senge, 1990), an LO can be the result of improved OL with subsequent potential advantages.

Barriers to OL

There are numerous impediments when it comes to OL. Everything that promotes OL could also, depending on the situation, be considered a challenge. For example, culture is seen as key for learning and innovation, but culture can also be detrimental, depending on its nature. Barriers to OL may not necessarily prevent all or any learning, but they will prevent desirable learning.

If an organisation fails to effectively utilise the loops of learning – indeed, many cannot identify that there is a gap between intention and outcome – this will act as a hindrance. In the same way, if the spiral process suggested by Nonaka cannot be supported, there is no real development in terms of knowledge and knowledge creation. Senge would say that insufficient understanding, drive, and support of the disciplines of personal mastery, mental models, shared vision, team learning, and systems thinking would make an organisation a less effective LO.

Another way to look at barriers is to start with the barriers suggested by Schilling and Kluge (2009) and their contribution to the 4I framework as developed by Crossan et al. (1999). The 4I framework consists of four social processes: intuiting, interpreting, integrating, and institutionalising. There are a number of barriers connected to each of these four social processes presented as actional-personal, structural-organisational, and societal-environmental.

According to Saskia Harkema (2003), most learning theories rest on a sender-receiver model of knowledge transmission and this affects how people learn within innovation projects. She (ibid) goes on says that "a complex adaptive approach offers an alternative perspective from which one can evaluate and analyse learning and innovation processes." This may be true in some cases, but what is equally important is not just the notion of sender-receiver, but that the dynamic interplay within an organisation that fuels the potential for learning is supported. As the organisation learns more about how it learns effectively, this knowledge is fed back into the organisation and implemented. This process includes questioning and modifying existing norms, values, goals, procedures, and policies. This may lead to a tendency

Organisational learning 85

towards systems thinking, a culture that resists blame, reduced bureaucracies, increased communication, and freedom to experiment. These are considered basic in terms of innovation. As such, it all starts with an intention and purposeful action.

Innovation as learning, learning as innovation

Learning represents a strategic element in any innovative process (Senge, 1990; Dhanaraj and Parkhe, 2006; and many others). Innovation and learning have a strong linkage (Cohen and Levinthal, 1989), and there is a positive relationship between OL and both performance and innovation (Jimenez-Jimenez and Sanz-Valle, 2011). Superior organisational performance depends on a firm's ability to be good at innovation, learning, protecting, using, and amplifying these strategic intangible resources (Campos and de Pablos, 2004). Indeed, OL is essential for innovation (Landry, 1992), and it can be seen as a bridge between work and innovation (Brown and Duguid, 1991). Although the relationship is neither obvious nor clear in terms of OL and organisational performance, an analysis of empirical studies allows one to assume that there is an essential correlation between the two (Zgrzywa-Ziemak, 2015).

There are three considerations worth mentioning here:

- Organisations do not always recognise that they create knowledge
- Learning is often assumed but it is not prioritised on par with other desired outcomes
- When a change occurs as the consequence of learning it does not automatically lead to innovation in a classic sense

The theory of organisations has long been dominated by a paradigm that conceptualises the firm as a system that solves problems or processes information (Campos and de Pablos, 2004). Nonaka and Takeuchi (1995) argue that organisations need to produce knowledge to adapt and be successful. Innovation as a process can be seen as problem-solving, but in order to do so, it is dependent on producing new knowledge. As a result, knowledge creation and exploitation are keys for an organisation's ability to innovate.

The study conducted by Jimenez-Jimenez and Sanz-Valle (2011) found that age, size, and environmental and industry turbulence temper the relationship between OL, innovation, and ultimately business performance. As complexity grows, culture and structure become more centred on conversing rather than adapting, and insights in one area of the firm do not necessarily generate new courses of action. Although the organisation may have learnt new things, nothing is actively done with the learnings to produce an outcome.

The innovation process itself is a very indeterminate process, requiring commitment and time. The process requires knowledge, skills, and capacity on behalf of the individual, group, and organisation. Lee and Davis (2016) accentuate "the importance of facilitating active feedback between consumers

86 *Organisational learning*

and producers as well as using that feedback for diversification." As seen in previous chapters, an environment supportive of innovation requires a willing and skilled culture, structure, and leadership. Learning "about" and learning "how to" become pivotal tasks for the organisation, and the effectiveness of the learning process stands in direct correlation to culture, structure, and leadership.

There are always some challenges when it comes to what to learn and how to learn. As seen in the previous sections, organisations learn in different ways, and learning is not just a consequence of planning to learn – it also happens spontaneously. That means that innovation offers direct opportunity to learn about what works and what does not work. Here, we can add to the Argyris and Schön's views on loops of learning: it is fundamentally important to understand why something actually works and not only be preoccupied with the gap between intention and result.

Learning shares an interesting trait with creativity in the sense that it happens and comes naturally to people. However, even if it is something one is born with, both can be improved. Even though we like innovation and innovation processes to be understandable and ideally predictable, learning and creativity – perhaps to an even larger extent than innovation – are messy and fuzzy. The question becomes: should organisations try to eliminate these "uncertainties," or should they encourage them since these uncertainties allow for the unpredictable? Two ways of looking at this are as follows:

- OL is more than the sum of its parts
- The "spill-over" effect of innovation is not predictable

Both Dodgson (1993) and Fiol and Lyles (1985) subscribe to the idea that OL is more than the sum of individual learning. That is, something greater than a sum of knowledge and skill available results from the learning processes. And attempts to identify and codify this learning only generate new learnings (which again aggregates something more undefined).

Innovation, then, can also have "spill-over" effects in other parts of the system, since other parts of the system may become aware, and view the world differently, as a consequence of innovation processes they have not been directly part of. This creates space for new ways of thinking and doing. This effect is not the same as planned knowledge transfer, since it is unintended. This "extra space" is an interesting way to think about triggers and stimuli for creativity, new ideas, and renewal: like a primordial soup between feeding the system.

The innovation process – even if it fails – offers rich sources of information that can be converted into knowledge, explicit knowledge, and tacit know-how. In other words, it results in learning and possibly also noticeable changes. Given our previous arguments, one can reasonably consider learning not only as a condition for innovation, but also as one of its outcomes. A challenge for organisations is how to pursue innovation in a way that renders learning as valuable – on par with other desirable outcomes. Indeed, in our complex and fast-evolving world, one could argue that it is learning that is the true testament to a successful innovation and that it is this capacity building that allows an organisation to innovate over and over again.

Summary

In this chapter, we have discussed OL and innovation. We have also indirectly argued that capacity building is dependent on learning. Capacity building as a process is ideally improved over time, and that suggests learning. Different areas such as goals and measurement, loops of learning, knowledge creation, transfer, retention, and management were discussed as aspects of learning. The LO was introduced as a concept to underpin the organisational-wide need for learning in the light of improved innovation capacity. Barriers to OL were presented before ending with a discussion of innovation as learning and learning as innovation.

As we now have covered innovation from different theoretical perspectives, from how we understand innovation to its spread and uptake, we will now turn our attention to another important area: what drives innovation?

Note

1 https://www.merriam-webster.com/dictionary/learning

7 The drivers of innovation

Introduction

So far in the book, we have looked at what innovation is and how it comes about. We have investigated innovation through the main theoretical challenges, from a conceptual understanding of innovation to the impact of organisational learning on innovation. The meaning of innovation has had different sources even if today we associate it to a large extent with economics and technology. Godin (2013b) shows that the linear model of innovation has two origins: one is management and economics, which focuses on the origins of invention, and the other is anthropology, which proposed innovation as a solution to the question of invention and its diffusion as a matter of cultural change. Over time, the two traditions have joined and certain approaches have favoured orientations towards invention, whereas others have favoured those towards diffusion. Today, we can see that when we talk about innovation, diffusion (that is, what sociologists call "adoption" and economists, "commercialisation") is often what is favoured over R&D (Godin, 2013b). Innovation is thus seen as the diffusion of invention. To that end, a third dimension of the innovation process can also be seen: its effects.

Understanding innovation as a process of achieving something new speaks in general terms to the idea of progress and prosperity. Innovation offers a perspective on these changes, as well as a reason for those changes to happen. Since Schumpeter (1939, 1942), the notion of creative destruction has served to explain innovation and value creation.

Innovation is connected to other areas of society apart from economics. The introduced qualitative change that comes with innovation may result in increased well-being, happiness, or general "societal value" as an alternative to mere economic outcomes. As such, the general goal of innovation is positive change: to make something better.

So far, we have yet to explore why innovation is essential or what drives it: we will turn to that in the next sections. After we discuss why we need innovation, five drivers will be introduced: technology, competition, globalisation, new business models, and self-actualisation. These are not exhaustive but cover the ideas we most often associate with innovation. They also

The drivers of innovation 89

drive each other, which means that globalisation may increase competition, self-actualisation may promote new technology, and so forth. Technology is a well-established driver of innovation both in literature and in policy and practice; as a result, it will be treated more rudimentarily than other drivers. Likewise, competition is a recognised driver of innovation, so only a few different frameworks will be presented. Globalisation offers a slightly different perspective as, on the one hand, it increases competition, but on the other, it also expands the potential market. New business models suggest that by re-thinking how to capture, create, and deliver value, more innovative solutions are available. Self-actualisation takes a different starting point as it suggests that people have an urge for the new and the valuable that cannot only be explained in terms of competition and new technology. Finally, the larger umbrella of change is introduced as innovation can be seen as a response to change as well as a driver of change. It should be noted that there are some inevitable overlaps with other sections (e.g. Chapter 2: The meaning of innovation) as the subject is contextualised.

Why do we need innovation?

As we have seen in the previous chapters, innovation has a long history and its meaning has changed over the centuries. Today, we most often think of it in terms of technological change and, indeed, progress: we see innovation primarily as an economic gain. Because of this, it is worth addressing the purpose of innovation and connecting it more clearly with economic progress and the imperatives that drive firms and organisations. But before we dive into that topic, let's address alternative purposes.

Innovation may have purposes other than purely economic advancement. As we have seen in the previous section, it also serves and has served as a political concept (Godin, 2013a, 2014b). Innovation has been synonymous with something that is good, desirable, and essentially right. Lepore (2014) talks about it as blind faith, the panacea to all challenges. But when something is almost beyond critique (who would argue that we do not need innovation, or that is preferable not to be innovative?), it becomes something that we would also like to be associated with. As such, innovation also legitimises (as the OECD legitimised it decades ago) a position, a brand, and an agenda. When innovation becomes a slogan (Godin, 2014b), it also detaches itself from being an indicator of progress. The purpose of innovation then becomes the creation of an image, more than real economical results or societal change.

Innovation as an indicator and driver of economic growth and progress is well established (e.g. OECD, 1966, 2005). In short, technological progress and innovation determine productivity and growth (Kaplinsky, 2007, 2011). However, in spite of its obvious importance, innovation has not always received the scholarly attention it deserves (Fagerberg et al., 2006). In the same way that innovation plays a role on the macro-level of our societies, it

90   *The drivers of innovation*

also plays a key role for firms. Numerous authors have established this, even though they tend to look at different facets of organisational success. The need for innovation in organisations is fundamental and imperative: organisations should innovate in order to renew the value of their asset endowment. Innovation adds value and sustains competitive advantage (Baregheh et al., 2009). It represents not only the opportunity to grow and survive, but also the possibility of significantly influencing the direction of industries (Davila et al., 2006). Moreover, businesses need to innovate to increase performance (McLaughlin et al., 2004).

In short, the purpose of innovation is increased or sustained profit and competitiveness, renewal, and fitness. Fundamentally, it is a sign of organisational and business vitality. One's understanding of the purpose of innovation sets the frame for an understanding of innovation itself and, vice versa, one's understanding of innovation fixes our perspective around its purpose.

Technology

According to Beinhocker (2006), global wealth has risen exponentially since around 1750. More so than any other reason, this growth resulted from technological advancements (Humbert, 2007). With reference to the evolutionary economist Richard Nelson, Beinhocker (2006) states that two types of technologies play a major role in economic growth: physical technology (e.g. steam machines) and social technologies (i.e. ways of organising people to perform tasks and activities). The development of new technologies of both kinds allowed for new ways of organising production and economic activity. Technological progress and the restructuring of production led to a cumulative acceleration of productivity development (Humbert, 2007).

It seems possible to discuss the development of the world through the lens of innovation. Revolutions have occurred throughout history (Schwab, 2017): new technologies and novel ways of seeing the world have sparked deep changes in our economic system and social structures. However, it is also worth noting that the industrial revolutions have not been evenly spread across the world. For instance, the Second Industrial Revolution has yet to be experienced by 1.3 billion people around world (ibid.). Many still lack, for instance, electricity. In terms of the Third Industrial Revolution, around half of the world's population still lack access to the Internet. Indeed, the imperatives of both growth and distribution raise issues of technology and innovation (Kaplinsky, 2011). Uneven distribution has an impact on, for instance, poverty reduction. What has changed is not only the content and consequences of the revolutions, but also the speed with which they spread. For instance, the spindle from the first revolution took almost 120 years to spread outside Europe, whereas the Internet spread across the world in less than a decade (Schwab, 2017).

One should not underestimate the systemic changes that technological breakthroughs offer. Their speed, scale, and scope are remarkable in terms of development and diffusion (just think of where companies like Google were 20 years ago, or where Airbnb, Uber, and others were 5–10 years ago). The idea of returns in terms of scale is both astonishing and challenging depending on one's perspective (Christensen, 1997), since digitalisation means automation and thus much smaller (trending towards zero) marginal costs. This makes it quite possible that businesses in the future will require fewer workers. The question of whether such innovations will generate new type of jobs is still unknown and may require that we reconsider the nature of work.

Insofar as technology is a driver for innovation, innovation in itself can serve as a spark for new technology. It is these aspects of technology – that it can be a manifestation of innovation, an enabler of innovation, and that it feeds into the larger ripple effect of innovation development – that tie it so tightly to the concept of innovation.

Competition

Michael Porter (1998) is an expert on competitiveness, and his Five Forces Framework was the definitive approach for decades. This theory hypothesises that there are five forces that determine the competitive intensity and appeal of an industry. These forces include the threat of substitute products and/or services, the threat of recognised rivals, the threat of new entrants, and the rivalry among existing competitors.

Obtaining competitive advantage is not the same as sustaining it. Indeed, changes in the marketplace generate a dynamism such that sustaining competitive advantage is impossible to guarantee. However, firms are not just victims to the marketplace; they can also influence it, as Davila et al. (2006) have observed.

A theory around how companies create competitive advantage was suggested by Utterback and Abernathy in 1975. They introduced the concept of "dominant design," in which they suggested that the emergence of a dominant design is a major milestone in the evolution of an industry. These milestones change the way firms compete in an industry and, as such, the type of organisations that succeed and prevail. They also win the loyalty of the marketplace. When a new technology comes forth, companies will often introduce a number of different designs. Over time, one design becomes more generally accepted (often after a number of incremental innovations) and a new industry standard may emerge. This new standard is not necessarily better than the alternative.

James Utterback defined three phases of innovation in the marketplace for any product and service (1996): the Fluid, Transitional, and Specific phases. When introducing a new product or a service to the market, we are in the Fluid phase, which is characterised by radical innovation and many different competing designs. At some point, there will often be consolidation around a dominant design, which will be adopted by all or by most actors. In the next phase – the Transitional phase – production innovation gives way to process

92 *The drivers of innovation*

innovation when the actors try to optimise processes, in order to improve the quality and decrease the cost of their products and services. In the Specific phase, the number of actors decreases because some will not be able to compete. They will move into other products and services or cease to exist as the prevailing ones focus on incremental changes to stay profitable.

After the last phase, the process essentially starts all over again as firms try to retain and develop their relationship with the market. As such, innovation becomes a series of Utterback cycles, almost like an endless spiral or an S-curve.

As firms compete and bring innovations to life, they can choose where to compete. Put differently, they can choose where to spend their R&D budget as they hope to capture returns and market shares. Kim and Mauborgne (2005) suggest that organisations should focus on "blue ocean" spaces in the marketplace that are free of competitors. This also indicates that defining a particular market can be seen as an innovative approach, if not an innovation in itself. Clayton Christensen (1997) introduces the idea of disruptive innovation and explains why the same management practices that cause some companies to become industry leaders also make it difficult for them to develop the kinds of disruptive technologies that start-ups may use to overtake markets. For example, the market leader becomes the market leader based on some sort of innovation or innovative approach to its business, and the new entrant finds an underserved segment and essentially pursues a variation of the blue ocean strategy, and from here "disrupts" the market.

As we can see, innovation, and how it is managed, is a key strategic issue, but the absence of a consensual definition is challenging. However, stating a purpose for innovation also helps to define it – or at least to render it more "tangible" by contextualising it.

Globalisation

Friedman (2006) states that the first era of globalisation lasted from 1492, when Columbus set sail and opened up trade between the New World and the Old World, until around 1800. The second era of globalisation occurred between around 1800 and 2000. This period was interrupted by the Great Depression and World Wars I and II. Where the first era was much about countries, the second was more about the multinational corporation. In the third wave of globalisation, it will be about individuals. Individuals now have the power and possibility to collaborate and compete on a global scale. In this new era, it is not only European and American corporations that are driving change: other countries, regions, and companies are entering the stage and shaping its course in a profound way. Furthermore, another defining characteristic of this development – strikingly different compared to previous periods – is the speed and breadth at which it is taking hold.

John le Carré once wrote, "The desk is a dangerous place from which to view the world" (quoted in Boyer, 2004). However, most leaders and

The drivers of innovation   93

managers are locked behind a desk, insulated by layers of organisational structures and full calendars (Boyer, 2004).

Christensen (1997) points out three predicaments for businesses:

- Leading companies listen to their best customers, but these companies are the last to adopt new and disruptive innovations and technologies
- Leading companies measure the size and growth of markets to understand customers better, but disruptive innovations are unpredictable and evade detection through traditional measurements
- Leading companies focus on the highest returns and large markets, but disruptive innovations are counter-intuitive: they start small and translate into lower profit margins in the early stage
- According to Adler (2007), the twenty-first century presents society with challenges that will determine the future of humanity as well as the future of the planet. She goes on to call for wisdom as a response. The study of wisdom in the scholarly management tradition is still very new.

Less privileged parts of the world are not just recipients of the creativity, inventions, and innovations from the west: they are increasingly recognised as areas of opportunity for innovation and growth. There is a huge market potential for a new class of consumers. The "bottom-of-the-pyramid" markets present significant challenges but also important growth opportunities (Webb et al., 2009). Prahalad and Hammond (2002), Prahalad and Hart (2002), and Prahalad (2006) point out that there are roughly 4 billion people living at incomes below $2,000 per year. They make three points to highlight the potential:

- Although incomes are low, many of these people are active consumers of goods and services
- Many of the products that the poor consume make intensive use of radical new technologies (as opposed to what is often highlighted in literature)
- These poor consumers represent a market of growing significance and provide the potential for highly profitable production

As we moved from a production paradigm characterised by mass-production (or Fordism) to a leaner, just-in-time production system, we experienced a new innovation challenge (Kaplinsky et al., 2010): increased flexibility and diversity were accompanied by smaller inventories and production to order as opposed to forecasting. All in all, these change reduced costs. However, the innovation challenge now is rapid production cycles and production innovations.

There are good reasons to believe that technological changes originating in the south will become a major driver of innovation in the twenty-first century (Kaplinsky, 2011). However, it is not just about excess production resources in the north that are pushing products to the south. Essentially, the

94   *The drivers of innovation*

less privileged also have the capacity to take part in the innovation process. In terms of innovation, demand has been under-recognised in economic theory (Kaplinsky, 2011). The global proportion of R&D occurring in low-income countries rose between 1970 and 2000 from 2% to 20%, but this does not necessarily mean that innovations meet the needs of low-income consumers (Kaplinsky et al., 2010). And it is innovation, not R&D, that really drives possibilities for poverty reduction.

In terms of entrepreneurial activities, in developing countries we must think differently about success (Webb et al., 2009). The dominant view is that entrepreneurial activities allow firms to create wealth. This remains true in developing countries, but there are other considerations such as societal and reputational gains that must be considered in conjunction with financial gains.

Kaplinsky (2007) pushes for a shift in strategy and policy from a focus on industrial development to one of innovation in all sectors for low-income countries. The focus on innovation capabilities opens up the challenge of moving beyond improvements in infrastructure and getting producers in low-income countries into global value chains. Focusing on innovation provides the capacity to learn, to operate on a continuously expanding global frontier. Porter and Kramer (2011) argue for the concept of "shared value" as a way to reinvent capitalism and unleash a wave of innovation and growth. Here the focus is on the connection between economic and societal progress. The ways that companies can create shared value opportunities are by:

- Reconceiving markets and products
- Redefining productivity in the value chain
- Enabling local cluster development

Innovation and technological change play an important role in poverty reduction through their contribution to growth, their use of factories for production, their environmental spill-overs, the social relations associated with production, and the characteristics of the products they produce (Kaplinsky, 2011). New business models must not disrupt local cultures and lifestyles. What is needed is an effective combination of local and global knowledge (Prahalad and Hart, 2002).

New business models

As we saw in the previous section, a redefined understanding of progress – as a combination of the economic and the societal – can trigger innovation opportunities. Another area where we see innovation taking a hold is public sector innovation. What distinguishes public sector innovation from simply innovation is its focus on generating new ideas that create value for society (Mulgan, 2007; Bason, 2010). Much attention is given to building capacity for innovation and co-creation. First used by Prahalad and Ramaswamy (2004), co-creation refers to a creational process where new solutions are designed *with* people and not *for* them. Co-creation is not just about finding solutions that deliver better services or generate intended outcomes, but rather about enabling public organisations to innovate and generate new value for less (Bason, 2010).

However, where the bottom line in business is essentially profit, how can that be understood in public policy and in reference to public sector innovation? Bason (2010) describes four public sector bottom lines: productivity, service experience, results, and democracy. Yunus (2007) states that if we describe our existing companies as profit-maximising business, the new businesses might be called social businesses. Entrepreneurs can then set up social business, not to achieve personal gain but to pursue specific social goals.

Whereas social or societal innovation can be explicit pursuits of certain organisations, private organisations can in theory have similar objectives. However, in reality, the societal benefits may be a consequence of private interests. There are companies that include societal objectives in their business model. Regardless of the type of organisation or the objectives one may pursue, there are more general reasons why an organisation would want to improve its innovation capacity. Drucker (1985) points out that there are many drivers for organisations to become more innovative. These include the following:

- The bargain power of suppliers
- The bargain power of customers
- The threat of new entrants into the market
- The link to an organisation's values and strategy
- Competitive rivalry within the sector

Changes in industry and market, as well as internal organisational changes, challenge the status quo and demand that firms change and innovate. But while this often leads to a drive towards integration and consolidation, there are other approaches as well. The open innovation paradigm, as suggested by Chesbrough (2006), can be understood as the antithesis of the vertical integration model. In the vertical integration model, internal R&D activities lead to internally developed products that are then distributed by the firm. In contrast, open innovation processes combine internal and external ideas into new types of architectures and systems. While the contours of the new model of innovation remain obscure, it is clear that any adequate understanding will require a more externally focused perspective, involving the actions of multiple actors in a far more distributed innovation environment (ibid.).

A new approach to developing custom products is to see customers as innovators (Thomke and von Hippel, 2002). Although many companies ask their customers what they want – and what they would like to see in new products and services –they go about it the wrong way (Ulwick, 2002). Thomke and von Hippel (2002) suggest to develop a user-friendly toolkit and essentially ask that companies be adaptable to what comes out of it. Developing a

96 *The drivers of innovation*

user-friendly toolkit and increasing the flexibility of the production process –
as well as being careful in selecting the first users or customers, developing
the toolkit continuously, and adapting the business practices accordingly –
may be a good prescription. Yet it does not prescribe where the value will
migrate or how to capture it (ibid.). That is, of course, crucial to the real value
of the approach.

Ulwick (2002) suggests an outcome-based methodology. Although his
approach follows very clear steps, it seems to be more valuable when the objective of the input is very clear – for instance, "decrease obesity." Thomke
and von Hippel (2002) are more open to the fact that there may be outcomes
that we do not know we wanted – indeed, that may be the whole purpose of
allowing users into the development process.

Some managers acknowledge that some parts of business are more art than
science. However, they often see this as a problem and not an opportunity.
Austin and Devin point out four characteristics of artful work that can help
managers of knowledge workers:

- Emergent yet reliable process
- Iterative, nonsequential, process shape
- Openness to uncertainty
- Failure as a step to valuable innovation

Hjorth (2005) argues that entrepreneurship cannot be instigated through the
strategies described in best-selling management books on the bookshelves of
airport lounges. In reality, there is no prescription for how to create opportunities out of occasions and create actualities out of opportunities, but there
are many good examples that can serve as inspiration.

Self-actualisation

Here we turn our attention to a driver of innovation that is often assumed,
but not always made explicit or articulated: the desire of individuals and
groups to engage in innovation because they like to work with innovation.
Often, one gets the impression that organisations are required to innovate,
given external forces. But in today's society – at least in richer countries –
people have choices about what type of education and work they want to
devote themselves to. Innovation may be an imperative for organisations,
but it is questionable if everyone needs or even wants to engage in it. But
there are certainly individuals who are drawn to this type of work. Often,
we think of them as entrepreneurs, but in reality, we also find them in organisations on different levels, engaged in different aspects of the innovation
process.

Much literature on this subject stems from the psychological field and areas such as motivation, personality types, and socialisation. Both Herzberg's
classical motivation-hygiene theory (1966) and Maslow's hierarchy of needs

(1943) offer insights into the claim of wanting to work with creating the new and the valuable.

Maslow and his hierarchy of needs were introduced previously in this book, so here we will just recognise the model as a possible diagnostic tool for discussing innovation in terms of human needs. We suggest that innovation is a consequence of an innate human desire to self-actualise. People engage in innovation because they think it is fun, stimulating, meaningful, and a way to grow, and because they see it as a means of obtaining something else. This does not rule out any of the other drivers; it simply deserves to be considered in its own right.

Innovation is relevant on all levels in Maslow's pyramid as it can help us solve problems that we encounter in each of those levels, but as we take a closer look at the top level of self-actualisation, it becomes clearer how it can be a driver for innovation. The top level of Maslow's hierarchy is about realising one's full potential. Maslow describes this level as the desire to increasingly become one's essence, to develop into everything that one is capable of becoming. For some people, innovation is an enabler of that development. Indeed, the words "creativity" and "problem-solving" are often used as examples of self-actualisation. As such, creativity and innovation become undertakings that drive ever more valuable results.

The concept of change

Drucker (1969) coined the phrase "the age of discontinuity" to underline the speed, uniqueness, and unpredictability of the changes that face organisations. Although his book was published in 1969, many of the underlying forces of change that he identified are still transforming the economic landscape and creating our society. The sources of these changes are multifaceted, and their impact is truly profound.

Drucker distinguished four major areas of discontinuity that underlie contemporary social and cultural reality. These are as follows:

- The outburst of new technologies resulting in massive new industries
- The change to a world economy from an international one – an economy that currently lacks policy, theory, and institutions
- A new socio-political reality of pluralistic institutions that poses drastic political, philosophical, and spiritual challenges
- The new world of knowledge based on mass education and its implications in work, leisure, and leadership

Although there have been contributions to our understandings of these discontinuities, they remain valid as they are neither resolved (i.e. we have found the answer) nor gone.

Change can be understood as a verb or as a noun. As a verb, it means to "make or become different" or to "take or use another instead of." As a noun,

98 *The drivers of innovation*

it refers to "an act or process through which something becomes different."[1] Change is about difference: between what is or was, and what is or will be. Drucker points to larger social-economical-technological forces shaping changes that have consequences for organisations.

For organisations, change can often begin with strategy. Changes in strategy may be triggered by changing realities in the external world or within the organisation itself. After setting new goals and allocating resources accordingly, new structures, systems, and procedures are introduced to support the new strategy. But history is full of examples of companies that have not survived because they have not adapted fast enough to changing conditions, which raises questions as to why.

The search for stability and certainty (which seems logical from an efficiency point of view) can lead organisations to adopt a mind-set that leaves them exposed to aggressive and innovative competitors [or entrants, following the idea of disruption as proposed by Christensen (1997)]. According to Hartley (1994), this particular mind-set is comprised of the following:

- Conceit (i.e. companies believe in their own invincibility and are disdainful of their competitors)
- Conservatism (i.e. companies are managed by executives too far away from the market and too steeped in conventional wisdom, not seeing new opportunities)
- Complacency (i.e. companies are self-satisfied, content with the status quo and no longer eager for growth)

While these three Cs can be effective when the strategy of the company is suitable for market conditions, they do not encourage initiative and ingenuity. In today's market, it seems very few companies can allow themselves the luxury of adhering to the three Cs for very long at a time. This means that the job of management is to institute some sort of rationality, narrative, and predictability out of the chaos and uncertainty that continuous change creates. The ability to manage change has been recognised by many, for instance, Peters and Waterman (1982), as key to corporate success and competitive advantage.

Lewin introduced the "force field model" in 1951 (Lewin, 1951), in which he suggests that change is a state of imbalance between driving forces (pressure for change) and restraining forces (pressure against change). There have been other frameworks for studying change. One of these would be Pascale's "7S model" (1991), a more holistic approach that is based on the premise that organisational effectiveness rests on the fit between strategy, structures, systems, style, skills, staff, and shared values.

A newer idea is that of "change readiness." This is derived from theories about organisations and organisational change (Lewin, 1951; Senge, 1990). Readiness is considered important because the members of an organisation work to sustain a situation that leaves them with a sense of security, control,

The drivers of innovation   99

and identity (Argyris and Schön, 1995). Change readiness can be understood as the extent to which members of an organisation are psychologically and behaviourally prepared to implement organisational changes (Weiner et al., 2008). In that sense, it is a two-dimensional phenomenon: whether the members are motivated *for* and whether they are capable *of* carrying through a planned organisational change.

Organisational readiness is a common psychological state in which members of an organisation feel committed to implementing an organisational change and experience a sense of reliability in their collective capacity to carry it through (Weiner, 2009).

The nature of change can certainly vary quite substantially. It can entail incremental changes as well as transformational ones. Where the first are often sustained, continuously experimenting with new ideas to improve performance, the latter are quite a different affair. Incremental changes often have only marginal consequences and rarely affect the underlying business models, or at least the philosophy of the organisation. Transformational changes produce a restyled type of organisation that has long-term consequences and often call for changes in culture and structure. Tushman et al. (1986) state that transformational change may be the response to three kinds of disruptions:

* Industry discontinuities
* Movements in the product life cycle
* Internal company dynamics

History has taught us that the changes that affect bodies of knowledge most profoundly do not as a rule emerge from within their own domains (Drucker, 1992). Appreciating and acknowledging new knowledge, or changes to it, is a strategic imperative. Miyazaki (1994) proposes that developing new technological competence in a company is also a cumulative process. Knowledge and intellect grow exponentially when shared (Quinn et al., 1996). This means that accumulating knowledge is a key capacity that can be increased and that the value of it increases as it is distributed and made communal.

Change in terms of organisations and firms is closely related to doing "new things." As such, it is directly related to the concept of entrepreneurship (i.e. moving resources from a less yielding area to a more yielding one). In Peters and Waterman's (1982) research, eight common themes were responsible for the success of the chosen corporations – hereunder autonomy and entrepreneurship – fostering innovation and nurturing "champions." Innovation can be seen as the "business of entrepreneurs" (Drucker, 1985). Collins (2001) found that companies that perform consistently do much better than those that do spectacularly one year and are feeble the next. As such, entrepreneurship and innovation follow Drucker's notion of (1985) the "business of entrepreneurs," and can be seen as a discipline, indeed as a means to meet or instigate change. We may define innovation as a diagnostic discipline

100 *The drivers of innovation*

involving the systematic examination of current changes, which in themselves may give space for entrepreneurial opportunity. Drucker (ibid.) articulates systematic innovation as involving the examination of seven sources of innovative opportunity:

- The unexpected (success, failure, outside event)
- Incongruity between the way things actually are and the recognition of the way they should be
- Innovation based on process need
- Surprise changes in industry or market structures (e.g. from the activity of free markets or government legislation)
- Demographic and sociographic changes (i.e. lifestyle changes)
- Changes in perception, mood, and meaning
- New knowledge (both scientific and non-scientific)

Cavé (1994) suggests that the choice of organisational structure may involve a set of compromises between the major organisational types (i.e. the functional, the adhocracy, and the professional bureaucracy) and the strategic forces driving the company (i.e. cost control, innovation, and quality).

In terms of bringing about change as innovation, Cavé and Peters and Waterman seem to be on the same page. When what is desired is innovation, a strict, rigid, and procedure-oriented form of organisation is less effective.

Godin (2010b) observes that early writers on innovation during the sixteenth and seventeenth centuries saw change as the antithesis to religious orthodoxy and authority. Change or novelty, as such, had nothing to do with technology. Innovation used to be understood as change (Godin, 2011), and it was not until the twentieth century that innovation became theorised explicitly as creativity (ibid.). Godin suggests that in studying innovation, researchers turned to the concept of change – cultural change (anthropology), technological change (economics), and social change (sociology). Change thus becomes the marker of invention and vice versa.

In economics, it is not enough that something is new or different only for the sake of change. The change, or what is new, must increase value of some kind. One way of interpreting Schumpeter is that innovation is essentially an effort by one or many to create economical profit through a qualitative change.

Invention and its successful introduction lead to increased productivity, which is the fundamental source of increasing wealth in an economy. It is this focus on what represents value or potential for better resource productivity that drives research and the development of new and innovative ideas for new products, services, and resources. Recognising and seeking change are the catalysts that drive the entrepreneur, and it is this drive for change that provides the opportunity for the new and different. Innovation, then, is a change that generates change.

Summary

In this chapter, we have looked at the rationale of innovation as well as different drivers for innovation: technology, competition, new business models, globalisation, and self-actualisation. We suggested that the purpose of innovation is increased or sustained profit and competitiveness, renewal, and fitness. We also introduced change as an overarching concept of innovation, and suggested that innovations are a driver of change and vice versa.

Change is hard to predict and difficult to cater for. Over the last decades, the classic positivist and reductionistic view and approach to the world has been challenged, as it has not been able to sufficiently describe the phenomena that shape our world. A new science started to become more popular in management literature throughout the 1990s, and it is that topic – complexity – to which we turn our focus now.

Note

1 These are my own definitions.

8 From chaos to complex adaptive systems – innovation as a complex adaptive system

Introduction

With the birth of the scientific revolution (Cohen, 1976) at the end of the Renaissance period, our notion of society and nature started to change. The mechanical ideas and principles that were discovered during this time came to influence not only our views of science, but also our understanding of virtually all facets of life in the west. This view of reality assumes a clear link between cause and effect (i.e. that the universe is orderly and follows laws, and that it is essentially a big, complicated machine), as well as that it is possible to understand things by taking them apart and studying their constituent parts (reductionism). Alongside new discoveries, we designed machines that seemed to reinforce the idea of the universe as a machine or clock, something with predictability and determinism. This understanding started to define work and knowledge in order to suit this worldview (Wheatley, 1992).

The impact of the Newtonian view of the world cannot be overstated. It has infiltrated and illuminated everything from our educational system to our views of organisation and management – it has even penetrated our language, our way of thinking, and our culture at large. Reductionism, the practice in which things are taken apart and examined individually so that we might understand and predict the whole, has prevailed to a large extent up to the present day. Even though scientists have started to abandon that worldview, many people still view the world in a mechanistic way. Indeed, many metaphors with roots in that worldview still live on in our everyday language (e.g. "what drives his behaviour," "we need to fuel the creativity," etc.).

New discoveries in physics at the start of the twentieth century contested and contradicted classical physics. Newtonian mechanics were overtaken by quantum mechanics (as pioneered by Bohr, Einstein, Heisenberg, Schrödinger, etc.) and by Einstein's theory of relativity. A new world was in the making.

The rise of computing power, an increasing interest in irregular phenomena (such as the spread of epidemics, random changes in weather, the metabolism of cells, changing populations of insects and birds, etc.), and the emergence of a new style of geometrical mathematics (non-Euclidean structures of fractal geometry) paved the way for chaos and chaos theory to became everyday words (Sardar and Abrams, 2004). That is, during the last century, a new science ushered a new understanding of the world. This is a world of chaos and complexity; of emergence; and of dynamic, self-organising systems.

The science of complexity has its roots in chaos theory. As the development of the different ideas and concepts was taken deeper into everyday situations, a new notion – the edge of chaos – took hold. Complex systems do not have a universal definition, but one way to conceptualise them is to examine their behaviour: if it is hard to explain, it is a complex system. Normally, for a system to be labelled complex, it needs to have numerous parts (or components) that have the capacity for structured interactions and which result in emergent phenomena. Ladyman et al. (2012) suggest five features: (1) an ensemble of many elements, (2) interactions (i.e. exchange), (3) disorder (parts), (4) robust order (overall patterns and structures are preserved), and (5) memory.

Ordering systems according to their complexity may be helpful, but this depends on the purpose of the ordering. In the "hard" sciences, it is helpful (and possible) to offer very precise meanings and definitions of phenomena, whereas in the "soft" sciences or other disciplines, interpretations will always be more contextual and rooted in tradition – and not easy to translate. One of the most fundamental understandings of the difference between the old paradigm and the new is offered by Mikulecky:

> Complex systems and simple systems are disjoint categories that encompass all of nature. The world therefore divides naturally into those things that are simple and those things that are complex. The real world is made up of complex things. Therefore, the world of simple mechanisms is a fictitious world created by science or, more specifically, by physics as the hard version of science. This is the world of the reductionist. It is modelled by the Newtonian Paradigm and simply needs sufficient experimentation to make it known to us. Those experiments involve reducing the system to its parts and then studying those parts in a context formulated according to dynamics.
>
> (2003)

The field of complex systems is today applied in all the classic disciplines of science, including engineering and management (Bar-Yam, 2002). Complexity can be viewed as a tool, or a lens, for understanding. It is in some ways a new science that echoes a new sensibility about the world around us. The roots of complexity as a science can be found in studies of chaos.

Complex systems, as a field of science, can be viewed as a discipline that is occupied with how parts of a system inter-relate and form relationships, resulting in (joint) behaviours of the system, and how that system interacts with its surroundings (Bar-Yam, 2002).

104 *From chaos to complex adaptive systems*

In this chapter, we will take a step back and investigate in more detail different important constructs so as to better understand complex systems. Chaos theory, systems, complexity theory, complex systems, and complex adaptive systems (CAS) will all be discussed individually. The chapter ends with a discussion of innovation as a CAS by comparing properties and characteristics between the two.

Chaos theory

In ancient Greek culture, where the first explanations of the universe emerged, the hymns of Orpheus were significant for introducing the term "Chaos."[1] Subsequent Greek philosophers reinforced the view that chaos portrays the shapeless and endless emptiness from which the universe is created (Theodossiou et al., 2012). The Merriam-Webster dictionary defines chaos as "complete confusion and disorder: a state in which behaviour and events are not controlled by anything" and "the state of the universe before there was any order and before stars and planets were formed."

Chaos theory is an area of study in mathematics, with applications and representations in a number of other disciplines, such as sociology and physics. It has its roots in the work of the French mathematician Henri Poincaré and his discoveries in the 1880s around the three-body problem,[2] where he found that there can be orbits which are not periodic (non-periodic), without either incessantly increasing or approaching a fixed point (Diacu and Holmes, 1996). That is, a general solution to the challenge of calculating the movements of three bodies (i.e. planets, stars, etc.) jointly attracted by gravity, based on their initial positions and velocities, is principally impossible. This is due to chaotic dynamics.

Chaos theory started to be recognised as a discipline after the 1950s, when scientists realised and accepted that the existing theoretical system (linear theory) could not explain what was being observed in certain experiments. What really fuelled this development was the computer. Now the time-consuming repetition of calculations could be done far more efficiently. Edward Lorenz, who worked on weather predictions, virtually stumbled upon one major insight: tiny changes in initial conditions can have large effects on the outcome over time. In effect that means, as a general rule, that even thorough atmospheric modelling cannot produce precise long-term weather forecasts (Lorenz, 1963).

Normally, trying to predict how phenomena will develop in nature depends on what is called "negative feedback." For example, thermostats react when the temperature is under a certain level, and then turn themselves off again when the desired temperature has been reached. Using positive feedback to describe the world, mechanisms that amplify a tendency rather than prevent it became possible with increasing computer power. Biologist Robert May was one of the first to develop such a model as a consequence of experimenting on his model for the development of fish populations (May and Oster, 1973).

In 1967, Benoît Mandelbrot published an article called "How Long is the Coast of Britain? Statistical and Self-Similarity and Fractional Dimension" (Mandelbrot, 1967; Gleick, 1987), in which he proved that the length of coastline alters with the scale of the measuring instrument. Furthermore, on all scales it resembles itself and is infinite in length for an infinitesimally small measuring device.

The Belgian chemist Ilya Prigogine was the first to introduce the idea of dissipative systems and self-organisation and to demonstrate that conditions that give birth to structures are "far from equilibrium." Irreversible processes are in fact the source of order (Prigogine, 1984).

In 1975, the mathematicians Tien Yien Li and James Yorke proved in their article "Period Three Implies Chaos" that it was not possible to set up a system that would repeat itself in a period of three oscillation without generating chaos. Li and Yorke are credited with coining the term "chaos" (Sardar and Abrams, 2004). And in 1987, James Gleick's book *Chaos: Making a New Science* (Gleick, 1987) introduced chaos theory to the public.

The theory of chaos was summarised by Edward Lorenz as follows: "Chaos: When the present determines the future, but the approximate present does not approximately determine the future" (quoted in Danforth, 2013). In short, one can say that chaos theory studies the behaviour of dynamic systems that are highly sensitive to initial conditions.

Systems

According to the Merriam-Webster dictionary, a system is a whole: a set of interacting or interdependent components forming an integrated whole.[3] Any entity that changes with time is called a system (Sardar and Abrams, 2004). The human body, a flu moving through the country, a school, and the population of penguins in the Antarctic are all examples of systems. A deterministic system is the one that can be predictable is stable and completely knowable (e.g. a grandfather clock). The difference between linear and non-linear systems is that in the first, the variables are simple and directly correlated, whereas in the latter, the relationships include more powers than one, which means that the output of a nonlinear system does not correspond directly in a proportional way to the input.

In a periodic system, a variable repeats exactly its past behaviour after a fixed interval of time. Aperiodic behaviour happens when no variable affecting the state of the system undergoes a completely regular repetition of values – visualise the flow of water as it goes down a sink. Chaos can be said to be the occurrence of aperiodic, apparently random events in a deterministic system (Sardar and Abrams, 2004). This can be contrasted with Kellert's characterisation of chaos theory as "the qualitative study of unstable aperiodic behaviour in deterministic nonlinear systems" (Kellert, 1993: 2).

A system can be closed or open – delineated by temporal and spatial boundaries – and subsequently more or less influenced by its surroundings.

106 *From chaos to complex adaptive systems*

As such, a system can be defined with respect to how it functions, its structure, its purpose, and how it changes over time.

In terms of systems, system theory and systems thinking are important developments. Systems theory is the science of comparing systems (Stichweh, 2011); that is, it is an interdisciplinary study that seeks to expose general principles that can be applied widely, regardless of the type of system. According to Capra (1996), it was Bertalanffy's concepts of an open system and the General Systems Theory that established systems thinking as a major scientific movement. Likewise, Bertalanffy's ideas were used by Luhmann in social systems theory (Luhmann, 1996).

Systems thinking, on the other hand, is the understanding of how systems affect and influence each other as part of a whole (Capra, 1996). In contrast with the scientific reductionism of Descartes, it suggests viewing systems holistically. Senge (1990) describes systems thinking as a discipline that integrates four other disciplines (personal mastery, mental models, building a shared vision, and team learning) in what he refers to as the "learning organisation." Systems thinking can be viewed as a way of solving problems by looking at them as part of a larger system, instead of concentrating and acting upon a specific issue.

Complexity theory

After the 1970s, scientists took the exploration of chaos deeper into everyday situations. In several disciplines, the concept of "the edge of chaos" started drawing more attention. The outline of a new science – complexity – was emerging (Sardar and Abrams, 2004). This was also reflected in book publications such as Roger Lewin's *Complexity, Life at the Edge of Chaos* (1992) and M. Mitchell Waldrop's *Complexity: The Emerging Science at the Edge of Order and Chaos* (1992).

Complexity can be viewed as a combination of order and disorder (i.e. the edge of chaos and order), but defining complexity is not a small task. Even scientists do not agree on its definition (Johnson, 2009). According to Johnson, it can be viewed as "the study of the phenomena which emerge from a collection of interacting objects" (Johnson, 2009: 3). A similar approach can be found in Arthur, who asserts that the common element of every study of complexity are systems: those with numerous parts reacting or adapting to patterns these parts generate (Arthur, 1999). Simon (1981) proposed defining complex systems as those that are "made up of a large number of parts that have many interactions." Others, however, doubt that there can even be a unified theory of complex systems (Horgan, 1995). Mikulecky (2003[4]) claims that complexity is the consequence of the Newtonian Paradigm and credits Robert Rosen, a Canadian biologist, with the following definition:

> Complexity is the property of a real-world system that is manifest in the inability of any one formalism being adequate to capture all its

properties. It requires that we find distinctly different ways of interacting with systems. Distinctly different in the sense that when we make successful models, the formal systems needed to describe each distinct aspect are NOT derivable from each other.

(Mikulecky, 2003)

The matter of understanding complexity, studying complexity, or using complexity challenges the extent to which understanding in one domain can be transferred to another. For instance, can complexity in innovation be regarded as the same as complexity in complexity theory? Bar-Yam (1997) states that:

- Complex = consisting of interconnected or interwoven parts/not easy to understand or analyse
- Complexity = the amount of information needed to describe it

The beauty of these definitions is that they can be applied in different domains. On the other hand, they may offer practical challenges of measurement, quantification, and predictability when they are applied to social systems. What information would be needed to portray the relationship between a leader and her peers? The challenge is that in order to fathom the performance of a complex system, it is not enough to understand the performance of the parts but rather how they jointly act to make up the performance of the whole. Yet the whole cannot be described without describing the different parts and each part must be described in relation to other parts – which accounts for why complex systems are hard to grasp (Bar-Yam, 1997).

According to Chu (2011), the notion of systems is commonly used in the sciences and usually refers to a distinct part of the world, to some extent separated from the rest. As the concept of complexity is often linked to the concept of systems, we can speak of complex systems as much as we can about systems that are "not complex" (Chu, 2011).

Complex systems

According to the *Business Dictionary*,[5] a complex system is one:

Consisting of many diverse and autonomous but interrelated and interdependent components or parts linked through many (dense) interconnections. Complex systems cannot be described by a single rule and their characteristics are not reducible to one level of description. They exhibit properties that emerge from the interaction of their parts and which cannot be predicted from the properties of the parts.

One can see that our understanding or definition of complexity depends upon our understanding of systems, or even the particular system in question. The

108 *From chaos to complex adaptive systems*

relationships between parts result in the collective behaviour(s) of a system, which interact and create relationships with their environment (Bar-Yam, 2002). The number of relationships and the nature of these relationships will be different compared to those outside the system. This also naturally positions views of complexity and simplicity as being relative and changeable over time. Ladyman et al. (2012: 27) suggest that "A complex system is an ensemble of many elements which are interacting in a disordered way, resulting in robust organisation and memory."[6] Simon writes (1962: 467–468):

> Roughly, by a complex system I mean one made up of a large number of parts that interact in a non-simple way. In such systems, the whole is more than the sum of the parts, not in an ultimate, metaphysical sense, but in the important pragmatic sense that, given the properties of the parts and the laws of their interaction, it is not a trivial matter to infer the properties of the whole.

Weaver (1948) suggests two positions: disorganised complexity and organised complexity. Disorganised complexity is a consequence of when a given system contains a massive number of parts (e.g. a gas container with millions of gas molecules) that can seem to behave randomly, but where the properties of the whole system can be understood (e.g. by using statistical models). With organised complexity, the correlation between the parts establishes properties not carried by individual elements and as such properties of the system may be viewed as emergent. An example of the latter may be a city, which Jacobs (1961) described as "organised complexity": the dynamic inter-relationships of systems, processes, and self-organisation.

Chaotic systems are not the same as complex systems. Chaos does not need to be seen as the non-appearance of order (disorder) as such, but rather as exceptionally complicated information (Hayles, 1991). The long-term behaviour of chaotic systems can be hard to foresee, even though they are deterministic. Complex (systems) are non-deterministic and cannot be predicted (Prigogine, 1997). While complex behaviour concerns how a huge number of very complicated and dynamic sets of relationships can create simple behavioural patterns, chaotic behaviour is the consequence of a relatively tiny number of non-linear interactions (Cilliers, 1998). Both chaotic and complex systems are sensitive to initial conditions, but whereas chaotic systems do not rely upon their history for their present behaviour, complex systems do. They have a history. This means that time cannot be ignored when analysing a complex system (Cilliers, 1998).

Another necessary distinction is between complex systems and complicated systems (Cilliers, 1998; Snowden and Boone, 2007). If a system contains a very large number of parts but can, even with difficulty, be fully described in terms of the individual parts – and as such the system as a whole – then it can be said to be complicated. An example might be a computer. In a system that is complex, the whole cannot be fully understood by examining its parts.

The interactions between the constituents in the system and the system and its environment do not provide a full understanding.

Ladyman et al. (2012) assert that there is no concise definition of complex systems. They offer the following quotations (except number 9) from a special issue of *Science* on "Complex Systems," featuring many key figures in the field (April 2, 1999). The following list is quoted verbatim from the issue:

1 "To us, complexity means that we have structure with variations." (Goldenfeld and Kadanoff, p. 87)
2 "In one characterisation, a complex system is one whose evolution is very sensitive to initial conditions or to small perturbations, one in which the number of independent interacting components is large, or one in which there are multiple pathways by which the system can evolve. Analytical descriptions of such systems typically require nonlinear differential equations. A second characterisation is more informal; that is, the system is 'complicated' by some subjective judgment and is not amenable to exact description, analytical or otherwise." (Whitesides and Ismagilov, p. 89)
3 "In a general sense, the adjective 'complex' describes a system or component that by design or function or both is difficult to understand and verify ... complexity is determined by such factors as the number of components and the intricacy of the interfaces between them, the number and intricacy of conditional branches, the degree of nesting, and the types of data structures." (Weng, Bhalla, and Iyengar, p. 92)
4 "Complexity theory indicates that large populations of units can self-organise into aggregations that generate pattern, store information, and engage in collective decision-making." (Parrish and Edelstein-Keshet, p. 99)
5 "Complexity in natural landform patterns is a manifestation of two key characteristics. Natural patterns form from processes that are nonlinear, those that modify the properties of the environment in which they operate or that are strongly coupled; and natural patterns form in systems that are open, driven from equilibrium by the exchange of energy, momentum, material, or information across their boundaries." (Werner, p. 102)
6 "A complex system is literally one in which there are multiple interactions between many different components." (Rind, p. 105)
7 "Common to all studies on complexity are systems with multiple elements adapting or reacting to the pattern these elements create." (Arthur, p. 107)
8 "In recent years the scientific community has coined the rubric 'complex system' to describe phenomena, structure, aggregates, organisms, or problems that share some common theme: (i) They are inherently complicated or intricate...; (ii) they are rarely completely deterministic; (iii) mathematical models of the system are usually complex and involve non-linear,

110 *From chaos to complex adaptive systems*

ill-posed, or chaotic behaviour; (iv) the systems are predisposed to unexpected outcomes (so-called emergent behaviour)." (Foote, p. 410)

9   "Complexity starts when causality breaks down."[7]

Cilliers (1998) suggests a description of the characteristics of complex systems, which can be used to explain a given phenomenon.

1   Complex systems consist of a large number of elements
2   In complex systems, its constituting elements interact dynamically
3   The behaviour of the system is not determined by the exact amount of interactions associated with specific elements
4   The interactions are non-linear
5   The interactions usually have a fairly short range; that is, information is received primarily from immediate neighbours
6   There are loops in the interactions. The effect of any activity can feed back positively or negatively (the technical term is "recurrency")
7   Complex systems are usually open systems; that is, they interact with their environment
8   Complex systems operate under conditions far from equilibrium. They require a constant flow of energy to maintain the organisation of the system. Equilibrium is another word for death
9   Complex systems have a history. Not only do they evolve through time, their past is co-responsible for their present behaviour
10 Each element in the system is ignorant of the behaviour of the system as a whole; each element responds only to information that is available locally

We can expand on two of the points mentioned by Cilliers above:

- No. 5: It is not so much that long-range interaction is impossible, but practical limitations normally stand in the way. This does not, however, prevent wide-ranging influence; rather, it is simply covered in a few steps. A consequence of this is that the influence becomes modified. It can be improved, repressed, or changed in many ways
- No. 7: It may be difficult to describe the border of a complex system, as the border is often not considered a feature of the system. One must also take into account the purpose of the description of the system, because it is often influenced by the position of the observer. This process is called framing

As we have seen, one can divide systems in different ways, depending on the purpose of categorising. Complex systems can be contrasted with simple, complicated, and chaotic ones (see, for instance, Snowden and Boone, 2007). However, there may also be a slightly different perspective from which the world is either complex or simple (Mikulecky, 2003), and where in reality, natural systems are always complex – simplicity is just a man-made construction in order to simplify our grasp of the world.

Complex adaptive systems

CAS represent particular cases of complex systems. The term was first used in its current meaning at the Santa Fe Institute[8] and is sometimes referred to as "Complexity Science." However, Walter Buckley (a systems-oriented social thinker) had already introduced it in 1968 in his article, "Society as a complex adaptive system," in which he used the term similarly to how it is understood today. He deliberately developed the expression to challenge a closed view of systems.

Complexity should be understood as associated with the sophisticated intertwining or interconnectivity of elements within a system and between a system and its context, and in this sense it is notable that Murray Gell-Mann (1995/1996) traces its etymology back to the Latin root "plexus," meaning "braided" or "entwined." From here "complexus" is derived: that is, braided together.

CAS are a combination of the phenomena (system) one is trying to understand and the systems hosting them. According to CAS, the main principle is that there are certain features (general principles) that run across all the actions within a system (Holland, 1993, 1996, 1999; Gell-Mann, 1995).

Many of our most troubling long-range problems – trade balances, sustainability, AIDS, genetic defects, mental health, computer viruses – centre on certain systems of extraordinary complexity. The systems that host these problems – economies, ecologies, immune systems, embryos, nervous systems, computer networks – appear to be as diverse as the problems. Despite appearances, however, the systems do share significant characteristics, so much so that they have been grouped together under a single classification at the Santa Fe Institute, which labels them CAS. This is more than terminology. It signals our intuition that there are general principles that govern all CAS behaviour, principles that point to ways of solving the attendant problems. Much of this work is aimed at turning this intuition into fact. (Holland, 1993: 1).

These systems are complex in the sense that they are dissimilar and made up of a multitude of connected components (agents). The key to understanding the system lies in understanding the aggregated behaviour of the agents, the consequence of the sum of interactions. Since these aggregated behaviours are non-linear, we cannot understand them only from understanding one or a few behaviours. Since the agents are diverse, if one is removed the system needs to reorganise, which implies changes. The consequence is the same if the systems context changes. In that sense, the system is adaptive; it can change and learn from experience. Another aspect relates to what guides the internal agent's behaviour. Gell-Mann (1995) calls this a "schema" and Holland (1993) an "internal model." It can be thought of as the number of rules – conscious or unconscious – that make it possible to "anticipate" the results of an agent's actions.

As CAS are dynamic, they can change, evolve, and adapt with their environment as it undergoes change. A consequence here is that the system is

112 *From chaos to complex adaptive systems*

not separated as such from its environment, but rather is closely linked. This means that change in one place or level must be viewed as a co-evolution in conjunction with other inter-related systems – not as a separate thing.

Holland (2006) offers a further list of properties that can help in understanding and controlling CAS:

1 CAS exhibit lever points – points where a simple intervention causes a lasting, directed effect. For example, vaccines cause lasting, desirable changes in an immune system
2 CAS have a hierarchical organisation of boundaries enclosing boundaries, with signals that are attuned to those boundaries. Without boundaries, there cannot be individual histories, and without individual histories, selection for fitness is not possible
3 CAS seem to evolve in an open-ended fashion, wherein an initially simple system exhibits increasing diversity of interaction and signalling

The most common definition of a CAS, based on the work of John Holland (1992), is "a dynamic network of agents acting in parallel, constantly reacting to what the other agents are doing, which in turn influences behaviour and the network as a whole." Another way of describing it would be as a way of thinking and analysing that appreciates complexity, patterns, and inter-relationships, rather than fixes on linearity and cause-and-effect. However, it should be noted that there are several definitions and descriptions, even if they tend to share some common characteristics (see, for example, Maturana and Varela, 1992; Svyantek and DeShon, 1993; Gell-Mann, 1995; Kauffman, 1995, 2008; Weick, 1995; Holland, 1996; Cilliers, 1998; Olson and Eoyongi, 2001).

CAS models represent a genuinely new way of simplifying the complex. They are characterised by four key elements: agents with schemata, self-organising networks sustained by importing energy, co-evolution to the edge of chaos, and systems evolution based on recombination (Anderson, 1999).

CAS are characterised by the following (Health Foundation, 2010):

- There are a large number of elements which interact dynamically
- All elements in the system are affected by other systems (CAS and others) that interact with the CAS and in turn affect those systems
- There is a constant flow of energy to maintain the organisation of the system
- There are non-linear interactions where small changes can generate large effects
- They are open, which can make it difficult to define system boundaries
- There is a history whereby the past helps to shape present behaviour
- Elements in the system are not aware of the behaviour of the system as a whole and respond only to what is available or known locally

The properties of CAS are (Health Foundation, 2010) as follows:

Emergence   The agents in the system interact in apparently random ways but from all of these interactions patterns emerge, which ultimately inform and change the behaviour of the agents and the system itself.

Self-organisation   CAS do not have a hierarchy of command. They constantly reorganise themselves to find the best fit with the environment.

Co-evolution   Systems are part of a broader environment, so as the environment changes, systems change to ensure best fit. This in turn influences the wider environment, and creates a constant cycle of change as the system develops to adapt to the environment and the environment changes as a result of system alterations.

Connectivity   How agents in a system connect and relate to one another is critical to the system's survival. As a result, the relationships between the agents are usually seen as more important than the agents themselves in CAS thinking.

Nested systems   Most systems are embedded within other systems.

Simple rules   CAS are not complicated and are often governed by simple principles.

Iteration   Small changes within a system can build like a snowball, leading to larger change.

Sub-optimal   CAS do not have to be perfect. Some go so far as to suggest that any energy used on being better than alternatives is wasted energy.

Requisite variety   CAS thinking suggests that the greater the variety within the system, the stronger it is, and the more likely it is able to create new possibilities and co-evolve.

Edge of chaos   Complex adaptive theory suggests that the most productive state for a system is the "edge of chaos," where there is maximum variety and creativity.

To clarify, despite all the CAS that have been investigated, we are still lacking general theories and models that can suggest how to identify or develop leverage points, or the mechanisms for making the boundaries or open-ended evolution.

Innovation as a complex adaptive system

A CAS is both self-organising and learning. Examples of CAS include social systems, ecologies, economies, cultures, politics, technologies, traffic, weather, and so on (Dooley, 1997). As such, we are all part of multiple CAS. A key point here is that principles such as emergence, co-evolution, and self-organisation are what separate CAS from other forms of multi-agent systems.

114 *From chaos to complex adaptive systems*

Two interesting questions then emerge: can CAS be used to explain innovation, and is innovation a CAS?

Innovation, management, and complexity have been addressed by numerous authors. Frenken (2005), for example, discusses three families of complexity models of technological innovation: fitness landscape models, network models, and percolation models. The systems of innovation approach have received considerable attention as a promising conceptual framework for advancing our understanding of the innovation process in the economy (Fischer, 2001[9]). Earlier approaches often focused more narrowly on R&D – often by analysing input with outputs from the system (for example, the OECD approach on technological change and innovation).

Below is a schematic presentation of characteristics of a CAS (taken from Health Foundation, 2010 – see the previous section) and a subsequent interpretation in terms of innovation characteristics (Table 8.1).

Furthering this schematic presentation, we turn our attention towards the properties of a CAS (also taken from the Health Foundation, 2010 – see previous section) and add innovation characteristics as well as implications for innovation – i.e. actions may be taken from an organisation to fuel innovation (Table 8.2).

Table 8.1 Complex adaptive systems and innovation characteristics

CAS characteristics	Innovation characteristics
A large number of elements which interact dynamically	Innovation does not depend on one thing, person, technology, process, etc. Each of these elements inter-relate and affect each other
All elements in the system are affected by other systems (CAS and others) that interact with the CAS and in turn affect those systems	Innovation does not exist in isolation, it is affected by everything from individual actions of individual people to larger systems, such as strategy or the organisation
A constant flow of energy to maintain the organisation of the system	Innovation requires outside-in flow of data, in the form of indications that point towards areas for change
Non-linear interactions where small changes can generate large effects	Innovation is affected not only by planned actions, but in principal by everything the system comes in contact with, and indeed, these sometimes have powerful implications
Openness, which can make it difficult to define system boundaries	Innovation borders depend to a large extent on decision-makers or leaders and their decisions about what to include or leave out
A history whereby the past helps to shape present behaviour	Innovation is a learnt behaviour. What has worked or not worked conditions current behaviour
Elements in the system are not aware of the behaviour of the system as a whole and respond only to what is available or known locally	Innovation is not a fully coordinated movement from ideation to endpoint utility. Instead, for example, an employee may neither know the totality of the process, nor necessarily how end users behave

Source: Author.

From chaos to complex adaptive systems 115

Table 8.2 Complex adaptive systems and innovation properties

CAS properties	CAS description	Innovation description	Innovation implications
Emergence	The agents in the system interact in apparently random ways but from all of these interactions patterns emerge, which ultimately inform and change the behaviour of the agents and the system itself	Innovation processes are often quite messy and unstructured – at least in the beginning – but often find a form and a format where the initial negotiations become agreements that then affect the people and possibly the organisation itself	Design for a situation where the agreements are changeable when they seem to stand in the way of creativity and productivity
Self-organising	CAS do not have a hierarchy of command. They constantly reorganise themselves to find the best fit with the environment	Innovation can be seen as having many hierarchies – starting with the customer and user, and leading up to management – but these are in effect more facilitators towards clinical endpoints	Designing for the best fit is often a matter of not imposing our own assumptions on a situation, but accepting the interplay between will, belief, and results
Co-evolution	This in turn influences the wider environment, and creates a constant cycle of change as the system develops to adapt to the environment and the environment changes as a result of system alterations	Innovation changes people's behaviour and indeed societies, but the multitude of changes taking place also requires new adaption from innovation and subsequently the actors engaged in making the innovation	Design for understanding what users and customers actually do, learn, and appreciate with regard to the innovation, and not just whether it lives up to pre-set targets. Ensure the organisation and innovation can adapt to new signals

(*Continued*)

116 *From chaos to complex adaptive systems*

CAS properties	CAS description	Innovation description	Innovation implications
Connectivity	How agents in a system connect and relate to one another is critical to the system's survival and so the relationships between the agents are usually seen as more important than the agents themselves in CAS thinking	Innovation depends on buy-in and support from a wide variety of people, systems, policies, and so forth – and innovation is often killed due to lack of anchoring, buy-in, and configuration to other parts of the extended organisation	Design for making alliances and support. Facilitate communication and connectedness across the organisation and beyond
Nested systems	Most systems are embedded within other systems	Innovation is (often) developed by a single organisation, but it can also involve others, such as other organisations or broader communities like cities or societies. This makes it hard to distinguish where innovation starts and where it stops	Design for innovation as being something also beyond the organisation as it is the system interaction that provides energy. Accept that it is less about full control as it is about nudging and facilitating
Simple rules	CAS are not complicated and are often governed by simple principles	Deconstructing innovation demonstrates relative user value, effective production, and marketing processes, as well as uniqueness and relevance of the idea as three basic governing principles	Design with clarity on direction, value, and values, and towards experimentation, learning, and improvement

From chaos to complex adaptive systems 117

CAS properties	CAS description	Innovation description	Innovation implications
Iteration	Small changes within a system can build like a snowball, leading to larger change	Alterations in the process of innovation often lead to very unexpected results	Design towards an appreciation of initial conditions and a devotion towards the question(s) behind the idea, as well as a malleable process structure
Sub-optimal	CAS do not have to be perfect. Some go so far as to suggest that any energy used on being better than alternatives is wasted energy	Innovation thrives in what can be called "creative friction," meaning that aiming for a process/state that has no limitations or challenges probably will have a decreasing return on investment	Design for getting it right, different, and productive, as there is no one way of being effective in the making of innovation. It is questionable if utilising more money and time than necessary increases the value of the output
Requisite variety	CAS thinking suggests the greater the variety within the system, the stronger it is, and the more likely it is able to create new possibilities and co-evolve	Innovation stifles without effort and the promotion of trying the new	Design for and reward on multiple levels as rewards condition behaviour
Edge of chaos	Complex adaptive theory suggests that the most productive state for a system is the "edge of chaos" where there is maximum variety and creativity	Innovation thrives in a space where structure and culture enhance each other – as opposed to pure anarchy or bureaucracy	Design for a space of diversity and chance encounters and a mix of methods, models, and views

Source: Author.

This relatively simple and schematic description of innovation that follows the descriptions of CAS shows that it is clearly possible to argue that innovation is a CAS. Innovation as a phenomenon – from the inception of a process to its successful adoption – can be explained by using the properties of a CAS. Indeed, innovation can be argued to be a CAS in the same way as other social

118 *From chaos to complex adaptive systems*

phenomena in that include many different agents, it adapts, and it is difficult to predict what it will lead to.

Furthermore, it is relatively easy to sketch out possible ways of going about innovation, given this interpretation. However, it is of course much easier to theorise about this than provide a prescription with some sort of certainty. Rather, it is better to view the description above as inspiration.

The world of innovation is characterised by non-linear dynamics: emergent properties, discontinuities, and self-organising patterns that once established become the platform for further disruptions. Larger organisations fulfil the criteria for being a CAS, smaller organisations less so. However, when we look at the full network even a small organisation is nested within, the complexity increases significantly.

Understanding CAS may also help us to improve our capacity for innovation, although it is difficult to do so within our traditional ways of working and our aptitude for control and planning. The science of complexity demonstrates that for a system to be innovative, creative, and changeable, it must be driven far from equilibrium where it can make use of disorder, irregularity, and difference as essential elements in the process of change (Stacey, 1995). But this makes it difficult to plan, monitor, and adjust since at a certain distance from equilibrium the links between cause and effect disappear. This is because positive feedback enables a system to intensify many small changes into globally different behaviour patterns. A consequence of this is that the nature of change in a CAS is not automatically a consistent pattern of change. Instead, it may be slow or fast, it may be resisted or encouraged, and so on.

When stakeholders demand the new, only those that are internally and spontaneously changeable – those operating at the edge – will survive selection by competition (Stacey, 1995). It is far more difficult to keep an organisation in this state than to allow it to move into stability or instability. As Kauffman (1995) contends, complexity itself triggers self-organisation, or what he calls "order for free." Complexity can also be understood on different levels. For instance, Frenken (2005) suggests that technology is a complex system *par excellence* since they made out of many interacting parts, and it is a collective process in which agents are engaged in a process of mutual learning. Some see similarities between the world of technology and the biological world in terms of evolutionary rules that govern origin, expansion, metabolism, and the decay of biological and technological ecosystems (for instance, Kauffman, 1995, 2008). The world of technology is full of self-organising dynamics and emergent properties. Complexity theory provides the language and an overarching framework with which to make sense of such organic development.

Margaret J. Wheatley (1992) describes innovation like so:

> The literature on organisational innovation is rich in lessons ... describes processes that are also prevalent in the natural universe. Innovation is fostered by information gathered from new connections; from insights

From chaos to complex adaptive systems   119

gained by journeys into other disciplines or places; from active, collegial networks and fluid, open boundaries. Innovation arises from ongoing circles of exchange, where information is not just accumulated or stored, but created. Knowledge is generated anew from connections that weren't there before.

At first glance, Wheatley's comment seems to simply describe the creation and inception of ideas, but looking deeper, she also suggests how an innovation develops from an idea to value delivered to users.

Summary

In this section, we have explored the concept of complex systems. We have looked at the history of the science of complex systems and investigated how they can be understood as well as their different characteristics. Today, we use the words "chaos" and "complexity" broadly in our everyday life. As our worldview shifted from the Newtonian, it is hardly surprising that an approach used in the natural sciences would emerge in the social world (Wheatley, 1992). One can certainly also hold a position that phenomena observed in the natural sciences cannot be assumed to be applicable in the social world. Here, however, we assert that the natural world and the social world are intertwined and characteristics and properties of complex (adaptive) systems can be seen as keys to understanding our social realities.

In sum, we can say that in terms of organisations, CAS offers interesting opportunities for new understandings of organisational work like innovation. It can help explain phenomena such as change and renewal, just as well as novelty, creativity, and innovation. But as we have seen, complexity theory has developed along a very interdisciplinary path, and as Anderson (1999) points out, in the end it may be so that organisation theory contributes as much as it borrows from the development of insight into the behaviour of complex systems.

CAS provide a new approach to innovation as well. Seeing innovation as a CAS offers a new understanding of innovation, one that allows us to approach it differently. Innovation in complex systems suggests that we have to consider a different sensibility in our endeavours, and different ways of doing so are the subject of the next chapter.

Notes

1 Note. A full presentation and explanation of all related concepts of Chaos theory is not possible in this thesis. A few significant strands and concepts are presented, as relate to the topic of this book.
2 This is the problem of finding the general solution to the motion of more than two orbiting bodies in the solar system (Ref. Wikipedia).
3 http://www.merriam-webster.com/dictionary/system
4 It is difficult to find a credible source when the writing was published, but 2003 seems to be the most credited by other sources.

120   *From chaos to complex adaptive systems*

5 http://www.businessdictionary.com/definition/complex-system.html
6 http://philsci-archive.pitt.edu/9044/4/LLWultimate.pdf
7 Editorial. "No man is an island." *Nature Physics*, 5:1, 2009, p. 12
8 http://www.santafe.edu
9 It should be noted that in this article the main departure is from the firm to the region, that is the system. In this chapter the system approach is considered more generally.

9 Innovation – between chaos and order

Introduction

> ... the point about complexity is that it is useful – it helps us to understand the things we are trying to understand.
>
> (Byrne, 1998)

As we have seen, the concepts of chaos and self-organisation have evolved from the physical sciences, whereas the idea of complex adaptive systems (CAS) has its roots in the biological sciences (Gell-Mann, 1994). The first managerial applications of complexity theory were proposed by Maturana and Varela's work on autopoiesis (Dooley, 1997). The theory of autopoiesis suggests that structural change occurs through self-renewal: replication, copy, and reproduction (Maturana and Varela, 1992). CAS has been used to examine organisations and leadership in a number of fields, including education (Mason, 2008; McQuillan, 2008), environmental science (Olsson et al., 2004), and health care (Fraser and Greenhalgh, 2001; Plsek and Greenhalgh, 2001; Plsek and Wilson, 2001; Wilson and Holt, 2001).

Organisation theory has historically borrowed from a number of parent disciplines (Anderson, 1999). The complexity of organisations is such that organisational studies scholars have searched for metaphors and models to help describe and explain the complex social phenomena observed in organisations (Weick and Sutcliffe, 2001; Lamberg and Parvinen, 2003). According to Reeves et al. (2016), companies are not like biological species or living systems (which would be more in line with, for example, Wheatley and Kellner-Rogers, 1998), but they are identical in one important aspect – both are CAS. As a result, the principles that generate robustness in nature could feasibly be transferable to business.

In CAS, order is emergent rather than predestined. Emergence results from the actions and reactions of the agents in a dynamic network. Things cannot be undone, so history is irrevocable. Since we cannot know what the reactions will be, the future is often unpredictable (Holland, 1996). Organisation theory has treated complexity as a structural variable that characterises both organisations and their environment (Anderson, 1999).

The science of complexity raises questions around the strategy process (Stacey, 1995). Here the questions revolve around (1) the system properties that make themselves capable of transformation and renewal, (2) intention versus emergence (i.e. considering the possibility of determining the long-term outcome of a changeable system), and (3) free choice versus determinism (i.e. whether agents are actually free to choose strategy and its outcomes, or if their choices are determined by the system itself).

Two fundamental dynamic properties from the science of complexity should be generally applicable to organisations (Stacey, 1995): (1) bounded instability and (2) spontaneous, self-organisation, and emergent order.

Jacobs (1961) speaks about the generative power of diversity as a source of innovation clustering. Here it could be argued that bounded instability (or strange attractors) is rooted in the differences between people and phenomena. Likewise, emergence – where local events and interactions among "agents" can cascade and reshape the entire system – is based on the positive feedback loop between the density of constraints.

This new system then influences and shapes the agents and their interactions – which again results in further changes in a continuously evolving process. A CAS can be seen as being nested in a larger business system, which again is nested in larger social systems and so on.

Reeves et al. (2016) suggest six principles that can help make CAS in business robust, derived from studies on features that distinguish dynamic systems that persist from those that collapse or decline:

- Maintain heterogeneity of people, idea, and endeavours
- Sustain a modular structure
- Preserve redundancy among components
- Expect surprise, but reduce uncertainty
- Create feedback loops and adaptive mechanisms
- Foster trust and reciprocity in the business ecosystem

The first three are structural and concern the design of systems. They are generally seen in nature. The other three are more managerial and have been recognised in a widespread diversity of managed systems.

A more recent field of interest in innovation studies is innovation and complex systems. According to Andriani (2011), the number of scholarly works that directly apply complexity to innovation is relatively small, although complexity theory provides conceptual tools by which to understand the world of innovation. Andriani (2011) groups the works into the following categories: (1) those that focus on self-organisation and emergent properties and (2) those that focus on networks.

The first is a departure from models that are based on the idea of balance (equilibrium), gradualism, and reductionism. The second is a departure in its focus from the firm and its boundary as the main subject of the innovation process.

Innovation – between chaos and order 123

This chapter contextualises innovation in the notion of complex systems, and the next sections address innovation from four different orientations, all of which make claims on the nature of novelty, change, and value creation – and also fit both of Adrianis' categories.[1] The four orientations are systems thinking, Complex Responsive Process (CRP), the Cynefin Model, and Chaordic.

Systems thinking and innovation

Systems thinking can broadly be seen as an orientation for understanding how elements of a given system influence each other, as well as how systems influence other systems as part of an even larger system. For example, in nature, there are ecosystems where biological entities interact with each other as well as with natural elements. When it comes to innovation and organisational studies, systems are considered to consist of people, structures, processes, and so on. Jackson (2000, 2010) demonstrates that there is not just one prefixed theory that describes systems thinking, but that the field is developing and that there are many variations of the theory. According to Skyttner (2006), a systems thinking approach includes several "theories":

- Interdependence of objects and their attributes – independent elements can never constitute a system
- Holism – emergent properties undetectable by analysis should be definable through a holistic approach
- Goal seeking – systemic interaction must result in some goal or final state
- Inputs and outputs – in a closed system, inputs are determined once and remain constant; in an open system, additional inputs are admitted from the environment
- Transformation of inputs into outputs – the process by which goals are achieved
- Entropy – the amount of disorder or randomness present in any system
- Regulation – a method of feedback is necessary for the system to operate predictably
- Hierarchy – complex wholes are made up of smaller subsystems
- Differentiation – specialised units perform specialised functions
- Equifinality – alternative ways of attaining the same objectives (convergence)
- Multifinality – attaining alternative objectives from the same inputs (divergence)

The systems thinking literature assumes that the concept of a system is useful in management and organisational research (Luoma et al., 2011). Peter Senge (1990) presents five disciplines that together encompass the art and practice of the learning organisation (see Chapter 6 for a more thorough presentation of the learning organisation):

- Personal mastery
- Mental models

124 Innovation – between chaos and order

- Shared vision
- Team learning
- Systems thinking

Systems thinking is the fifth discipline of organisational learning. To some extent, Senge considers systems thinking to surpass the other four disciplines, but all are seen as essential components that work together. Others who begin with systems theory as a way of understanding organisations are Argyris and Schön (1995). Jackson (2010) has critiqued many of the variations of systems thinking – for instance, the fifth discipline theory, living systems theory, autopoiesis, complexity theory,[2] and postmodern thinking. He sees them as responses to the "failure of the traditional approaches when confronted with extreme complexity" and argues for a pluralist orientation in critical systems thinking. Although all systems theories have their strengths and weaknesses in given situations, but appropriately attuned they have the potential to address the complexity of managerial problems and situations. Furthermore, "a diversity of theory and methods could be seen to herald not a crisis but increased competence and effectiveness" (Jackson, 2010).

Systems thinking has not been immune to a broader critique (Stacey et al., 2000; Mowles et al., 2010). Still, most management literature is underpinned by systems thinking (Mowles et al., 2010) and together with scientific management, it is the dominant discourse within management of human organisations (Stacey et al., 2000: 56). Jackson (2003: 125) says that this view is no real challenge to systems thinking, it just "simply follows a path already well-trodden by system theorists." Zhu (2007) follows the same line as Jackson, suggesting that systems should be viewed as "a dynamic web of the tensions, reciprocalities and transformations between various aspects of organisational life, each differentiated from and connected with, depending upon and affecting, each other" (Zhu, 2007: 460). Luoma et al. (2011) argue that systems thinking and the theory of CRPs (i.e. the theory of Stacey et al.) are complementary perspectives.

Galanakis (2006) claims that systems thinking can be used to make sense of the innovation process and he points towards the "systems of innovation" approach (Edquist, 1997). A system of innovation (SI) can be defined as "all important economic, social, political, organisational, and other factors that influence the development, diffusion, and use of innovations" (ibid.: 14). As such, the SI approach is about the determinants of innovations, instead of their consequences (in terms of growth or quantity of employment) (Edquist, 2001). While this may appear to undermine its position in relation to systems thinking (because SI is not focused on outcomes or goals), in reality, that is a misunderstanding since the goal is still innovation, regardless of what type of innovation it might be.

The systems thinking framework accepts the social as equal to the technical. It also accepts uncertainty and complexity as part of the management of the tasks, planning and control (Saad et al., 2002). According to

Kapsali (2011), systems thinking methods that are used in innovation project management provide the flexibility to manage innovativeness, complexity, and uncertainty in innovation projects more successfully. Much of the research on the organisation of project management has separated strategy development from execution (Artto et al., 2004). This division between strategic decision-makers and project managers results in two different managerial systems: one that is formal and used to comply with external demands, and one that is informal, based on the intuition of the project managers and the group dynamics within the projects (Jaafari, 2001). A systems thinking approach is synthetic and integrative (Pourdehnad, 2007). Through it, we can gain understanding of individual and collective behaviours that cannot be gained by analysis alone. As such, systems thinking is the right conceptual frame within which to pursue this kind of conditional managerial design in both practice and theory (Kapsali, 2011).

CRPs and innovation

The theory of CRPs has gained popularity in the last two decades. Ralph Stacey and his colleagues (Stacey et al., 2000; Stacey, 2007, 2011) developed the theory in opposition to systems thinking. Whereas systems thinking fundamentally considers the idea of a system valuable to management and organisational research and development, Stacey and others do not. Their central proposition is that it is not possible to develop, structure, and work on an organisation-wide level.

Systems theory underpins most management literature (Mowles et al., 2010). That means that theories of organisational change support the idea that change can be "wholesale, linear and predictable." Even though Jackson (2000) asserts that no single systems theory exists (but rather, many variations of it), Mowles et al. (2008, 2010) respond that they share common characteristics. They see organisations as an "idealised whole" (i.e. that borders exist to differentiate between internal and external) consisting of parts. Since these parts stand in a direct causal relationship with the whole, working on the whole can affect the parts and vice versa. This indicates that complete organisational change is possible.

Mowles et al. (2008) state that systems thinking developed into system dynamics and beyond to incorporate theories of emergence and complexity as described by Kauffman (1995), Holland (1999), and Jackson (2000). The unexpected (Senge, 1990) and mistakes (Weick and Sutcliffe, 2001) can be seen as information generated from positive and negative feedback (Argyris, 1982; Schön, 1983; Senge, 1990). Information is thus seen as an opportunity (Mowles et al., 2010) to improve the systemic model.

Rooted in CAS, others have furthered this thinking accordingly (Mowles et al., 2008; Mowles, 2010). Wheatley (1992; Wheatley and Myron-Kellner Rogers, 1998) states that members of organisations should operate according to simple rules, which warrant creativity and improve results through the

126 *Innovation – between chaos and order*

power of complexity. This thinking comes from the notion that organisations are like (or at least could and should operate like) natural living systems, which emerge and grow according to simple rules in their environment. The ability to identify (either by finding or developing) these rules would make organisational change easier.

Griffin (2002) has put forth an extensive critique of this line of thought. Here, complex and paradoxical phenomena are drawn into a systemic understanding of organising which then decreases the complexity of the phenomena in question.

According to Stacey et al. (2000), there are two different notions of teleology (or causality) when it comes to the notion of novelty and change within organisational development: (1) natural law teleology (scientific management), where change is caused by natural laws, and (2) formative teleology (systems thinking), where certain qualities in combination lead to various expressions (e.g. the acorn becomes the oak). Both could be considered as rationalist teleologies (where change is a result of human choice and action). Ideas are born in the minds of people (i.e. managers) and then promoted into the organisation. Following the thinking of Stacey et al. (2000), this causality does not allow free will for anyone in the organisation beyond the manager, and participation simply means maintaining the organisation.

Stacey et al. (2000) argue for a teleology that is transformative, where novelty is understood to emerge through human interaction. This is why they call their theory of complex responsive processes of relating (CRP).

CRP rejects any separation of subjective and objective understandings of human action and draws attention to the innately paradoxical and transformative nature of everyday experience (Stacey et al., 2000; Stacey, 2007). It therefore claims to offer a more radical understanding of the relationship between human action (and organisational life) and complexity theories. The theory emphasises power relations, communicative interaction, and the unprompted and improvisational nature of human action (Mowles et al., 2008).

Stacey et al. take a more absolute stance than the teleology of systems thinking in that they assert that global patterns emerge only as a consequence of the interaction of local actors (or agents). Everything these local agents do (even if that is nothing) has an effect on emerging patterns over time. The effects do not go in the other direction (i.e. no one controls the turn of events). At the same time, even though patterns of relating lean towards a certain direction, the precise global patterns that emerge are unpredictable. The global patterns are paradoxical in that they are formed by local agents and, at the same time, form the local agents. As such, they both constrain and enable what is possible for local agents to do.

CRP draws upon the theories of the American pragmatists – primarily George Herbert Mead and his theory of language and the mind – and the social theories of Norbert Elias, which focus on the relationship between power, behaviour, emotion, and knowledge.

Mead (1934) contended that the self is not so much a substance as it is a process. In this process, the conversation of gestures has been internalised within an organic form. People are then engaged in constant repetitions of gestures and responses with others, forming an ever-evolving, emerging social pattern. This becomes a constant process of negotiation and adjustment, shaping the intentions and communication of the generalised other, in which the meaning of one gesture cannot be understood outside the context of its response.

A single individual does not simply "have" an intention; rather, the intention an individual expresses emerges from his or her conversational interaction with others. Intention and choice are not lonely acts but rather themes organised by and organising relationships at the same time. (Stacey, 2007: 281).

As such, CRP offers a different way of understanding what happens between people. This retrospective sense-making process stands in contrast to the idea that it is possible to design solutions in advance of action (Mowles et al., 2010).

Norbert Elias (1939/1991, 1939/2000), like Weber (Elwell, 2013),[3] tries to bridge the gap between micro- and macro-sociology, by focusing on how structural and individual personalities interact with one another in social change. According to Elias, personality and social structure are closely interrelated. When the social structure changes, so does the individual personality structure, which causes further change to the social structure. People only exist in interdependent relationships, oriented by both nature and nurture. Individuals define themselves and their world, as well as orient their thought and actions through these interdependencies (figurations). The individual and the society are therefore indivisible, part of a single whole, impossible to understand in terms of individual singularities. According to Elias, our relations with others are conditioned by power relationships. We act within a web of the intentions of other people, and because of this, we cannot forecast what the outcome will be. As such, Elias argues against the tendency to reduce processes to states, to separate actor and activity, structures and process, agency and structure, objects and relationships.

Both Mead and Elias see human nature as social and our sense of self as arising through social interactions. These interactions are iterative and reflective. Change is the result of interdependent actions and is informed by past actions (i.e. not simple causality). It is not planned, nor is it foreseeable. We make sense of our world through reflection and reflexivity.

Stacey sees consciousness as arising from the communicative interaction between humans (following the traces of Mead and Elias). In our vocal gestures or actions to another, we evoke our own responses. Our actions are not isolated; they are formed by the other as well as our appreciation of that other and the action itself. It follows that consciousness, knowing, and the mind are social processes in which meaning emerges in the social act of gesturing and responding (Mowles et al., 2008), whereas gesturing cannot be seen independently from responding (Stacey, 2001, 2007).

128 *Innovation – between chaos and order*

In order to produce change, managers can make gestures towards a desired future for the organisation, which will trigger responses in the different actors through local interactions. These local interactions will decide if the desire (e.g. a new strategy) will actually be turned into practice. This change cannot be planned as such, since so much is happening at local levels (both internally and externally) that will shape the course of events.

Working with ambiguity and complexity is not easy for people steeped in linear thinking (Mowles et al., 2008). As a consequence of Stacey and his colleagues, Aasen and Johannessen (2009) approach the management of innovation as a communicative process (2009) and Buur and Larsen (2010) suggest a new way of understanding innovation as the emergence of new meaning in conversations.

Where Stacey and others claim their positions and approaches to be radical departures and rejections of systems thinking, others do not (Jackson, 2000; Zhu, 2007). Furthermore, some see them as compatible (Luoma et al., 2011). Regardless of how different CRP may be, it has undoubtedly gained much traction and popularity among scholars and practitioners. Examples of the use of the theory can be found in organisational and leadership writings (Simpson, 2007; Aragón, 2012), health practice (Mowles et al., 2010), NGO work (Mowles et al., 2008), leadership development evaluations (Jarvis et al., 2013), analysis church leaders' narratives (Simpson, 2012), and understanding of ERP usage (Christensen et al., 2012), among others.

Cynefin and innovation

Cynefin is a framework for helping leaders make decisions. *Cynefin*, pronounced ku-*nev*-in, is a Welsh word that signifies the multiple factors in our environment and our experience that influence us in ways we can never understand (Snowden and Boone, 2007). More specifically, the Cynefin framework helps leaders determine the prevailing context so that they can make suitable choices.

According to Cynefin creator David J. Snowden, the development of the Cynefin framework has its roots in his work on understanding how informal networks and supporting technologies allow greater connectivity and more rapid association of unexpected ideas and capabilities than formal systems (Snowden, 2012). It draws on ideas and theories from the knowledge management complexity sciences, and takes off from the distinction of what is known, knowable, and unknown. Knowledge management started around 1995 with the popularisation of the SECI model (Snowden, 2002). SECI focuses on the movement of knowledge between tacit and explicit states through the four processes of socialisation, externalisation, combination, and internalisation (Nonaka and Takeuchi, 1995; Nonaka and Konno, 1998). Snowden (2002) refers to Stacey (2001) and points out that not everyone considers knowledge a "thing" or a "system" but more of a process of relating. This is a departure from a Kantian worldview (or epistemology) where knowledge is something absolute, awaiting discovery. Snowden (2002) considers knowledge both a thing and a flow.

The Cynefin framework provides a structure in which to discuss different forms of uncertainty, such as deep uncertainty, the growth of knowledge as we learn about the world, stochastic behaviours, and randomness (French, 2015). The framework also offers a further perspective on the relationship between scenario thinking and decision analysis in supporting decision-makers (French, 2013).

Snowden and Boone (2007) believe the time has come to broaden the traditional approach to leadership and decision-making and form a new perspective based on complexity science. The Cynefin framework allows leaders to sort the issues they are facing into five contexts defined by the nature of the relationship between cause and effect. Four of these – simple, complicated, complex, and chaotic – require leaders to diagnose situations and to act in contextually appropriate ways. The fifth – disorder – applies when there is no clarity over which of the other four contexts is predominant.

The model suggests that there is a way to act given the situation one finds oneself in:

- *Simple* suggests a best practice orientation with the steps of "sense", "categorise," and "respond."
- *Complicated* suggests a good practice with the steps of "sense", "analyse," and "respond."
- *Complex* suggests an emergent (practice) with the steps of "probe"," sense," and "respond."
- *Chaotic* suggests a novel (practice) with the steps of "act", "sense," and "respond."

Cynefin has been used in a range of contexts to support decision-making and strategy development in dynamic and challenging situations (Gorze-Mitka and Okreglicka, 2014). It has also been used (and suggested) in other areas such as health promotion (van Beurden et al., 2013), information services (McLeod and Childs, 2013), and statistics and decision analysis (French, 2013).

While the Cynefin framework can help organisations understand their context, it may also be helpful in understanding and organising for innovation. Innovation is, as we have seen, not a simple, straightforward process. It requires a departure from business as normal to pursuing something new, different, and valuable. The Cynefin model suggests how one can go about it: how to act and respond when leaving the known.

Where the Cynefin framework can easily come out as a categorisation framework, it is also more than that. Certainly, it offers a lot of value as an aid to categorisation, but even more so it is a dynamic sense-making framework. Sense-making should be understood as the complex process by which people make sense of the situation in which they find themselves. When categorising, say, a company in one of the given domains, often it is not emphasised

130 *Innovation – between chaos and order*

that the position is not static or single. In other words, categorisations can change and, moreover, a complex entity may occupy more than one position simultaneously depending on the enforced boundaries of interpretation (e.g. the competitive market may be "complex," but the internal situation could be labelled "complicated"). Because the framework is contextual, how people perceive and interpret the world becomes the key to utilising it.

There is a difference between some theorists' orientations on systems thinking and Cynefin. System thinkers orientate themselves towards an ideal future and then develop strategies for how to get there from the present. Because it is rooted in complexity, Cynefin focuses on the present, identifying what can be changed and then taking small steps in a positive direction without assuming a final destination. Snowden and Boone (2007) are less convinced than many other thinkers that human complex systems can be easily modelled from those found in nature. They point to some distinct differences between people and animals:

- People can have several identities
- People make decisions based on past patterns of success and failure, rather than on logical, definable rules
- People can, in certain circumstances, purposefully change the systems in which they operate to equilibrium states (think of a Six Sigma project) in order to create predictable outcomes

As such, leaders who want to utilise and apply the principles of complexity need to go about it differently than just merely assuming a one-to-one relationship between natural and human-created systems. One can argue that this is precisely what complexity theory teaches us: we cannot assume the same result from one system to another.

Chaordic and innovation

"Chaordic" (Hock, 1999) was invented by Dee Hock, the founder of the VISA card. It is a combination of the words chaos and order and suggests the ability to be both at the same time. Hock based his thoughts on his experience with creating the VISA card and also his views on complexity. Hock also suggests a very social view of the world as he says that organisations are fictions of the mind – they cannot really be directly experienced by our senses. They have no smell, no taste, and so forth. We experience them indirectly.

The Chaordic model can be explained as a path with stepping stones through which an organisation changes. It is a model that suggests that an organisation needs to be integrated from its aspirations and ideals to its practice. It also suggests that changes happen through mutual agreements that occur in sequential order. It does not, however, suggest that an organisation can ever be fully finished. Instead, the process is cyclical: after completing all the steps, one starts all over again. As such, this process requires organisations to be in constant introspection and in contact with its environment. As well, the process is not prescriptive and could potentially incorporate many different methodologies in each step.

The Chaordic design process has six dimensions, beginning with purpose and ending with practice. Each dimension can be considered a lens through which participants in the design process study the conditions giving rise to the need of a new organisation or reconceiving the existing one, as well as actually defining it. It is important to stress that defining one stepping stone may require taking one step back to reconsider it. For instance, an agreement on principles may call into question the purpose.

The dimensions are described in detail below:

Purpose The reason for being. It is understood as something very deep, something providing meaning, and which binds the community or organisation together.

Principles After the purpose has been lucidly stated, one needs to define the principles that will guide and steer the work done in pursuit of the purpose. Principles can be seen as values, but they are agreed-upon values – not just all or any values held by individual members. They are formulated to bind the community together and describe what is believed to be true and can be used to judge actions and decisions.

Concept The third step is about developing a concept for the organisation, ensuring that the entity is effective in accordance with its purpose and principles. Questions around legal structures, governance, and ownership – as well as discussion around industry – are often considered here, but it is to a large extent an overall envisioning step.

People The key here is to identify the relevant participants (i.e. those who are affected and needed). These participants can be seen as individuals and/or groups, and can include other organisations.

Structure The actual organisational setup and operations are articulated in the form of a composition (i.e. often referred here as a constitution) and by-laws. It essentially incorporates all previous steps with more detail and precision.

Practice According to the theory, this step is a naturally evolving consequence of the previous steps. By thinking through the previous steps clearly and effectively, practice should unfold in an effective way. It is often described as a situation that blends competition and cooperation in a beneficial way – realising the purpose of a self-organising, self-governing system that is positioned for continuous learning and evolution.

> Purpose and principle, clearly understood and articulated, and commonly shared, are the genetic code of any healthy organisation. To the degree

132 *Innovation – between chaos and order*

that you hold purpose and principles in common among you, you can dispense with command and control. People will know how to behave in accordance with them, and they'll do it in thousands of unimaginable, creative ways. The organisation will become a vital, living set of beliefs.

– Dee Hock

When considering the theory behind the Chaordic model, one has to separate its higher aspirations regarding how organisations should work and be structured (i.e. ideals such as justice or equity) and the actual model. For the purposes of this book, we are more concerned with the actual model and to what extent it is helpful in terms of innovation. Although the model is an organisational development, Hock argues that it is also firmly rooted in a contemporary worldview on systems thinking and complexity. On the one hand, the model can appear very sequential, with a clear taxonomy. On the other, it can also be an approach to developing an innovation organisation.

Towards a theoretical foundation of innovation in, as, and of complex systems

As seen in this chapter, finding common ground around the applicability of these theories is not so easy. There are both similarities and differences in the four lenses on innovation introduced in this chapter. Even though scholars may disagree on some points, others see ways of bridging these disagreements. While there seems to be agreement on the characteristics of a CAS, and that a CAS is an adequate way to understand the world (or at least those parts of the world that fulfil the criteria of a CAS), there is disagreement over the use of CAS for understanding social systems. Stacey (2007, 2011) and Snowden and Boone (2007) are more sceptical about applying CAS wholesale when it comes to social (man-made) systems, whereas Reeves and others are more in favour of such approaches.

Another disagreement concerns whether the future should be "designed" and whether one can affect systems as a whole (i.e. in a top-down approach) in pursuit of a desired, future state. Unfortunately, scholars from different camps do not fully agree here, either. System thinkers such as Senge (1990) and Jackson (2000, 2010) maintain the possibility of a "designed" system change, but this has been rejected by Stacey and others.

According to Luoma et al. (2011), CRP "illuminates many of the micro behavioural, local interaction and creativity-related organisational phenomena whereas the systems perspective is useful for other purposes." Systems thinking can support research in several ways by suggesting different levels of analysis and synthesis for different problems, as well as theories and methods (Kapsali, 2011). There are some areas where systems thinking and complexity theories share beliefs and approaches:

- Reductionism (the belief that everything can be reduced to individual parts)

- Determinism (the misbelief of complete control)
- Analysis (breaking down systems to their smallest constituents to obtain understanding)
- Cause and effect logic (closed boundaries, linear thinking, and absence of circular feedback loops)

Businesses today face a different reality compared to that of the past: environments are often tougher, more ambiguous, and more malleable (Reeves et al., 2012, 2015, 2016). Technological innovation has increased the pace and effect of change. The diffusion rate of products – that is, from invention to saturation – has intensified dramatically. As a consequence, companies move through their life cycles twice as fast as compared to 30 years ago. This requires them to adapt much faster than before, since their products, services, and business models become outdated more rapidly. Another development is the growth in interconnectedness. Activities are linked across the world, often in particular ecosystems that foster interdependencies between participants. But where connections generate vitality in the economy, they also increase the risk of shock events cascading through the system (Reeves et al., 2016).

The Cynefin framework offers a way to articulate the reality of an organisation or particular events within or without the organisation. Principles from CAS help us to determine the nature of the phenomenon in question and, if it fits the criteria, how one can work with it. Systems thinking can help us look at and understand social phenomena that occur both within and without organisations, and the interaction between the organisation and its context. CRPs focus more on what actually happens in the particular, local interactions that help shape the course of events.

One strength of the Chaordic model, similar to the Cynefin framework, is its relative ease in terms of comprehension and communication. Organisational and business developments often rely on simplistic models, not because they are considered exhaustive or assumed to be eternal truths, but because of their approximative value. In the end, it comes down to how well an organisation uses the given theory, framework, and model, and how it adapts the frameworks to their lived reality – as opposed to simply considering one model's relative theoretical strength over another. That is also unfortunately why complexity theories often are disfavoured in comparison with classical reductionist models.

Innovation can be argued to flow out of interactions between people. Essentially, it is the unpredictable multitude that nourishes the creative process. As the innovation (as a CAS) within a larger CAS (i.e. the wider organisation) develops, the multitude and complexity changes as the form becomes clearer. Decisions are made, processes are designed, and structures are imposed, making the innovation process less malleable. As the innovation process leads towards spread and uptake, the system becomes bigger due to increasing interactions beyond the bounded idea of the organisation. Throughout its non-linear journey, learnings are available, but often it is

134 *Innovation – between chaos and order*

only when we see how an innovation performs in the market that learnings become more concrete. Innovation, then, can be seen as a CAS that occurs out of complex systems, in complex systems.

Summary

In this chapter we have taken the idea of innovation as a CAS and provided four orientations – theories, frameworks, and methods – that can help us better to understand innovation and how it can be addressed. In addition to being useful analytical frameworks for assessing the innovation process, these orientations are helpful when designing and undergoing those processes.

In the next chapter, we turn our focus towards capacity building: that is, how to generate the power to innovate.

Notes

1 It should be noted that complexity theories have been applied in quite a number of fields within management. For illustrative purposes, some literature is referenced and described to provide a more comprehensive idea of the field. Also, much that has been written on this topic has not been necessarily empirical, but rather the result of opinions and analyses of the individual authors.
2 That is, some authors see complexity theory as part of systems thinking and vice versa.
3 Elias's "civilisation process" can considered to share aspects Weber's concept of rationalisation, having similar origins in the changing character of interactions between social structure and individual personality.

10 Capacity building

Introduction

Capacity building is a relatively new concept that has started finding its way across organisational life and action. It has roots in a number of disciplines that in the 1970s promoted empowerment in areas such as community development, international aid and development, public health, and education (Crisp et al., 2000). Capacity, in our current understanding of the word, has a number of synonyms such as faculty, power, ability, or capability. For instance, the President's Emergency Plan for AIDS Relief (2012) defines capacity as "the ability of individuals and organisations or organisational units to perform functions effectively, efficiently and sustainably."

The use of the phrase "capacity building" is quite widespread in the NGO sector, where it often means providing or improving the skills of people, organisations, or communities to achieve their objectives. This often requires overcoming certain obstacles to ensure particular qualities, such as inclusion or democracy, are developed. For instance, the President's Emergency Plan for AIDS Relief (2012) defines it as "capacity building is an evidence-driven process of strengthening the abilities of individuals, organisations, and systems to perform core functions sustainably, and to continue to improve and develop over time."

The NGO sector is quite outspoken about the fact that capacity building is one of their main objectives in, for example, developing countries. In this book, however, we will treat capacity building as an internal quality and focus area for securing growth and success. Ignoring capacity development can bring about, at best, mere optimisation of operations with regard to existing resources and objectives and, at worst, eventually lead to an organisation's demise.

According to Wikipedia, capacity building (or capacity development) is "the process by which individuals and organisations obtain, improve, and retain the skills, knowledge, tools, equipment, and other resources needed to do their jobs competently."[1] Growing this quality is therefore about the power of individuals as well as organisations to do more or better.

Kaplan (2000) claims that developing capacity in organisations involves building an organisation's tangible and intangible assets. Although he refers

136 *Capacity building*

specifically to NGOs, there are compelling reasons for organisations at large to consider his suggestion of starting with intangible qualities. He (ibid) goes on to argue that organisations (NGOs) focusing on developing a conceptual framework for capacity building need to start with an understanding of the world, the organisation's attitude or view of itself, its vision, and its strategy. Organisations that can do this properly are more skilful at being self-reflective and critical, two qualities that facilitate more effective capacity building.

These qualities do not occur all at once; rather, they are improved over time and on an on-going basis. Similarly, capacity building is not a one-time effort to improve short-term efficiency or effectiveness, but a continuous effort towards the creation of resilient and sustainable (i.e. successful) organisations.

In this chapter, we will look more closely at capacity building for innovation and expand upon Tidd et al. (2005) and Prajogo and Ahmed's (2006) respective views on innovation capacity. The first section addresses the topic of innovation capacity building in more depth. A discussion on some challenges and opportunities with respect to innovation capacity building follows, before we suggest a model for organisational capacity building. Finally, a discussion of measuring innovation capacity building is offered.

What is innovation capacity building?

A specific aspect of capacity building concerns the capacity to innovate. According to Tidd et al. (2005), innovation capacity is "the ability of enterprises to identify trends and new technologies, as well as to acquire and exploit this knowledge and information." Smith et al. (2011) state that we must clearly distinguish "capacity" from dynamic innovation "capability." The latter deals with the firm's specific ability to continuously transform knowledge and ideas into profitable innovations.

It may be helpful to articulate differences between capacity, ability, and capability. Distinguishing between the three can be difficult as they are synonyms in many ways. For example, all three are often used to indicate one's power to perform an action, but capacity is a broader term than capability or ability. In organisms, capacity is inborn whereas abilities are learned. Even though organisations are social systems, one can say that all of them have the capacity to be innovative, but all must also learn the ability to innovate. Capability can be seen as something more specific. An organisation may claim the ability to innovate, but they may not have the capability to innovate a new high-tech medical device. Where capabilities are often seen as either-or propositions, ability is normally measured in degrees[2].

Following this logic, innovation capacity can refer to something more or different than abilities and capabilities. It is often helpful to distinguish between certain terms because terms can overlap depending on the specific context of their use. This monograph takes a wider and more fundamental approach to the concept of innovation capacity and sees organisational innovative capacity as the power of an organisation to potentially produce and successfully introduce new innovations repeatedly. This power then is the result of the combination of organisational knowledge, skill, attitude, and other resources.

A study performed by Prajogo and Ahmed (2006) suggests that innovation stimuli do not directly affect innovation performance. Rather, its effect is mediated through an organisation's innovation capacity. The direct consequence of these findings is that improved innovation performance requires improved innovation capacity. The authors (ibid.) suggest that an organisation must develop the behavioural and cultural contexts and practices to attain desired outcomes and high performance in the area of innovation.

It is not only a question of stimuli, but of what an organisation does with it. But what are stimuli? A general way to view stimuli is as "available information." The pertinent question is about the ability to detect, process, and apply stimuli towards organisational gains that determine the innovation capacity of an organisation. Specifically, what constitutes right or good behavioural and cultural contexts and practices is debatable, as is the question of developing said behaviour, culture, and practices. What makes one organisation successful in how it processes stimuli may not be the same for the other. Local qualities that make one organisation effective are often nested and culturally dependent, making them difficult to isolate and replicate. We're not arguing against trying to learn from others; rather, complexity theory suggests that outcomes can be different, even given the same stimuli.

Innovation performance is the true preoccupation of organisations. It is also the true test of capacity building. But as previously discussed, having the capacity is not the same as exercising it. Still, without the capacity to innovate, innovating cannot happen. It is an important distinction, and it points to another important aspect: having the capacity for something points towards opportunities and possibilities, but only those within reach. It is a resource and strength, but for various reasons, it may not have been exercised (or exercised properly). Capacity, then, refers to a particular strength to obtain something. We can have or exercise capacity at the individual level as well as with constellation of actors (e.g. organisations or even societies).

Following the logic introduced in Chapter 1 on the theoretical challenges in terms of innovation; organisational capacity building for innovation can thus be defined as "the activities and processes undertaken to improve a system's innovation qualities."

Two challenges and opportunities with innovation capacity building

Capacity building poses several theoretical and methodological challenges – some more obvious than others. The need for an innovation strategy (Pisano, 2015; Vindeløv-Lidzélius, 2018) is one. A strategy offers direction and focus. And without one, it is questionable how efficient one's capacity building

138 *Capacity building*

efforts can be (i.e. one may spend a lot of resources on less yielding efforts.) But the absence of clarity in terms of the direction of innovation does not mean that nothing can be achieved. Indeed, openness in the early stages may result in an unexpectedly fruitful turn of events. Likewise, strategy may shift given new market signals and rewards.

Measuring innovation capacity building is also uncertain because it can often be unclear what should be measured. Sometimes the chosen criteria may simply be too narrow to capture the full value of an effort. It is relatively easy to measure in terms of input factors (e.g. expenditure), intermediate outputs (e.g. establishing an innovation model), and actual outputs (e.g. number of successful introductions of new products). It is far more difficult to capture the full range of effects, as there are effects in a system that are hard to assume before a given action and remain hard to identify afterwards.

Two of these challenges also represent opportunities: the spill-over effect and the two uncertainty types.

The spill-over effect suggests that one change or action impacts other areas. For instance, developing a new system for capturing and developing ideas in the front-end of innovation could potentially generate a number of related (or possibly unrelated) effects: the system could be expanded to include later stages in the innovation process, the capability of creating such a system may increase the ability to make other systems (e.g. feedback systems on managerial communication), there might be an increased focus on creativity and ideas in general, or it might build engagement and community through participation in the development and use of this new endeavour. In general, the development of specific capabilities also leads to a general increase in abilities.

The uncertainty types draw upon the argument from Chapter 1, and the taxonomy on the four stereotypical positions of an organisation can be in (i.e. knowing or not knowing what and how). There are essentially two types of uncertainties. The first concerns identified uncertainties, in which one may not know what will happen, but questions can be asked to generate potential scenarios. The second are unidentified uncertainties (i.e. uncertainties we have no awareness of). Obviously, in this case, questions cannot be asked, nor scenarios developed. The second type of uncertainty is the more difficult one and is also the one organisations need to prepare for. To deal with this type of uncertainty, capacity building may have a positive effect as it generates just that – capacity.

In short, one can say that: whether we build capacity towards something specific and tangible (e.g. delivering more of a specific product) or towards something fluid and ambiguous (e.g. developing a more resilient culture), a focus on one or the other may have a positive reciprocal effect.

The 6P model

Rooted in Kaplan's (2000) proposal of beginning with intangible assets, a 6P model is suggested below for organisational capacity development. The

Capacity building 139

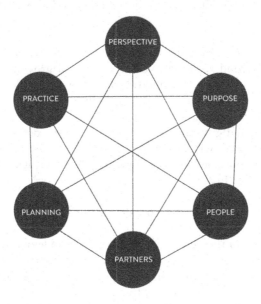

Figure 10.1 The 6P model.
Source: Author.

model can help to guide efforts for building capacity. The 6 Ps are perspective, purpose, people, partners, planning, and practice, and they are described in greater detail below (Figure 10.1):

Perspective Everything starts with how we see and think about the world. The way we think about the world and the lenses we use to interpret it define to a large extent what we see. For example, if we see new technology as unimportant, we will act accordingly. Or if we consider strategy to be best developed by a few top managers, rather than something that many should build together, we will design accordingly. A key point for developing capacity is therefore the ability to remain conscious about how we think about and see the world. If we do not recognise our own convictions, values, and truths, these will reinforce our blind spots and will stand in the way of looking deeper and wider.

Purpose Clarity on why capacity building is needed may sound banal, but quite often it is so taken for granted that we miss the opportunity to focus. Instead, we plant the seed for future confusion and mistakes. Purpose is not useful only for very clear and tangible capacity building efforts, but can also serve as a guiding star for more ambiguous ambitions, such as developing a problem-solving culture. Even when we are unaware of what problems will arise, we need to develop the capacity to solve problems. These resources may

140 *Capacity building*

include resources and collaborations beyond the borders of any one individual organisation.

People The heart of organisations are people. As a result, even if capacity building goes beyond working with, helping, and growing people, people are still the main focus. Continuously investing in people (as opposed to, say, money) and their growth is key to organisational capacity building. Towards that end, an organisation can "up-skill" or "re-train" staff, or they can support learning and growth even without a specific, defined application of those new skills or knowledge. Indeed, learning something new, even if it is not necessarily applicable here and now, may boost creativity and ideas not initially considered. In addition, just encouraging people to learn something new has the effect that people become better at learning, and that skill may be subsequently applied when a more defined need arises.

Partners Many of the perceived or identified problems and opportunities for organisations today require something more than the organisations themselves to resolve. Instead, they might require university collaborations, private R&D institutions, new sub-contractors, or marketing bureaus. Again, it may be easier to develop partnerships when we know exactly what capacity must be developed, but in principle it goes beyond the defined and points towards the potential. Partnership strategy and structures can also serve as a vehicle for addressing issues we cannot anticipate.

Planning Capacity building does not happen by itself or, at the very least, one cannot assume an unplanned process will be sufficient. The quality of the plan depends on the quality of the planning. There is a need to thoughtfully select priorities. No organisation can improve its capacity in all matters simultaneously. As such, taking into account strategy, each organisation will have to assess their situation and design the course of actions needed in a logical and coherent manner.

Practice Process refers to how things are done. Often when we think of how organisations differ, we think about what they do, their size, and so forth. But how they do things is just as an important source of understanding their effectiveness. Methodologies, procedures, and policies that help to steer organisational life are ultimately measured in the light of their effect on practice. When building capacity, the right practices determine the outcome. It is insufficient to identify a capacity need and make a plan if the practices, or the lack thereof, stand in their way. Our organisational worldview and purpose come to life through practice.

This model should not be seen as a one-time process, but rather as a continuous effort where the six domains help us navigate decisions in terms of designing the right mix of capacity building initiatives.

Implicit in the model lies the important recognition that the system is at once interdependent on other systems, as well as self-consistent, self-referential, and self-organising. This (also called the second order of cybernetics[3]) means that any assessment of the model must consider not just feedback, but also the system facilitating the feedback. To put this in a simplified way: when a group of people assess an organisation and its landscape, they need to factor in how they obtain information, how they process it and make decisions about it, and finally how they communicate it.

Measuring capacity building

Knowing if one has actually developed capacity is an important but difficult question. Depending on the mix of capacity building strategies and initiatives that an organisation undertakes, one may have to look at a combination of assessment techniques and unique criteria (Poole, 1997).

First, there should be agreement on what is to be measured. As an example, up-skilling staff may suggest an assessment of what people have learnt and how efficient this was done, perhaps in relation to an assumed outcome and expenditure. This is normally then done on an individual basis, with the results aggregated at the end. However, we would measure differently from an organisational view (i.e. where the whole is greater than the sum of its different parts).

The real results of up-skilling are evident in terms of increased productivity, new products, better sales, fewer sick days, and so forth. But the ability to draw a clear line from a specific initiative to an absolute outcome may be tricky as development is a nested affair, and there could be other factors that impact the end result. This is not to say one should avoid assessments, but rather that we should conduct them with care – balancing immediate outcomes with more long-term effects.

The second consideration concerns *how* to measure. Capacity building is a process that generates change as it unfolds (as opposed to solely at the end). This provides us with the opportunity to investigate the changes during the process as well. As such, we can use different techniques and focal areas as we measure. Indeed, as measurement can be a form of intervention, it may actually support the capacity building itself.

Finally, capacity building may have a spill-over effect since building capacity in one area may have consequences – positive and negative – in other areas.

We can therefore see that it's important to move beyond merely measuring *if* a capacity program has been implemented; rather, we should measure the *quality* of that implementation in the light of what it rendered (that is, not only if it delivered what we expected).

Summary

Building capacity is an essential aspect of organisational and business success. In this chapter, we have discussed what capacity building is, and more

142 *Capacity building*

specifically what innovation capacity is as well as some of its opportunities and challenges. We offered a 6P model to guide efforts for building capacity. The 6 Ps are perspective, purpose, people, partners, planning, and practice. This represents a starting point for the following three chapters on strategising, leading, and organising. Although these are interdependent, they are discussed in different chapters to ease the reading experience. We will include additional findings and ideas form complexity theories and methods to situate these ideas.

Notes

1 https://en.wikipedia.org/wiki/Capacity_building
2 This argumentation draws from the logic in: https://grammarist.com/usage/ability-capability-capacity/
3 The second order of cybernetics is the recursive application of cybernetics to itself. See this link for more details: https://en.wikipedia.org/wiki/Second-order_cybernetics

11 Strategy

Introduction

According to *Harvard Business Essentials* (2003), there are two schools of thought when it comes to strategy in relation to value creation. The first suggests that the road to value creation lies in driving out the old-fashioned practice of relying on gut instincts and replacing it with strategy based on rigorous, quantitative analysis. That is, the basis of thought is analytical thinking, aimed at providing certainty. The other school favours creativity and innovation, and is more rooted in the idea of intuitive thinking. In reality, though, the strategy process tends to favour a "both-and" approach, in which one does not rule out the other, but rather is supportive of the other. Although many have suggested the importance of innovation strategies, many organisations still lack one (Pisano, 2015; Vindeløv-Lidzélius, 2018).

Newer theories, like Cynefin (Snowden, 2002, 2012; Snowden and Boone, 2007) and Complex Responsive Processes (Stacey, 2000, 2007, 2011; Stacey et al., 2000), offer different schools of thought in which strategy is emergent (Holland, 1992, 1993, 1999) and cannot really be designed. Complex Adaptive Systems and Systems Thinking also offer interesting perspectives for how to develop and deploy strategies for greater success in complex systems. The underlying organisational dynamic needs to be taken into account if a change strategy is to be effective (Van Dijk and Peters, 2011). Stavros and Hinrichs' (2009) SOAR (strengths, opportunities, aspiration, and results) framework is a strengths-based appreciative inquiry (Cooperrider and Srivastva 1987; Cooperrider et al., 1995; Cooperrider et al., 2000; Cooperrider and Whitney, 2001) orientation towards strategy development.

Innovation strategy is in many ways a subset of business strategy, but merely reducing the conversation to applying tools and practices on a different level is a bit too haphazard as the nature of innovation requires a focus in its own right. Innovation may actually be a defining factor in strategy delivery, and even crafting strategies, as it may drive a change in strategic goals or focus.

In the next section, we turn our attention towards understanding what an innovation strategy is. Following that, we will discuss the complexity approach to strategy as it requires a more communal and interactional approach

144　*Strategy*

than the classic strategic planning approach. When we look at capacity building, we can simply say that organisations have a few choices. We often think of what is happening and what can be done within the organisation in question. This may be relevant on one level as we should expect that any course of action that an organisation takes would require at least some sort of configuration (or adaptation) on behalf of the organisation. However, it is helpful to consider three overall approaches that are available to organisations: capacity building can occur through mergers and acquisitions (M&As), by creating partnerships, or through the development of the internal organisation. These three overall approaches are discussed more in detail in the following three sections. Clearly, what works in one situation may be totally inadequate or even counterproductive in others (Van Dijk and Peters, 2011).

Innovation strategy

The word strategy is widely used in virtually all aspects of human affairs. Far from its original use in the military, we now speak about career strategies and even "strategies" for our holidays. However, strategy still remains a dominant part of business life and a main concern of c-suite management and executive boards. Innovation strategy is still a relatively new topic and not much has been written on the subject. This is partly due to the fact that innovation itself is a fairly new phenomena and a relatively fuzzy topic. However, the absence of an articulated innovation strategy does not necessarily mean that there has been no consideration, plans, models, resource allocations, or problem identification. Rather, so far we have shown that there has been considerable thought and work done on the subject of innovation. Innovation strategies, as an organisational focus, seem like a natural consequence of the growing attention given to innovation and the need to ensure more value out of innovation efforts.

Strategy has a number of definitions and subthemes, and our understanding of it has changed over the years. In the most simplistic terms, a strategy is a general plan. In 2001, Collins proposed a move away from a production and customer focus (i.e. what we make and for whom) towards the question of why we exist. The intersection and overlap of the following three questions form the basis for defining the strategy: what are we passionate about? what can we be best in the world at? and what drives our economic engine?

Rumelt (2011) proposed that a good strategy has a fundamental rationale or structure. He called this the "kernel." The kernel consists of three parts: a diagnosis that defines the challenge (or problem), a policy for how to go about this challenge, and a set of coherent actions designed to carry out the guiding policy.

Because of this, it is key for obtaining commitment and cross-functional support across the organisation in order to reach its goals.

Innovation in this aspect can be seen as how we move from where we are to where we want to go, spanning the entire organisation and its effort to reach its vision and goals. But taking a slightly more modest approach to innovation would suggest that it is a subset of business objectives.

According to Pisano (2015), the problem is that an organisation's capacity for innovation stems from an innovation system: "A coherent set of interdependent processes and structures that dictates how the company searches for novel problems and solutions, synthesises ideas into a business concept and products, and selects which projects get funded." Here, it is worth raising a word of caution. A system of sort suggests that it is something that is planned, structured, and somewhat efficient and ideally effective. But a system is often not just the consequence of rational planning, choices, and actions. In terms of organisational matters, there is always chance, irrationality, and contradictions. Innovation systems in general are more a result – a combination – of what is planned and what is actually happening. As such one may ask what the point then is to direct so much attention towards purpose, planning, and coordination, when things turn out differently anyway? That is, however, too much of fatalistic view. Strategy does matter. Without a strategy, innovation efforts can quickly become simply the result of existing practices, ideas, and products that might be counterproductive, or at the very least harnessing strengths and resources ineffectively.

The matrix offered by Pisano (2015) displays the choice organisations have about how much focus they should place on technological and/or business development. The matrix can facilitate perspectives around the fit of a potential innovation in relation to a given organisation's technological capabilities and existing business model. For instance, a new coffee beverage for Starbucks would leverage existing technical competencies and business model (this can be seen as routine innovation), whereas an office delivery service would require a new business model but still leverage existing technical competencies (this can be seen as disruptive innovation). If Starbucks would develop a clothing line, this would require new technological competencies and would not necessarily require a new business model (this can be seen as radical innovation). If, however, Starbucks would only become an online subscription model, this would not only require new technological competencies but also a new business model (this can be seen as architectural innovation).

The key questions in terms of innovation are as follows: how will this innovation create value, and for whom? and what is needed for this to occur? From here, making plans and allocating resources, managing changes, and other related tasks become the key managerial activities.

Crafting an innovation strategy

As illustrated in the previous section, drawing from the rich resource of research, models, and experiences from the domain of strategy is absolutely possible, but we must adapt it to the innovation domain without losing sight of the business strategy and landscape.

146   *Strategy*

Complexity theories offer several takes on how to craft strategies. Instead of focusing only on strategy, the Chaordic approach is a sequential model for developing an entire organisation, but its emphasis on purpose and shared values clearly speaks to a combination of emergence and decision-making. Indeed, systems thinking would argue that there must be a design position, normally considered a managerial job, whereas Stacey and others would reject such an idea (or, at very least, reject it as an ideal). Somewhat surprisingly, the "realised strategy" as described by Mintzberg et al. (1998) results in a combination of the planned and what actually happens.

Following Snowden (2002, 2012) and Snowden and Boone's (2007) proposition that change and strategy development depend on the level of complexity an organisation finds itself in, one also has to consider the culture of the organisation. Culture is a key determinant of how successful the analysis of the complexity will be, as well as how well the development and implementation of the strategy will be. A polarising aspect of strategy development is about using problem-based business improvement methods, or strengths-based constructionist methods. These are stereotypically seen as an either-or proposition, therefore accepting as a predicate of a field-limiting separatist paradigm (Cooperrider, et al., 2000).

In complex systems, strategy development is definitely important, but there must be sensitivity to change and existing conditions in the organisation. The classic ideas around strategic planning function best as propositions, rather than as fixed views and approaches. In contrast, complexity would call for a more relational approach. Appreciative inquiry was developed by Cooperrider and Srivastva in 1987, suggesting that successful change most easily accomplished when people share views and when that change is built upon stories of successes and strengths, rather than failures, flaws, and weaknesses. The classical 4-D model has four stages: Discover (what gives life and the best of what is), Dream (envisioning what might be), Design (co-constructing what should be), and Destiny (deliver and sustain).

In 2009, Stavros and Hinrichs created the SOAR model (or tool), which draws very heavily upon the 4-D model. SOAR is often contrasted with the classic SWOT (strengths, weaknesses, opportunities, and threats) analysis. While it is arguably as much a strategic planning tool as many other classic ones, it focuses on an organisation's strengths and vision of the future when developing strategic goals. The four stages of SOAR are strengths, opportunities, aspiration, and results.

Interestingly, the dominant view of the organisation is that it already "has the answers," as opposed to "finding" answers externally. Of course, there is no reason for not using a combined approach. Indeed, in this book we would recommend innovation strategy as being a combination of strategic thinking and strategic planning – including strategic investigating and strategic dreaming. The strategy development process can do more than simply result in a good strategy – that is, a strategy that has focus, direction, and commitment – it can also build culture and learning as well.

Mergers and acquisitions

The first general way to build capacity is through M&As. In general, M&A is a term for describing the consolidation of organisations (mostly in the form of companies) or assets. This is done through a financial transaction. M&As are in reality two separate actions, but in terms of capacity building, they should accomplish the same thing: the joining of two organisations into one.

It may be useful to distinguish between the two. Mergers refer to the decision between two organisations to join as one. Acquisitions occur when one organisation takes over another, where the acquired organisation ceases existence. Acquisitions can be friendly (i.e. the organisation wants to be over-taken) or hostile (i.e. the organisation does not want to be taken over by the purchaser).

There are several variations within M&A, such as the acquisition of assets (i.e. does not involve buying the shares of another organisation), manage-ment acquisition (i.e. also known as management-led buyout, and therefore private), consolidation (i.e. creating a new organisation), and tender offer (i.e. one organisation offers to buy another at a given price, communicating directly with stockholders).

Over the decades, mergers have followed different types of logic, such as horizontal to vertical mergers, and taking into account diversification strat-egies and globalisation. In last couple of decades, cross-sector convergence (Lachapelle, 2018) has become more usual. This is a clear indication of capac-ity building through M&As. For example, a retail company could buy a tech or e-commerce firm to keep up with the transition to a more digital market-place, acquire new markets, and generate new revenue streams.

Whether or not mergers or acquisitions payoff is not fully clear. One of the challenges is how to assess success. Straub (2007) suggests three different ways to best measure post-M&A performance: synergy realisation, absolute performance, and relative performance.

According to Rumyantseva et al. (2002), from a knowledge perspective, firms can generate greater values through the retention of knowledge-based resources which they generate and integrate. Due to organisational dif-ferences, it continues to be an ongoing challenge extracting technological benefits during and after acquisition. Ranft and Lord (2002) suggest five components for their grounded model of acquisition:

- Improper documentation and implicit knowledge transformation make it difficult to share information during acquisition
- For the acquired firm, symbolic and cultural independence –based on technology and capabilities –is more important than administrative independence
- Detailed knowledge exchange and integration is difficult when the ac-quired firm is large and high performing

148 *Strategy*

- Management of executives from the acquired firm is critical in terms of promotions and pays incentives in order to best utilise their talent and value their expertise
- Transfer of technologies and capabilities is the most difficult task to manage because of the complications associated with acquisition implementation. The risk of losing implicit knowledge is always associated with fast-paced acquisition.

Partnerships

Partnerships are a normal and common way of building capacity. Organisations do this for a variety of reasons, and at times do not consider doing so as capacity development. Indeed, in our everyday language we often speak of partnerships, even when describing customers and subcontractors.

Partnerships come in many different forms, but they all involve collaboration or the intention of collaboration. Joint owners of a business entity often refer to their business as a partnership because they share profit and losses according to an agreed-upon schema. A very basic and general way to think about this is that a partnership requires that both parties have something to gain and something to lose. Often, one can assume a partnership is directed towards the following:

- Developing new products and services
- Increase market positioning
- Adhering to regulations

Within these three areas are several applications, such as research projects, branding initiatives, and different forms of compliance. Partnerships also have indirect applications, such as outsourcing production or marketing and sales, as well as taking advantage of specialised knowledge.

When considering why partnerships are a logical way to build capacity, many reasons arise but in general we can say it is done either to prevent or ensure an action. In other words, partnerships are about reducing risk, improving performance, and/or acting on opportunities.

There are a number of challenges when it comes to partnerships that need to be overcome in order to realise an agreement and ensure it lives up to the original aspirations. The goal of the partnership, what each party will invest, how to make decisions, how to solve problems, and how to share results are all important factors.

One consideration around partnerships is that although they are in general made for specific reasons at specific times, those decisions can also be made to build general readiness for what's coming (i.e. developing capacity). In today's volatile world, the future is unpredictable. Also, developing partnerships take time. Trust, understanding, and collaboration require mutual and purposeful adaptation and learning. This may lead to insufficiently effective

Strategy 149

partnerships that may not be capable of responding to changing conditions in the market. Whereas there is no way to fully overcome this challenge, organisations can acquire diverse sets of partners and invest in mutual exploration and exploitation.

Internal development

Internal development is frequently what people think about when we talk about capacity development. And obviously, some internal initiatives and change management may be needed for making M&A and Networks/Partnerships doable. As a result, internal configuration to a new operational mode is always required on some level.

Internal development can occur in different ways, but it often occurs through one or more of the following, which are generally considered when talking about internal capacity development:

- Acquiring new staff with the same skills as existing staff (i.e. producing more)
- Acquiring new staff with different knowledge and skills (i.e. producing something different or in a different way)
- Developing the existing workforce (i.e. the ability to produce more)
- Developing the existing workforce (i.e. producing something different or in a different way)
- Changing policies and procedures
- Changing resource allocation and organisational design
- Obtaining new tools, technology, and production and services artefacts

(Note that this list does not separate managers and managerial practices from other people.)

One might wonder why a change in culture is not mentioned here. The reason is that changing culture is not a stand-alone area, but rather a coupled consequence of several actions. For instance, changing culture may require up-skilling, introducing a reward system, and changing workflows.

Changing the strategy is not in itself capacity building, but rather a prerequisite for effective capacity development. A change of strategy will require changes internally.

Relocation of activities – in the sense of physically moving departments within the organisation to be more centralised or decentralised – could be seen as one method of internal development, as well as of increasing effectiveness in terms of partnerships. In practice, though, relocating brings forth several internal development requirements.

As an example, here is how the United Nations Development Programme (UNDP), "Supporting Capacity Building the UNDP approach," outlines their model. The UNDP promotes a capacity building approach at the

150   *Strategy*

institutional level and offers a six-step process for systematic capacity building (UNDP, 2011). The steps are as follows:

1 Conducting a training needs assessment
2 Engage stakeholders on capacity development (i.e. participation by all those involved)
3 Assess capacity needs and assets (i.e. prioritise and make the chosen initiatives more contextualised)
4 Formulate a capacity development response (based on the core issues of institutional arrangements, leadership, knowledge, and accountability)
5 Implement a capacity development response
6 Evaluate capacity development (that should be based on changes in performance around the core issues of institutional arrangements, leadership, knowledge, and accountability)

The UNDP model does not fully cater to changing policies and procedures, technology, organisational design, and so forth. It is quite standard in that it focuses on needs and supports the idea of engaging the relevant/affected stakeholders by conducting assessments and formulating ways to enable capacity building.

Human development is at the core of internal capacity building. Heslop (2010) defined human resource development as "the process of equipping people with the understanding and skills, and access to the information and knowledge to perform effectively."

A very particular and important aspect is the role and responsibility of leadership (which is addressed more in detail later in this book). Regarding the relationship between management capabilities and innovation, Eisenhardt and Martin (2000) argue that the capabilities of management allow them to set strategic goals and design strategies for achieving these goals, which leads the organisation to innovation and higher performance. Organisational development focuses on the process (i.e. how things are done) and promotes an examination of why that is and how that can be improved.

It is important to consider internal development as something that consists of more than people, but that also includes them. There are many good arguments why internal development should be the first priority of any organisation. M&A and partnerships present more accentuated and unfamiliar risks to any organisation. Internal conditions are more known by the organisation and, at least in theory, are more in the domain of managerial influence. In practice, though, organisational change may prove to be quite difficult, and this is why some organisations sometimes establish new organisations, distancing themselves from the existing culture and structures.

Summary

In summary, in order to have success with M&As, partnerships, and internal development, one must carefully analyse the situation and organisation. Why are we doing this and what do we want to get out of it? What is needed for us to be successful? What can and should change for this to work?

Understanding strategy and particularly innovation strategies is an increasingly important task for any organisation. In terms of how to develop innovation strategies, combining a more classic problem-based orientation with a strength-based orientation seems to be the more potent option in complex systems. It would be easy to view the three options (i.e. M&As, partnerships, and internal development) as inherently different and discuss them independently. Although there is some merit to that approach, it represents a very linear way of thinking. In reality, most organisations end up with a mix of these three strategic choices, and as such, they need to develop an organisational setup that effectively encompasses all three possibilities. Leaders are a major driver of strategic development, and leadership as a construct is closely related to strategy. Leadership is the subject of the next chapter.

12 Leadership

Introduction

Bringing innovation, as Van de Ven et al. (1986) point out, requires managers at all different levels to be involved. Innovation needs to be not only sanctioned but also led from the top.

There is a growing interest in understanding and increasing competence in the ability to lead innovation, and capacity building for innovation has resulted in different orientations on behalf of organisations. One way this has manifested is in a fairly new role that is emerging in organisations: Chief Innovation Officer. This, more than anything, is the recognition that (1) innovation is important and (2) someone must be responsible for and prioritise it. The question of how to lead innovation inevitably depends on so many different factors and circumstances that it is fair to assume that there are a myriad of possible approaches.

Leadership comes in many shapes and forms. Ridgeway and Wallace (1994) offer a model that maps the leadership role to leadership qualities. On an overall level, Drucker's notion of "effectiveness" (1967) seems to be paramount. This is leadership that delivers results. According to Collins (2001), this is a kind of leadership that blends extreme personal humility with intense personal will. The characteristics they describe in this kind of leader are humility, will, ferocious resolve, and a tendency to give credit to others while placing blame on oneself. This type of leadership stands in contrast to the oft-stereotyped leader, who more often than not is portrayed as charismatic, energetic, and equipped with a fair amount of ego.

Innovation is hard to distinguish from entrepreneurship. As Drucker (1985) points out, innovation *is* the business of entrepreneurs. As such, entrepreneurship is also critical for large, established companies, not only for start-ups and growing companies. Entrepreneurship also stands for renewal and improvement. Still, it is not enough that the leader displays entrepreneurial qualities or is an entrepreneur: today, there is a need to bring entrepreneurial qualities and innovation out of employees.

Since innovation does not happen in isolation, the question of team becomes important. In an echo of Dee Hock (1999), Bens (2006) suggests a "delegative" leadership style, since employees today more often than not have the necessary skills and knowledge about the best way to move forward. As Hjorth et al. (2011) point out, because of the increasing complexity of the tasks we face, the focus for leadership has shifted from leading creative individuals to leading creative groups.

An innovation process has a lot in common with that of a more general change process. It can be described as a cycle whereby one moves from motivating change, to envisioning that change, to building coalitions, to managing the change, and, finally, to learning. Cummings and Huse (1989) identify three activities that successful leaders of change should undertake:

- Envisioning, which involves conveying a belief in a brighter future for the company
- Energising, where the chief executive generates enthusiasm for the new venture and communicates early successes to maintain enthusiasm
- Enabling, where the leaders provide managerial, operational, and financial resources for the changes

For this reason, it is worth discussing leadership in terms of change and also offering some insights as to the tools that are being used by leaders to pursue innovation.

In this chapter, we will specifically look at a few aspects of leading capacity building and innovation. The role and responsibilities of the leader are changing with complexity and new demands. Afterwards, we will look at the construct of competence. Following this, methodologies and skills will be explored, and finally, a new take on innovation leadership in complex systems will be introduced.

The role and responsibility of leadership

The responsibility of a leader can, in simplistic terms, be defined as "getting the job done," "developing competence," and "building relationships." Whereas the first arguably encompasses the latter two, these also suggest something additional: competence development and relationship building are key responsibilities regardless of how well it suits more narrowly defined metrics. It is simply the way one can build capacity towards the unknown (Figure 12.1).

Innovation in complex systems seems to call for leadership that is able to reconfigure existing characteristics in a system (Cilliers, 1998; Arthur, 1999) by probing, sensing, and responding (Snowden and Boone, 2007). This can be traced back to acting by making "gestures" (Elias, 1939). Van Loon and Van Dijk (2015) state that coping with complexity, global interconnectedness, and continuous change are the greatest leadership problems of today.

Complexity leadership is a new orientation portrayed by Mary Uhl-Bien et al. (2007) that uses complex adaptive system (CAS) as a lens. It contrasts

154 *Leadership*

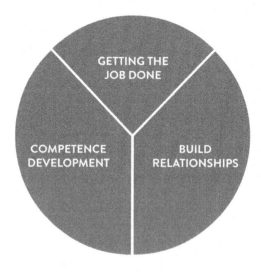

Figure 12.1 The responsibility of a leader model.
Source: Author.

more traditional views of leadership (Yukl, 1994; Grint, 2011) in the following ways:

- Align and control versus Interaction and adaptability
- Change efforts driven top-down versus Change is emergent (contextual)
- Relies on leader vision, inspiration, and execution versus Seeds the organisation with generative (i.e. adaptive) properties and uses for day-to-day performance

The conceptual framework of complexity leadership includes three entangled leadership roles (i.e. adaptive leadership, administrative leadership, and enabling leadership) that reflect a dynamic relationship between the bureaucratic, administrative functions of the organisation and the emergent, informal, dynamics of CAS (Uhl-Bien et al., 2007).

While conventional contingency theories suggest that accurate accounts of the context are a critical element in decision-making, Grint (2005) states that decision-makers are far more active in defining the context than conventional contingency theories allow. This then suggests that a persuasive rendition of the context legitimises a particular form of action that is in line with the leader's preferred mode of engagement, rather than with what the situation requires. As such, leadership becomes political in the sense that certain worldviews are preferred and define the context. However, as leadership is not value-free, it does not happen in isolation. It is essentially relational and contextual (Van Loon and Van Dijk, 2015).

Leading innovation and capacity building for innovation therefore becomes a multifaceted role. On the one hand, the leader is responsible, but the ableness

Leadership   155

for responding to a large extent depends on other people and indeed on the system itself. The leader can affect, but not necessarily predict, control, or guarantee. That change is emergent does not rule out pointing out a direction, generating a strategy, and so forth. In this book, we lean towards an "and" type of approach rather than a "versus" one. Understanding leadership in complex systems, and indeed innovation efforts, follows the findings of van Dijk and Peters (2011): it is seemingly more a question of "how" than of "what."

Leadership becomes a question of adding to the situation what the situation calls for. However, this is a balancing act between navigating the present and considering the long view of the innovation process. Often it can be about setting the frames and creating the conditions in which propositions or questions are offered to different groups within an organisation. That generates proactive answers which, after calibrating understandings, can be pursued. The absence of leadership vision or strategy is rarely good for innovation efforts.

Skills and style

Ridgeway and Wallace (1994) developed the Potential Competency Model, which combines leadership roles with leadership qualities. In their model, the hexagon represents the six basic competencies (intellectually curious, assertive, proactive, well-adjusted emotionally, flexible and open to others, and tolerance for ambiguity), which themselves are contained in three broad domains (intellectual skills, influencing skills, and counselling skills):

Leading innovation or the capacity building for innovation process requires both intellectual and emotional resources. It is partly about getting people onboard, but it is equally about being continuously open to changes and adjustments. But what type of leadership is needed when the leader does not have the answers, indeed when the answer or the best way forward is spread out among many different stakeholders or people within an organisation? One possible answer is the facilitative leadership style.

The task of leadership has changed over the last decades when it comes to innovation. The personal qualities (Van Loon and Van Dijk, 2015) and inter-personal skills are more desired and demanded, often placing the leader in a facilitative role in which he coaches (Flaherty, 1999) and becomes an expert in helping (Schein, 2009b, 2013). Bens (2006) asserts that leaders who operate in today's networked world of projects and teams find themselves in a dynamic environment that didn't exist even a few decades ago. Today, leaders are expected to manage people with skill sets and expertise that are unfamiliar to them and over whom, in reality, they have little or no authority. But facilitation is not simply repeating the same thing over and over again (Ghais, 2005). Every situation is unique and calls for a different sensibility. The four-level empowerment ´grid model below gives prominence to the leader's ability to accurately assess the given situation and then apply a suitable response (Table 12.1).

One of the challenges in terms of group processes is that there are many different individuals involved, each with their own perspective and objectives.

156 *Leadership*

Table 12.1 The four-level empowerment grid model, Bens (2006)

	Management style			
Description	Level I Directive style	Level II Consultative style	Level III Participative style	Level IV Delegative style
	Management decides and then informs the staff	Management decides after consulting the staff	Staff recommends and acts after receiving approval	Staff decide and act (preapproval)
Appropriate situations	Information is sensitive, staff lack skills or experience, or accountability can't be shared	Accountability can't be shared but management wants input from staff	Staff ideas and active participation are desired, but risk is high or members lack experience to go it alone	Staff have the necessary skills and can assume full accountability for outcomes
Effect	Management control and accountability; staff are dependent	Management benefits from staff ideas; staff are more involved than at level I	Staff take initiative and implement outcomes; management and staff are interdependent	Staff take responsibility and are independent

Consensus (that is, the assumption that the group must make a decision or recommendation as a group) is therefore difficult (Ghais, 2005).

Of all the skill sets and roles that support the shift from traditional management to a more collaborative approach, none is more relevant than that of the facilitator (ibid.). Although the art of asking questions is not limited to the leader as facilitator, it is a requirement of the role. Questions catalyse insight, innovation, and action. Engaging the best thinking from various individuals around complex issues that don't have easy answers is key to creating the futures we want rather than being forced to live with the futures we receive (Vogt et al., 2003). But as leaders, we affect situations in myriad ways; it is unavoidable. In the end, it is not only about authenticity and confidence, but also about being aware of the presence we bring into a room.

Methodologies and tools

There are many methodologies and tools that are often mentioned and used in relation to innovation, such as Design Thinking, Waterfall, Stage

Gate, and others. One of the challenges is actually distinguishing between a methodology and a tool. Although we use them interchangeably, one could argue that methodologies are broader in that they contain many tools. Another challenge is that many methodologies and tools are not domain restricted: they can easily be used somewhere else in terms of business or organisational development. For instance, the concepts of value proposition, the customer journey, and techniques for idea development are used much more widely even if they are considered indispensable in terms of innovation. Moreover, the tools and methodologies associated with innovation are predominantly used in the front-end side of innovation, with the obvious exception of methodologies that facilitate the entire innovation process or steer decision-making in the later stages of the process.

There are some interesting methodologies and tools worth mentioning here as they tend to draw more upon systems thinking and the notion of complexity. Clearly the previously mentioned Chaordic model by Dee Hock and Cynefin by Snowden would belong to this group of methodologies and tools, but since they have already been introduced, we will discuss some others worth mentioning.

Again, the following are not explicitly considered "pure" innovation methodologies and tools, but deserve to be mentioned as they have been used by several people and organisations. These methodologies are helpful in our complex and networked world, where both individual and collective qualities are necessary. What separates them from classic strategic planning or business development tools is the absence of an analytical framework. They are far more conversational and relational, delivering on the need for togetherness and meaning. On the belief side, there is a strong inclination towards the belief that "the answers are present" and "more heads think better than one." Those assumptions also point to the inherent dangers with these types of methodologies. On the other hand, they do deliver when it comes to creating commitment and engagement, which are indispensable.

A number of new methodologies have gained ground in the last couple of decades, such as Open Space Technology (Owen, 2008); Graphic Facilitation, pioneered by David Sibbet and the Grove Consultants (Sibbet, 2009); The Art of Hosting,[1] pioneered by Toke Møller and other practitioners (Scordialou, 2005); and the World Café developed by Juanita Brown and David Isaacs (2005).

Graphic Facilitation or Visual Collaboration (Qvist-Sorensen and Baastrup, 2019) draws our attention to expanding our language for collaboration to tackle complexity. This way of working is often used in combination with other methodologies, for example, Open Space Technology.

Open Space technology is based on four principles:

- Whoever comes are the right people
- Whenever it starts is the right time
- Whatever happens is the only thing that could have
- When it's over it's over

158 *Leadership*

Art of Hosting is a methodology to leadership and collaboration that scales up from the personal to the systemic. It uses personal practice, dialogue, facilitation, and the co-creation of new ways to tackle complex challenges.

A World Café is a structured conversational process for knowledge sharing. Groups of people discuss a topic at several tables. Through the process people switch tables periodically allowing the conversation to grow and findings to be shared, connected, and developed.

What ties these methodologies together is that they are all essentially based on conversations around building relationships that shape new worlds. For example, the World Café is about "shaping our futures through conversations that matter." In the foreword to *The World Café* (ibid.), Margaret Wheatley outlines some elements that underpin the process:

- The belief that everybody has the capacity to work together
- That diversity, and how to do it well, is necessary to achieve an accurate picture of any problem
- That invitation is key (a belief rooted in the notion that everyone is needed)
- That listening is crucial
- That movement generates new perspectives and connectedness
- That good questions open up new insights and understandings
- That the process generates energy, from playfulness and laughter, as we relish being together

Together, these methodologies can be considered participatory, co-creational, and facilitated processes. Buur and Larsen (2010) state that in the co-design processes, it is widely understood that innovation is a planned, goal-oriented activity that can be propelled through well-facilitated events in which conversations aim at consensus on new product and service ideas. They suggest that bridging differences can create new insights and that innovation can be considered the emergence of new meaning – oftentimes through conversations that involve conflict. Buur and Matthews (2008) outline a proposal for an integrated approach to user-driven innovation that aims to overcome some of the practical organisational difficulties encountered when applying user-centred development practices in industry. There is a need to focus not only on questions like, "How do we translate participants contributions into innovative products?" but also on questions like, "What resistance to user involvement will we encounter in the organisation?" and "How can we utilise different groups and departments in the organisation without usurping their sense of control and expertise?"

Buur and Mitchell (2011) present a set of techniques and an overview for modelling business in rich, tangible formats. These formats have proven successful in initiating conversations on innovating business with cross-disciplinary and cross-functional groups of participants. Examples of such techniques are

Value Network Mapping[2], using tangible material, as well as Picture Cards[3] to compare business relations.

Numerous other techniques and methodologies can also be used: for instance, Lego Serious Play (Roos and Victor, 1998) and Osterwalder's Business Model Canvas (Osterwalder and Pigneur, 2010).

Of course, the key questions are as follows: do these methodologies or tools really work? and if so, does any one work better than others? Can we outline situations in which one (or more) of these tools are more suitable than the others? Often these tools can help us engage in different ways that generate new and original thinking. In Buur and Mitchell's study (2011), the models and techniques presented here kept participants busy and allowed them to be less stressed by the need for verbal articulation. Buur and Sitorus (2007) suggest that ethnography can provoke perceptions of design by giving individuals space to rethink and reframe their understanding of problems and solutions. Moving beyond textual material allows us to understand that insights are not bullet points, nor necessarily the result of logical reasoning. However, there is a need to "prove" that these concepts of tangible modelling have actual merit for industry; that is, they actually deliver results (Buur and Mitchell, 2011).

Leading innovation in complex systems

The need for leadership cannot be overstated when it comes to innovation in complex systems. Complexity emphasises the non-manageable aspect and suggests interactions as co-creation. As we can see, leading innovation processes can be viewed as a subset of leading change. These leadership roles and qualities require a change in our understanding about the nature of leadership. Leading change and innovation is not just about formulating plans and implementing them; it is also about being enterprising and ensuring action on creativity. Said differently, the post-industrial economy requires a reduction in the management component of leadership so that the entrepreneurship component can be given more space.

Entrepreneurship, like leadership, is not primarily an economic act but rather a creative one (that, of course, also creates economic opportunities). Entrepreneurship and innovation both require creativity, but eliciting creativity out of people is not necessarily straightforward, as many have been trained to think and see differently. Adriansen (2010) sees creativity as a step towards innovation and states that thinking creatively and thinking critically are not at odds with each other. Rather, the challenge is that in our school system we are normally trained and rewarded for our critical thinking skills. As Adriansen says (ibid., 82) "… the cultural norms in academia is not cultivating creativity."

Given the increasing complexity of the tasks we face and the possibilities we envision, the focus for leadership has shifted from leading creative

160 *Leadership*

individuals to leading creative groups (Hjorthet al., 2011). This requires a different sensibility to group process and questions around motivation and norms. Instead of talking about skills and competencies required out of a leader, we suggest more of a systems approach, where it is the system that must embody certain qualities. Naturally, the leader or leadership group should also embody many of these qualities; there is no opposition to the idea that they can fuel or funnel the energy that goes into the innovation effort as opposed to driving it. Leadership is about showing the way, but that can be done in many different ways.

In this book, we propose the following qualities for leading innovation efforts:

Building relations   The innovation effort starts and ends with people. The nature of these relationships to a large extent sets the bar for the innovation result.

Generating meaning   Understanding why this is important and why this is relevant for the organisation, as well as the individual, is a crucial trigger and rationale for engagement.

Enhancing motivation   Motivation is not something you simply possess. It is something that must be nourished. The greater the motivation, the greater the ease and resoluteness when confronting obstacles.

Setting the direction   Choosing to do something as opposed to something else requires a connection to what is to be accomplished, or at least to the criteria that will guide decisions on what to leave out and what to leave in.

Framing the challenge and the opportunity   Innovation is not just creativity and an aspiration; it is working with real needs and wants. Grasping the connection with the user and the problem to be solved is crucial.

Creating the conditions   Oftentimes, the leadership role is not about providing solutions, but more about ensuring that the right conditions exist for the solutions to emerge. This requires sensing the people involved and the larger context in relation to the direction.

Crafting cross-boundary spanning   The innovation effort needs to be protected but it is difficult to confine it (and it rarely benefits from that). There is a need for balancing disturbance with new input, going beyond the beaten track.

Facilitating   The ability to learn is the key to unlocking a successful future – beyond one or two innovations. Learning and learning how to learn is a crucial leadership focuses.

Bridging creative tensions Handling paradox is a consequence of accepting complexity. Smart individuals, creative teams, and great ideas may sometime be at odds with each other. That can be detrimental but also fuel for something great.

Configurating to the current reality Always stay in touch with the current reality. It is what it is. As we interact, reality is interpreted by the people involved, not the least the customers and users.

Summary

We have discussed the role and responsibility of leadership with an emphasis on innovation and complex systems. We then suggested that leadership style and skills can take as a starting point what a given situation demands, although in terms of innovation and complexity, there is a strong tendency towards a facilitative style. We presented different methods and tools with an emphasis on those that are more relational, co-constructive, and contemporary, in the same tradition as appreciative inquiry. Finally, we proposed ten qualities for leading and leadership innovation in complexity. As leadership, considered separately from strategy, is closely connected to organisation, we turn our focus to that in the next chapter.

Notes

1 More can be found about the Art of Hosting here: http://artofhosting.ning. com/u
2 https://en.wikipedia.org/wiki/Value_network_analysis
3 https://www.cetic.be/IMG/pdf/slides-2003-12-09-unisys-3.pdf (as an example)

13 Organisation

Introduction

Organising is an interdependent facet of strategy and leadership. Leaders show the way, and organising effectively is a de facto consequence of their efforts to accomplish something. The same goes for strategy: implementing strategy requires the organisation of resources. As Czarniawska-Joerges (1992) points out, organisations – at least large ones – are complex. And they are political systems. As a result, it's difficult to research organisations and fully understand how they organise for innovation. To say it is only due to one department, unit, or group is simply too simplistic. It may help to view a unit (for instance, an R&D unit) as a system, but that system is interdependent on other systems within the larger system of the organisation – and, indeed, inter-connected with systems that span beyond organisational boundaries.

Given the focus of this book, there are two interconnected organisational aspects:

- Organising the capacity building effort
- Organising the innovation effort

These two aspects could be approached independently, but that would somewhat undermine the message of this book. Both of these two organisational efforts are interdependent. Organising the innovation effort requires some form of capacity building, as it is a question making something new. Organising the capacity building effort in pursuit of innovation may require an innovative approach in the sense that the effort may be new, and it must be valuable and socially acceptable.

One of the big challenges in modern organisations pushed by the demands of efficiency is generating the opportunity to actually work with innovation. Creating space is becoming an increasingly challenging task of management. Space can be understood as both physical and mental, as well as inside organisations, outside them, or inter-organisational. In terms of innovation and innovative organisations, the sense of autonomy and identity seems to play a huge part. This suggestion is echoed by Ackoff (1981), Morgan (1996), Schein

(2010), Amabile (1998), and Amabile et al. (2002). Leonard and Strauss (1997) state that companies with strong cultures can indeed be very creative, but within predictable boundaries (e.g. clever marketing or imaginative engineering). This is because strong cultures can be very homogenous, which results in efficient functioning but limited approaches to problems or opportunities. As a result, even if space can be created for innovation both within and without the organisation, networks as well as knowledge cannot be separated from issues of power and politics.

Organisational culture is a very important aspect of creating capacity as well as succeeding with innovation. The popular idea of innovation culture is widely shared in business. Culture virtually becomes a condition – albeit one that can be altered – for how much success one can have. The complex mosaic of individual, group, and organisational characteristics creates the organisational context – the creative situation – within which individual and group behaviours are played out. As such, there is a need to re-describe our existing procedural skills on successive representational levels so that we can transform them in different ways (Boden, 1991).

Knowledge, then conceptualised in terms of tacitness and explicitness, is an important factor in determining whether members of networks can effectively share information and skills (Powell and Grodal, 2006). Another challenge is developing the capacity for increasing the flow of information between participants and open up to new entrants to these networks.

According to Schön (1986), problem setting (i.e. what we view as problem identification, interpretation, definition) matters when trying to understand what is supposed to be solved (or innovated, if one prefers). Conflicting frames are not problems. Each story constructs its view of reality through a complementary process of naming and framing.

March (1976) points out that there are dangers in imitation, coercion, and rationalisation. Values develop through experience. The evaluation of social experiments need not be in terms of the degree to which they have fulfilled our *a priori* expectations. Rather, we can examine their effect in terms of what we now believe to be important. Furthermore, it is our presumptions that inhibit the serendipitous discovery of new criteria.

Amateurs are not a major source of the world's most important innovations. Leonard and Strauss (1997) state that to create an innovative organisation, leaders need to hire, work with, and promote people who make them feel uncomfortable. An understanding of one's own preferences is necessary so that weaknesses can be complemented and strengths exploited. Rightly harnessed, the energy released by the intersection of different thought processes will propel innovation.

In the following sections, we will address three different areas when organising capacity building and innovation. First, we will explore the idea of creating space for innovation. Next, we will have a wider conversation around organisational culture. Finally, in terms of structural setups, we will introduce the relatively new concept of The Moonshot Factory.

164   *Organisation*

Creating space for innovation

Aasen and Johannessen (2009) state that industry leaders encourage innovation based on expectations of improved business performance. Nevertheless, they argue that such processes are more often than not met with opposition, possibly because the development and adoption of novelty also involves risk. Thompson and Purdy (2009)[1] point out that to fully understand curricular innovation, one must consider the context into which an innovation is introduced, the tactics actors use to support or resist the innovation, and how these actors interact over time. In short, a good idea is not enough (Van de Ven, 1986; Thompson and Purdy, 2009).

While it can be argued that creating space for innovation falls under the work of innovation management, it should also be recognised that organisational culture and individual inclination will highly influence what can be managed. We can observe that creating space for innovation does not occur only within organisations; increasingly, it also happens between organisations (Powell and Grodal, 2006).

Pfeffer (1992) states that organisations (particularly large ones) are like governments in that they are fundamentally political entities. He refers to the political scientist Norton Long, who wrote: "People will readily admit that governments are organisations. The converse – that organisations are governments – is equally true but rarely considered" (Long, 1962: 110). Mintzberg (1985) considers the political environment of organisations to be one among various systems of influence, which include systems of authority, ideology, and expertise. All of these are considered to be legitimate in some sense. Mintzberg sees political behaviour as neither formally authorised, widely accepted, nor officially certified. As a result, political behaviour is typically diverse and conflictive, often pitting individuals or groups against formal authority, accepted ideology, and/or certified expertise, or else against each other. The views that come to dominate can be attributed to the notion of power.

Power is the secret of success (Salancik and Pfeffer, 1977). It may be difficult to fully define it, but it is easily recognisable: those who possess it bring about the outcomes they want. However, there is a challenging aspect of power when it comes to organisational performance. According to Salanick and Pfeffer (1977), that challenge is that the way power is used and developed always results in sub-optimisation. Increasing one's own power, decreasing the power of others, or merely maintaining one's position are all different positions relative to power. Aasen and Johannessen (2009) argue that communication can be seen as a joint patterning process of power and identity, influenced by all those involved, although undoubtedly certain individuals always have a larger say.

Another way to create space for innovation is to stretch the space outside the boundaries of the classic notion of the organisation. As we saw while describing the different innovation models, a bias towards networks has grown.

According to Powell and Grodal (2006), this contributes significantly to the innovative capabilities of firms by exposing them to novel sources of ideas, enabling fast access to resources, and enhancing the transfer of knowledge. Furthermore, formal collaborations may allow for the division of innovative labour to accomplish goals that are not possible otherwise, such as mutual learning and increased patenting. Dhanaraj and Parkhe (2006) observe that innovation networks can often be viewed as loosely coupled systems between autonomous firms. Orchestration comprises knowledge mobility, innovation appropriability, and network stability. Cooke et al. (1997) advocate for a strengthening of regional level capacities for promoting both systemic learning and interactive innovation.

Politics is not just internal for organisations. Hislop et al. (2000) examine the highly political nature of innovation appropriation processes and conclude that knowledge and networks have a dual character: on the one hand, they can provide access to relevant knowledge and artefacts, but on the other, they can also be used as political tools in support of particular interests.

Borum and Christiansen (1993) move away from the political perspective and see higher value in the network perspective where pre-existing end emerging relations between individuals govern processes. If problems arise they attribute this to the absence of motivated, resource- and information-controlling actors or insufficient strength of relations between actors.

Mintzberg (1985) points out that where the dysfunctions of politics are fairly recognised in terms of divisiveness and costs, the functional role is less often considered. That role can correct deficiencies and dysfunctions in systems of influence, providing a certain flexibility. It can also ease the path for the execution of decisions, promote necessary organisational changes, allow all sides of an issue to be fully debated, and promote the strongest individuals to power. Hislop et al. (2000) suggest that examining the decision-making processes at early stages, when the character of change is still open to negotiation, reveals the political nature of networking and knowledge utilisation practices undertaken by various interest groups. This reveals how power and politics shape a wide range of issues, such as the framework of the scope of change discussed, general issues of agenda formation, the type of people involved in (and excluded from) the decision-making process, the value attached to particular bodies of knowledge, and the way meaning is managed to justify the decisions made. When making decisions, Pfeffer (1992) points out that the decision-making process in itself changes nothing; instead, we need to know something about implementation science. Further, he notes that when decisions are made, we cannot know if they are good or bad, since it is only through results that we can view and assess their quality. And finally, he observes that we almost always spend more time living with the consequences of our decisions than we do making them.

In terms of decision-making, March and Olesen (1976a) pointed out as early as 1976 that even if organisational participants are problem-solvers and decision-makers, they find themselves in a more complex, less stable, and

166 *Organisation*

less understood world than in the past – they are placed in a world over which they have only modest control. Organisational choice often involves a curious paradox: the process is both surprising and not. Beliefs and preferences appear to be the results of behaviour as much as they are the determinants of it.

According to Borum and Christiansen (1993), three perspectives on implementation can be derived from the literature: administrative, political, and network. These reflect different assumptions about the nature and control of implementation processes. Where neither the imposed formal structure nor the political configuration governs the process, network analysis goes beyond the structural language of the interpretations offered by the other two by putting focus on actors and their construction of the organisation.

Organisational intelligence, like individual intelligence, is built upon two fundamental processes (March and Olesen, 1976b). The first of these is rational calculation, by which expectations about future consequences influence the choice between existing alternatives. The second is learning from experience. Through learning, feedback from previous experiences is used to inform choices between present alternatives.

Learning represents a strategic element in any innovative process (Senge, 1990; Dhanaraj and Parkhe, 2006 and many others). But learning to improve under ambiguity is complex because a shared view of what events occurred, why they happened, and whether they are good or bad does not exist (March and Olesen, 1976b).

Although innovation can be seen as a continuous process within the organisation, the process of innovation is still often organised in projects (Darsø, 2003; Austin and Darsø, 2009; Van de Ven et al., 2008, and many others). As such, the people involved are by definition part of temporary groups. Meyerson et al. (1996) investigate swift trust and temporary groups. Temporary groups turn traditional notions of organisations upside down. They often work on tasks with a high degree of complexity, yet lack the formal structures that facilitate the work. They know little about other people's skills, expertise, and background. In short, trust is less about relating to others than it is about doing. Both Meyerson et al. (1996) and Mønsted[2] (2006) arrive at similar conclusions: they view trust as a necessity and a practical approach or strategy for handling uncertainties generated by complex systems invented to perform complex interdependent tasks using the specialised skills of relative strangers. Given those complexities, unless one trusts quickly, one may never trust at all.

Organisational culture

Whenever we speak about organisations and organisational conduct or performance, we also speak about culture. What we refer to changes: it can be "what separates one organisation from another," what drives success (i.e. because of the culture), or why something is not succeeding (i.e. the culture is broken or dysfunctional). Cummings and Worley (2005) state that the topic of organisational culture has become extremely important to American companies in the past ten years. Interest in the subject has spawned a number of best-selling books such as Peters and Waterman's *In Search of Excellence* (1982), Collins and Porras' *Built to Last* (1994), and Collins' *Good to Great* (2001). Nevertheless, Watkins (2013) asserts that "while there is universal agreement that (1) it exists, and (2) that it plays a crucial role in shaping behaviour in organisations, there is little consensus on what organisational culture actually is, never mind how it influences behaviour and whether it is something leaders can change." The rest of this section will examine culture as both an enabler and hindrance to innovation.

According to the online business dictionary,[3] organisational culture is comprised of the "values and behaviours that contribute to the unique social and psychological environment of an organisation."

Schein defines culture as:

A pattern of shared basic assumptions learned by a given group as it solved its problems of external adaption and internal integration, which has worked well enough to be considered valid and, therefore, to be taught to new members as the correct way to perceive, think, and feel in relation to those problems.

(2010: 18)

Schein (2009a, 2010) makes a distinction between espoused values and underlying beliefs. Underlying beliefs may or may not be conscious to the organisation and may or may not be consistent with its espoused values. In fact, it is not uncommon that espoused values fail to truthfully reflect the culture of an organisation. For example, an organisation may embrace the idea of risk-taking, but when mistakes are made, they are not celebrated or rewarded, and the individual who committed the mistake may even sanctioned against (e.g. by being given less trust, freedom, and opportunity when a new idea or project arises). According to Schein it is often difficult to get beneath the artificial level of espoused values to uncover the beliefs and assumptions that truly underlie the organisation (of which the organisation itself is sometimes unaware).

If these assumptions that make up the culture are essentially learnt responses to external adaption and internal integration, then it makes sense that certain cultural assumptions survive: they have proven effective.

Culture, according to Schein (2010), can be said to start with an originating event. For example, an originator might assemble a group of people together for some purpose. Individual assumptions, values, and behaviours eventually form a shared mission as the individuals start to understand each other. Yukl (1994) points out that one of the most important elements of culture in new organisations is the set of beliefs about the distinctive competence

168   *Organisation*

of the organisation that differentiates it from other organisations: that is, a belief in the superiority or uniqueness of their particular products and services. Furthermore, the culture in a young, successful organisation is likely to be very strong because it is key to its success.

Interest in organisational culture probably comes from its assumed link to organisational performance. Conceptually, it is not difficult to identify the contribution innovation can make for competitiveness (Tidd, 2001). Cummings and Worley observe that a "well-conceived and well-managed organisational culture, closely linked to an effective business strategy, can mean the difference between success and failure in today's demanding environments" (2005: 482). Furthermore, they state that evidence suggests that corporate culture can affect organisational performance. If culture is seen as key to performance, it is not far-fetched to consider culture an important aspect for innovation. According to Aasen and Johannessen (2009), the obvious challenge is to create an environment of perpetual innovation, where everyone is committed to excellence, resulting in growth and sustained competitive advantage. Yukl (1994) considers changing culture as one "indirect" effect of the decisions and actions leaders make (e.g. by strengthening values such as concerns for quality and continuous improvement, concerns for teamwork and cooperation, and loyalty to the organisation). The difficulty is that organisations are by their nature – and often by design – oriented towards stabilising and routinising work (Schein, 1988b). In addition, not everyone considers culture as "something that requires fixing," but rather that cultural change is what happens when new processes or structures to tackle business challenges are put in place (Lorsch and McTague, 2016). One challenge in researching the relationship between innovation and culture is the multitude of cultural variables under investigation. This has led to a fragmented concept of culture for innovation, and its inclusion into management theory has yet to occur (Büschgens et al., 2013).

Many of the findings by Collins and Porras (1994), who studied 18 companies, point towards cultural traits and organisational behaviours as among the distinguishing factors for continued success. In particular, the installation of a core ideology (i.e. values and purpose as principles for guiding decisions and inspiring employees) stands out in terms of culture. A similar orientation is suggested by Hock (1999), and Laloux (2014: 33) states that "company culture is king." In certain very successful companies, culture comes before strategy and end execution. In this type of company, CEOs view promoting culture and shared values as their primary task.

Collins continued this research in *Good to Great* (2001), which focused on enabling companies to be "great." Again, culture comes out as a main differentiator between those that make it and those that don't. For him, the focus on a disciplined culture is key.

Collins emphasised that success relies on a particular form of leadership, which he calls level 5 leadership. This leadership has certain characteristics, such as a focus on "who" before "what," an ability to confront brutal facts about the organisation, and the ability to build a hedgehog concept (i.e. the intersection of what we dream about, what we are best at, our financial engine, and the establishment of a culture of discipline and technological acceleration).

Bennis and Nanus (1985) performed a five-year study of dynamic, innovative leaders, including 60 top leaders from the corporate sector and 30 from the public sector.[4] Even though there was great diversity among the leaders, the interview protocols revealed insights about the nature of effective transformational leadership. Essentially, it involved:

- Developing a vision
- Developing commitment and trust
- Facilitating organisational learning

Schein also puts a lot of emphasis on leadership. He argues that:

> 1) leaders as entrepreneurs are the main architects of culture, 2) after culture is formed it influences what kind of leadership is possible, and 3) if elements of the culture become dysfunctional, leadership can and must do something to speed up culture change.
>
> (Schein, 2010: xi)

From a leadership perspective it is relevant to examine what facilitates and limits innovations, or how to best organise to bring about innovation (Van De Ven, 1986). Given the above arguments, culture could be considered either an enabler or a hindrance to innovation. According to Yukl (1994), a major function of culture is to help us understand the environment and determine how to respond to it. To some extent, it can be said that culture shapes how the organisation actually sees and interprets its situation. Managers of innovative organisations are most likely to implement a developmental culture that emphasises flexibility and an emphasis on the external (Büschgens et al., 2013). In short, culture affects the effectiveness of the innovation tools used (Davila et al., 2006).

Schein (1988b) hypothesises that in order to be innovative an organisational culture must assume:

- That the world is changeable and can be managed
- That humans are by nature proactive problem-solvers
- That truth is pragmatically arrived at
- That the appropriate time horizon is the near future
- That time units should be geared to the kind of innovation being considered
- That human nature is neutral or good and is, in any case, perfectable
- That human relationships are based on individualism and the valuing of diversity

170   *Organisation*

- That decision making is collegial/participative
- That diverse sub-cultures are an asset to be encouraged, but that sub-cultures have to be connected to the parent culture.

Kim et al. (2006) argue that innovation happens in dynamic, entrepreneurial, and creative places, where individuals take risks and leaders are considered innovators and risk-takers. The glue that holds these organisations together is a commitment to experimentation and innovation. According to Davila et al. (2006) these organisations must embrace balance and disequilibria: on the one hand, a balanced culture permits the peace that creativity and value creation require, but at the same time, only challenges and surprises move the company forward. This suggests the presence of paradoxes such as risk-taking and conservatism at the same time, as well as discipline and surprise, and so on.

Moving one step away from culture to take a closer look at the individual, Amabile (1998) states that a high degree of inner motivation brings forth far more creative solutions and, as such, it must be assumed that higher levels of autonomy stimulate inner motivation and lead to higher degrees of innovative behaviour. Kanter (1988) concurs, saying that flexibility and autonomy are important for members of the organisation to engage in creative problem-solving.

A different approach to innovation and culture is offered by Fonseca (2002). Here the classic view of innovation (Peters and Waterman, 1982; Schein, 1988, 2009, 2010) as a somewhat planned process, and of culture as something that leadership must identify and manage in order to secure desirable organisational behaviour is rejected. Likewise, Kanter (1988) and Van de Ven (1998) reject the idea that innovation is a political and uncertain process yet nevertheless subject to contextual conditions that can be managed. Instead, they consider innovation to be a new patterning of our experiences of being together, as new meaning emerges from ordinary, everyday work conversations. As such it is echoing the idea of complex responsive process as proposed by Stacey and others.[5]

Moonshot factories

Whereas culture and space can be seen as something cross-organisational and indeed, inter-organisational, there are also more functional and dedicated structures setup by organisations. Often this takes the form of innovation units, products and service development, R&D, and so forth. Sometimes these setups live in relative reclusiveness in larger organisations; other times, they are more closely connected with the different business units and their client needs. To some extent, this depends on the nature of what function these units perform. The more hypothetical and experimental, the further away these units exist from the realities of the other business units.

In recent years, a new phenomenon has started to emerge, primarily in the public media and as part of the vocabulary within business. This phenomenon is called "moonshots."

The term stems from the Apollo 11 spaceflight project, which landed the first human on the moon in 1969 and has come to signify a bold effort to achieve a seemingly impossible task (Casadevall and Fang, 2016). "Moonshot" may also reference the earlier phrase "shoot for the moon": that is, to aim for a lofty target.[6]

The term gained attention and traction as Google launched Google X in January 2010, which was renamed X as part of the restructuring of Google into Alphabet in 2015,[7] but it had been used by management thinkers prior to that (for instance, by Hamel, 2009). X is an attempt to go about solving huge problems, as opposed to merely big problems (Rowan, 2013; Gertner, 2014). It is a "shoot-for-the-stars-ideas" factory (Miller and Bilton, 2011). The X stands for ten – making a problem ten times better, within a timeframe of about ten years.[8] Even though not all moonshots at Google are part of X (for example, their life-extension program Calico is not), several have gained massive media attention. Examples of moonshot projects within X are self-driving cars, Loon (Internet access to everyone through the use of balloons in the stratosphere), Wing (which is about delivering products using flying vehicles), and Google glass (augmented reality head-mounted displays). An example of a project that has left X is the Google brain (deep learning), and an example of a project that has been shelved is the space elevator.[9]

Google lists three criteria for a project to be labelled a moonshot project (Gertner, 2014):

1 It needs to address a huge problem
2 It needs to propose a radical solution
3 It should use breakthrough technology

In a technology context, a moonshot is an audacious, experimental, and revolutionary project that is undertaken without any definitive expectation of success or profit in the near future. This does not mean, however, that it does not aim for future success.

The notion of moonshots has started to find its way into areas other than technology. For instance, the Obama administration called for a moonshot to cure cancer (Casadevall and Fang, 2016). It is important to note that while Google may be the company most renowned for working with moonshots, it is far from the only one. Many of their projects have counterparts in other companies. For instance, Google Glass has a counterpart in Microsoft's Hololens. Google Wings has a counterpart in Facebook drones, and Loons at both Facebook and Microsoft (although here they are focused on using radio white spaces). When it comes to autonomous vehicles, virtually every large carmaker is testing in that space as well, with probably Tesla as the most notable (consider Tesla's work with hyper-fast trains in California). Google's space programme has competitors in Virgin Galactic and Space X, to mention just two. As a result, what may really stand out with Google X is their ability to organise around a project, attract talent, and create attention (i.e. brand build).

Other companies, such as Danske Bank in Denmark and Telefónica's Alpha in Spain, are also using the moonshot metaphor. What separates the approach of Danske Bank from, for instance, that of Google and Alpha is that the "moonshot unit" within Danske Bank is more of an actor within the company's perceived core business (i.e. banking and financial services).

In order for moonshots to be successful, Casadevall and Fang (2016) consider it important to have an appropriate knowledge of "the basic science underlying a problem in question so that efforts can be focused on engineering a solution." They do admit, though, that history has proven that massive research often leads to conceptual and technological discoveries that have provided society with unforeseen benefits. The classic experimental research facilities, such as Thomas Edison's Research Laboratory, Bell Labs, and Xerox PARC, easily come to mind. Moonshots are about exploring big questions and experimenting through the creative work of a diverse set of people. As such, moonshots are about R&D, but perhaps they represent more of an aspirational and directive variation of the classic workshops of at Edison's Lab in Menlo Park, New Jersey.

Moonshot factories can be seen as the progression of strategy work on behalf of the company that concluded that today's volatile and fast-moving business environment needed a radical approach – or at least to supplement other initiatives (Vindeløv-Lidzélius, 2018). As such, one can think of moonshot factories as part of a strategy-portfolio (i.e. a company should move on several fronts at once) and a contemporary option theory, in which uncertainty about what will win markets, products, and services in the future is unknown (i.e. there is a need to test several ideas, including ideas that involve technology that may not necessarily be within our scope today). Another way to look at it is that this type of initiative is a departure from the classic line of thinking of risk-management towards uncertainty-opportunity. By reaching beyond the scope and range of existing the business of the enterprise, these companies hope to counter limitations in existing markets and reap the benefits of creating new markets (ibid.).

Moonshot factories help companies move from what could be considered a risk-management orientation to reap the benefits of uncertainty. To some extent, uncertainty points towards unidentified and unutilised markets and needs. From leadership, organisational, and strategy perspectives, what stands out is the new assumption that there is a need for a new type of culture (i.e. not dominant in the mother company today) – something that is more entrepreneurial and based on Internet (or digital) thinking. This culture is then assumed to require a different organisational structure in order to thrive. Leadership in moonshot factories is very much seen as a balancing act between being distributed and centralised, and between being a visionary leader and a curator of creativity, ingenuity, and motivation. Given the

Organisation 173

particulars of the company, the leader is also a very political person in that he or she must anchor the company within its mother company in order to obtain support and traction. To some extent this is done by gaining recognition from individuals and organisations outside the company. This balancing act often appears in conversations that are situational and culturally dependent, since moonshots often have very different cultures. As such, when it comes to innovation strategy – as with strategy in general – culture is the enabler and the limiting construct.

Alpha can be seen as an innovation unit, but given its explorative and experimental nature, it leans towards the very early phases of innovation as described by Godin (2006, 2013b). It is therefore more appropriate to view it as an R&D unit – but not R&D as understood in a classic setting. Instead, this is R&D arriving as a consequence of realising that the world is complex and the business environment is unstable and fast-moving. Moonshot factories essentially invent new markets where the company has a natural competitive advantage for exploiting it. The market and opportunities are "out there," but they are created by combining data and creativity to "re-configure" the company's understanding of those same markets and opportunities.

Summary

In this chapter, we have investigated the last construct of the three suggested for capacity building for innovation in complex systems: organisation. We started by exploring space and how to create space for innovation. Then we turned our focus towards culture as an enabler or a hindrance for innovation capacity. Finally, a specific focus was given to a relatively new phenomenon– The Moonshot Factory – as a new take on R&D and innovation capacity building. In the final chapter of this book, we will bring the different chapters together and look onwards to a holistic approach towards capacity building.

Notes

1 Although their work is in the area of education, it is not far-fetched to apply the same findings in this book.
2 This is more focused on the borders of the formal organisation rather than inter-organisational collaborations.
3 http://www.businessdictionary.com/definition/organisational-culture.html. Accessed 02.06.2016.
4 Also referred to by Yukl (1994).
5 See Chapter 8, where complex responsive processes are dealt with in more detail.
6 http://whatis.techtarget.com/definition/moonshot
7 https://en.wikipedia.org/wiki/X_(company)
8 http://www.bbc.com/news/technology-25883016
9 See https://www.solveforx.com/about/ for more info.

14 The innovation imperative – towards a holistic approach for developing innovation capacity

Introduction

Based on a theoretical analysis, supported by explorative qualitative and quantitative research, Vindeløv-Lidzélius (2018) suggests that organisations develop the capacity to generate innovation in a multifaceted way. Strategy, organisation, and leadership are all interrelated constructs that cannot be separated from the notion of innovation and how it unfolds in local realities. From a systems perspective, local constructs are nested and embedded in larger systems, while dominant discourses around the value of innovation, what innovation is, and how to best go about it frame local and provisional conceptions around innovation. Essentially, then, organisations face a choice between becoming better at utilising resources to excel in innovation activities and trying to break new ground. While this choice calls for different orientations around leadership, organisation, and strategy, both options entail a number of methodological, theoretical, and cultural challenges that require perceptual and conceptual changes on individual and group levels.

In the end, there are many answers to why an initiative becomes an innovation and why certain organisations are better at innovation than others. However, none are in themselves a guarantee for success when transferred to another organisation and its reality. One image that can illustrate this enigma is that of a jigsaw puzzle. We seem to have many of the right pieces to the puzzle, and we might even have an idea of the image itself. However, there is no how-to book on how and in what order to place the pieces; as soon as it is laid down, the other pieces and the image itself change – sometimes in ambiguous ways. Furthermore, while other players are working on their puzzles, ours may become obsolete or at least altered due to others' manoeuvres. Innovation is, it seems, an elusive promise of success and an imminent risk of being outdated.

Innovation appears to be the mantra of our time regardless of the problem. But what innovation is, how it comes about, and how to be effective at it attracts numerous interpretations, theories, and practices that obscure or enrich the field – depending on one's preferences. The Cox Review (2005) offers a setup that connects creativity, design, and innovation.

> Creativity is the generation of new ideas – either a new way of looking at existing problems or the discovery of new opportunities. Innovation is the exploitation of new ideas. Design is what links creativity and innovation – it shapes the ideas so they become practical and attractive propositions for users and customers.

But design also has role in supporting creativity and making ideas come about. Design, then, can be seen as a concept of human endeavour for solving problems.

The search for new knowledge to help alleviate our organisational challenges as well as deliver upon our aspirations calls for research concerning innovation. But given our challenges in agreeing on what innovation actually is, we are faced with a dilemma: how can we become better at something whose definition which we do not fully agree and which we cannot prescribe how to do? This is an important conundrum to resolve.

Ackoff (1981) defined a dilemma as "a problem, which cannot be solved within the current world view." A dilemma and combinations of dilemmas demand and generate new ways of thinking about and resolving them. Metaphors play a significant role in how we comprehend management and organisations (Morgan, 1996). In principle, one can use the same argument when it comes to our appreciation of the world in general. If metaphors guide and shape our thinking and subsequently our actions, then it is important to understand and perhaps challenge these metaphors if we seek change.

Most of our metaphors in organisational life today still stem from a mechanistic view of the world. Our view of the world impacts our understanding of a given situation (e.g. a leadership challenge or business opportunity) and the assumptions that we make about that situation. Our understanding of the world is then a product of historical circumstances – relational circumstances – that make a connection with social constructionism. Innovation thus can be seen as both a metaphor in its own right and as being dependent on other metaphors. Innovation can be a transformational tool for individual and systemic change, towards a more sustainable future and a higher quality of life. Because we understand many phenomena – such as innovation, strategy, leadership, and organisation – by examining them through various metaphors, we should also approach problems from more than one worldview or methodology.

The kernel of innovation

According to the *Harvard Business Essentials* (2003), there are two schools of thought when it comes to strategy in relation to value creation: the first suggests that the path lies in replacing the old-fashioned practice of gut instincts with strategy based on rigorous, quantitative analysis. The other favours creativity and innovation. Another polarising approach in strategy development concerns using problem-based business improvement methods

176 *Holistic approach to develop innovation capacity*

and strengths-based constructionist methods. These are stereotypically seen as an either-or proposition, therefore accepting as a predicate the assumption of a field-limiting separatist paradigm (Cooperrider et al., 2000). In practice through, most organisations would combine problem-based and strength-based methods, as well as gut feeling and data.

The kernel is a term I have borrowed from professor Rumelt (Rumelt, 2011), who used the word to distinguish between good and bad strategies. He asserts that the kernel consists of three parts: an overarching policy, a well-defined situational analysis of challenges, and an outlined set of actions to overcome these.

To a large extent, this theory can be applied to the concept of innovation and innovation strategy. Innovation efforts require a direction, an understanding of challenges that follow, as well as a clear plan on how to do this. It should be noted that we do not assume a positivist and linear approach, but rather we see strategy as a proposition, a "gesture," in the words of Elias (1939/2000), that calls for a reaction. That reaction subsequently impacts the initial proposition before a renewed gesture sees the light of day. And like so, it continues. There is nothing inherently wrong with a more overall proposition, but it must be sensitive to the signals it generates.

Let's turn our attention to the three parts of Rumelt's idea of the kernel (ibid.).

If we look at what an overarching policy would mean in the context of innovation, it is important to understand innovation as a subset of business strategy. Essentially, innovation is not just a "what" but also a "how." It is a way for us to ensure that we end up with a desired future, rather than a default one. As such, an innovation strategy must support business strategy. If not, very quickly we end up with scattered efforts and uncertain results, and we run the risk of missing out on what a company requires to thrive. An overarching policy then is directional, and it provides the organisation with a decision-making framework. The principles and criteria serve as rules and guidelines for the organisation to reach its long-term objectives.

One interesting aspect concerns the lack of clarity around the business strategy. If the business strategy is not sufficiently clear, what then? Again, innovation efforts may be lost as it is unclear how to act upon them. There is an opportunity for innovation efforts to define and drive the business strategy, primarily in smaller organisations. But this is a challenging approach. It may sound promising and be filled with the potential of success, but in general, leaving innovation to chance does not really fit our understanding of how organisations should be run. Rather the question is about how we can create a good match and dynamic interaction between the business and innovation strategies.

"A well-defined situational analysis of challenges" then offers an interesting conceptual challenge since even though innovation obviously has a strong focus on ideas, it also focuses more on problems, opportunities, and value-creation. Challenges come in many forms and shapes. Depending on

Holistic approach to develop innovation capacity 177

the scope and range – and the clarity – of the overarching policy, challenges should be properly articulated. As we saw earlier in this book, they can exist on several levels, such as on a theoretical, methodological, structural, and cultural level. At the same time, there is a question of time involved. Even though we may not see innovation as a linear process, our understandings change over time. Indeed, in terms of innovation, we must assume that our situational analysis will change as time passes. As we impose our framing onto the challenges and start to work with them, they change (i.e. they might be resolved, be transformed, or made obsolete). This requires a temporary approach to the situational analysis.

Ideas are part of innovation, but innovation is more than ideas. Indeed, when working on opportunities, they too often become formulated as problems or challenges in the pursuit of action. As well, the concept of creativity is similar in this respect. By contrasting innovation and creativity, there seems to be a difference in terms of ideas and problems. Creativity can be argued to be more oriented towards ideas, even if our creative work is often situated around a problem. Innovation can be argued to be more oriented towards problems, in the sense that innovation must be valuable and doable.

When we look at actionable steps, we find ourselves in an interesting conundrum as one could argue that these should be derived from the intention and the problems. This view leans towards a project, or novelty, view of the innovation process, culture, and structure. However, this may be problematic on two levels. First, we normally cannot just shift or change existing structures, culture, and processes so easily or effectively. Second, organisations to a large extent are in the business of "normisation" and standardisation because the cost side of replication is simply lower than continuously starting from the scratch. It seems that businesses are therefore drawn to a paradox: on the one hand, they would like universal cures (i.e. a recipe or prescription on how to do this), whereas on the other, they want their approach to be unique and subsequently harder for others to replicate. In reality, this creates an interplay between ideals, setups, resources, and constraints. This entire situation is simply too complex, so we end up with simplifications in order to explain, design, and enact. However, this does not mean that creating actionable steps is a waste of time, quite the contrary.

Using the metaphor of the kernel, innovation thus consists of a few crucial elements:

- A well-articulated business strategy to steer the innovation direction
- A thoughtful description of what the innovation effort will result in
- An allocation of resources, support, demands, and mandate

When considering these parts, one can see that they either feed into an existing innovation model and innovation process, or they effectively call for a model and a process. What is sometimes experienced is that even when an organisation changes its strategy and aspirations, the organisation itself does

178 *Holistic approach to develop innovation capacity*

not really change accordingly. In other words, our innovation model does not change even when we want something new to result from it. This is not inherently wrong, as the innovation model and innovation process may be equipped to take into account a change in input factors and output expectations. However, this is very often not the case. An effective orientation towards innovation also calls for an innovative approach towards the model and process – innovating your innovation effort, if you will.

Beyond the organisation – a systems view

A holistic view of organisations may make intuitive sense, but in reality, it goes beyond organisational borders. Our perceptions of organisations are often constrained by our assumption of a physical presence, such as production facilities, offices, or stores. But an organisation is not really a physical entity; rather, it is a construction of the mind. That is, one cannot taste, smell, touch, hear, or see the organisations.[1] But the consequences of an organisation are often very impactful in our everyday lives, even if we cannot experience organisations directly through our senses. We experience them indirectly and, as we have seen, they are a very powerful abstraction given their artefacts.

Over the last several decades, digital realities and the online world has shown us something else. Organisations have influence and affect us far beyond their normal physical artefacts. Of course, this has always been true. A simple case would be IKEA. Where does IKEA start and end? Perhaps at its stores and other offices? Perhaps in their parking lots? Perhaps with the buses that take you to their stores? Or with the catalogues that you read in your living room? Or as the established response to a more or less conscious desire lurking in the back of your head?

In terms of innovation, many theories speak to the idea of an extended organisation. This may be open innovation, user-driven innovation, or others. The more modern models also call for embracing feedback loops from the market in different ways. A grey zone would be the intention an organisation has when it establishes new initiatives with the purpose of being separated from the organisation as a whole. Of course, in most examples, this would still speak to the notion of an organisation as a unit since it would still exist under the umbrella of a larger construct. The simplest example would be different forms of outsourcing, where the organisation does not necessarily own or control the other unit, still depends largely on it. As such, the organisation would try and indeed demand some adherence to its needs and wants.

We should understand the organisation as a system that consists of a number of sub-systems, which are themselves nested within and interact with other systems. Those systems may be similar (e.g. other organisations) or very different in size, shape, and nature (e.g. a conglomerate versus a start-up or museum). The system is also part of larger systems as well, such as the market or society as a whole. As an organisation looks to develop its innovation capacity, the larger system must also be considered. As we have argued so far, an innovation system within the organisation must not be understood as existing in isolation. Instead, it is affected by the organisation at large and it affects the larger organisation. In a similar way, the organisation and its innovation capacity and potentiality go beyond organisational boundaries. A contemporary approach must consider a broader view.

For instance, when an organisation lacks the necessary resources to go about a certain task, challenge, or idea, they may partner with another organisation(s). This might imply full outsourcing (such as giving an R&D assignment to a university) or a partnership that requires the establishment of a new joint venture. The logical course of action will change from one situation to another. Indeed, an organisation often finds a preferable course and follows that model as new challenges and opportunities arise.

Another side to a systems view beyond the organisation is about how we think of value creation, business cycles, and life cycles. If we reduce our thinking around innovation capacity to a single organisation, we lose out on the idea of the innovation system. As systems interact, an improvement in one system can affect other systems as well. In short, if an organisation helps a subcontractor to improve some element of their business (for example, their business process and logistics), this will improve their output in terms of price, service, and product characteristics, thereby generating an improved situation for the business itself. Although this is not a completely new idea, we argue for an improved organisational competence for detecting the most cost-effective way forward. For example, an organisation might recognise that its ability to create a new product aimed at a new target group is hampered by existing organisational politics, processes, and experiences – and as a result, decides to invest in a new start-up instead. Alternately, an organisation might realise, after acquiring a number of start-ups to obtain new products and customers, that it doesn't have the capacity to leverage on this and decide to build a new R&D from the scratch.

Furthermore, as organisations and their situations become increasingly complex, organisations must test different ways forward and learn and improve from those tests. In reality, organisations try to affect the systems around them so as to better suit their goals, and vice versa. Since organisations all have limited power to influence and shape others, and since all forces are influenced by other forces, this process is in effect perpetually forming. Thus, the true merit of an organisational effort is if it is more effective than other alternatives at hand.

An integrative approach

An integrative approach suggests that in order to be effective in developing capacity for innovation, one must bring together all aspects of an organisation into one framework. One definition of integrated management says it is the "effective direction of every aspect of an organisation so that the needs and expectations of all stakeholders are equitably satisfied by the best use of all

180 *Holistic approach to develop innovation capacity*

resources" (Dalling, 2007). An integrative approach is by and large a conse-quence of a systems approach where two assumptions come into play: (1) that one can encompass the system, and (2) that intended change can happen as a consequence of planned action. However, this is not a reductionist approach, but rather understood as a non-linear process that recognises connectivity be-tween problems (Bizikova et al., 2011). According to Dalling (2007), features of integrated management are consensus-based decision-making, search-ing for effectiveness, and the co-existence of both uniformity and diversity within systems.

Integrative thinking can be seen both as a variation of integrated man-agement and also as something more particular. According to the Desautels Centre at the University of Toronto's Rotman School of Management (2019), "integrative thinking" is the

> ability to constructively face the tensions of opposing models, and instead of choosing one at the expense of the other, generating a creative resolu-tion of the tension in the form of a new model that contains elements of both models, but is superior to each.

Here, an integrative approach essentially suggests a combination of integra-tive thinking and integrated management. This approach is characterised by being:

- Theoretically inclusive: it allows for paradoxes, allowing for more than one truth to exist
- Boldly practical: "what works" is the steering principle for development
- Transdisciplinary: it focuses on problems that cross the boundaries of disciplines
- System sensitive: it takes into account the larger context and its implica-tions on the organisation
- Multi-value oriented: it takes into account different forms of value creation
- Opportunity oriented: it encourages a generative take on results, events, and challenges

An integrative approach is needed for a holistic approach towards developing capacity because it promotes a localised, coherent, and cohesive anticipa-tory design – allowing for uncertainty, chance, and the unknown. It assumes effective capacity building as nested challenges requiring communal engage-ment rather than only top-down prescriptions.

The lifeworld of innovation

As seen in this monograph, the evolution of innovation has revealed that it is a socially embedded process (that is, a complex adaptive system in its own right)

Holistic approach to develop innovation capacity 181

in a larger complex system including the organisation as well as its surrounding environment. As context plays a huge part in understanding and developing innovation, there is a duality and an interplay between the understood and organised, and the undefined and the generative. On the one hand, this duality speaks to the ideal of being able to prescribe innovation, turning it into a system that can be replicated. On the other hand, it also speaks to the ideal of the unknown and unpredictability. Defining innovation as "the making of new meaning in dissipating structures" (Vindeløv-Lidzélius, 2018) echoes this dynamic and highlights the challenge of an either-or orientation.

The concept of "lifeworld" was introduced by Edmund Husserl in *The Crisis of European Sciences and Transcendental Phenomenology* (1936) and was further developed by Jürgen Habermas in his social theory (1981). For Habermas, the lifeworld comprises socially and culturally sedimented linguistic meanings. It is where human's primary socialisation and language development happen, and it is a place of negotiated realities and communal accommodations. For Habermas, the lifeworld is based on non-purposeful interaction, which is contrasted by the system, which is based on purposeful and outcome-oriented action. Basically, his view is that the lifeworld of organisations is being "rationalised" and colonised by the system world – i.e. the instrumental rationality of bureaucracies and market forces.

Innovation is fuzzy concept that can be seen as caught between the system and the lifeworld. There is a strong push towards incorporating the lifeworld into the systems world by academics, organisations, and practitioners alike. Indeed, the logic behind that push is that by doing so, one can successfully create an "innovation engine" – a more or less predictable mechanism that can be dealt with as any other that has a complicated setup. But there is an obvious problem with this: if one subjects what is to some extent a creative action or experimentation to the same type of rationalisation and bureaucratic logic that drives modern organisations in pursuit of efficiency, one may very well kill the innovation sought after in the first place.

Complexity theory would point to the ludicrousness of assuming that one can actually reach such a situation where innovation comes down to a simple prescription; therefore, attempts towards a systems world approach can only lessen the uncertainty at best. But as Habermas points out, as the colonisation happens as a consequence of the organisation in the first place, the real question may very well be: How do we ensure that innovation does not become trapped in a myopic logic where what we see up close is the full and only picture?

This discussion should not be understood as a call for a non-systemic approach to innovation. To the contrary, as the book has argued the entire way, a holistic approach towards capacity building is necessary for getting the most out of the capacity building effort. This includes the need to understand and accommodate the necessity of the unpredictable and chance. Instead, this is a call for an ambidextrous organisation (Duncan, 1976; March, 1991), capable of balancing exploration and exploitation while simultaneously efficiently

182 *Holistic approach to develop innovation capacity*

meeting today's business requirements and remaining adaptive to changes in the environment.

This calls for a new type of orientation towards strategy, organisation, and leadership. As we have discussed, these three represent overarching constructs that can be used to analyse, understand, and affect innovation. Changes in any of these constructs can have a significant impact on the innovation development process as well as innovation in the market space (e.g. marketing, branding, etc.). Indeed, having a new understanding of these constructs may be more important for success than having better ideas, inventions, or even innovations. A singular focus on ideas and innovations that disregards possible changes in the support system may quickly turn out to be the reason why a great idea fails.

Future areas of research

There are many subjects that require further research when it comes to developing capacity for innovation in complex systems. Some of the main propositions in this monograph are also far from definitive and call for further research.

The first areas concern complex adaptive systems, in which the two most important topics revolve around (1) the applicability of the characteristics of complex adaptability in a social system, and (2) what that does to our practices around decision-making and problem understanding.

The other area concerns developing capacity – or capacity building – for innovation. As we have seen in this monograph, capacity building is very orientated around gap analyses. Gap analyses are not in themselves a problem; rather, they are problematic when considering time, uncertainty, and flexibility. In terms of innovation and innovation capacity it is to large extent a matter of framing a moving target.

Assuming the actual identification of what is needed (far from a trivial exercise) is done well, this identification is still based on what we know at the current moment. As this may quickly turn out to be wrong, we are left with a couple of options:

- We could shorten the time between the identification of a need to the implementation of a solution to that need
- We could put a greater focus on general and generic improvements rather than locking into something specific – which may take into account a nimbleness and agility

Conclusion

The world is currently experiencing massive changes on many levels: global, national, regional, local, organisational, and personal. Global challenges are very present in our everyday lives and changes, ranging from political

Holistic approach to develop innovation capacity 183

interests to technological breakthroughs, seem to come from everywhere. Already in 1969, Drucker coined the phrase "the age of discontinuity" to emphasise the uniqueness, unpredictability, and speed of the changes facing today's organisations. However, it is important to remember that not all changes are unwelcome or come as a surprise. Change also holds the seed for new opportunities, and, indeed, some changes are planned and are within the power of organisations to design and initiate. Strategies, re-organisations, and new products are among the decisions that an organisation can make, even if success cannot be guaranteed. This uncertainty and turbulence can be hard to fathom through classic worldviews and tools. Instead, complexity theories are helpful. In these theories, organisations are viewed as combinations and collections of structures and strategies. The structures become dynamic webs of interactions, and behaviour is considered adaptive. The collective as well as individuals transform and self-organise.

Systems thinking points to how "the parts" affect "the whole" and, as Ackoff (1972) observed, "a system is more than the sum of its parts; it is an inseparable whole." These new sciences can help us understand organisations, as well as strategy and leadership in new ways.

Innovation itself can be explained through the lenses of a complex adaptive system. As seen, many of the properties and characteristics we associate with innovation seem to find an echo in those of complex adaptive systems. But complexity and its root theories also suggest that we should be careful when applying ideas rooted in physical and biological systems into our social spheres.

Moreover, just as with complexity theories, innovation can also be used to understand how we got to where we are today in our world. Global wealth has risen exponentially since around 1750 (Beinhocker, 2006). According to Humbert (2007), this growth was due to technology more than any other cause. Invention of new technology made new ways of organising production and economic activity possible. Productivity development and acceleration was made possible by the technological progress and the restructuring of production. Schwab (2017) points out that revolutions have happened throughout history (i.e. new technologies and novel ways of seeing the world) and that these revolutions have generated deep changes in our economic system and social structures. Innovation therefore goes beyond the mere techno-economical view and is a development from the Schumpeterian view of innovation.

The shift from an Industrial Age to an Information Age marks a transition in terms of value: that is, from physical to intellectual resources. This is a fundamental change whose full consequences we have yet to see. The last decades of the twentieth century have been characterised as a period of disruption and discontinuity in which the structure and meaning of economy, polity, and society radically altered. And there is nothing that suggests that this pace and magnitude will slacken. To the contrary, they will likely accelerate. Given this, one should not underestimate the systemic changes that technological

184 *Holistic approach to develop innovation capacity*

breakthroughs offer. Their speed, scale, and scope are remarkable in terms of development and diffusion. Companies like Google barely existed 20 years ago. Spotify, Airbnb, and Uber were founded roughly ten years ago. Today, all of them have changed their industries and how we as consumer behave. But even though all of these examples have been very innovative and created value, it is important to remember that their remarkable returns have also created negative impacts for some people in our societies. The benefits of innovation are not equally distributed.

As changes pave way for innovation, innovation also drives change. Some organisations are fortunate and are placed ahead of these changes. Still, over time, innovation is a consequence of one's own deliberate and disciplined effort (Drucker, 1985). In the words of Jim Collins (2001), "Greatness is not a function of circumstance. Greatness, it turns out, is largely a matter of conscious choice, and discipline."

But as innovation is very much a moving target, organisations are left with the challenge of making decisions about something that quickly can turn out to be obsolete. While patience is a virtue, breaking new ground successfully is an irresistible managerial dream. Seeing the train pass by – or, worse, not even being on the platform – is almost seen as a mortal sin in today's reality. Here, the idea of capacity building finds additional value beyond just building capacity towards something concrete. Whereas no one argues against thoughtful analyses to understand a situation – that is, the problems and opportunities – and to devise the correct initiatives for overcoming obstacles and delivering on desired objectives, doing so is not always easy. Our understandings are at best approximations and our predictions are always uncertain. Building capacity, then, can also be directed towards a more general readiness for change and innovation.

As such, capacity building must encompass uncertainty and negotiations about the current reality. It needs to be addressed holistically – through the constructs of leadership, organisation, and strategy, on an overall level as well as on a very concrete, relational level. These two levels will often generate friction. As managers design and plan, the execution depends on others and those two worlds often collide for different reasons. However, this friction is not necessarily negative; rather, it can represent an opportunity to learn and grow. A bottom–up approach certainly generates many qualities for an organisation, but there is also a need for an outlook and foresight that transcends the individual or smaller self-governing groups. Engaging in capacity building provides that interface which allows for the strategic to meet the operational, the concrete with the abstract, and the best practices with next practices.

Innovation does not exist in isolation; rather, it is an interdependent construct. The same goes for the constructs of leadership, organisation, and strategy – they are not only conditions for innovation, but also shaped by innovation. Yet when organisations want to work on their capacity for innovation, they address that capacity through those three constructs.

As such, developing the capacity for bringing about innovation means developing and implementing more effective forms of strategy, leadership, and organisation.

Note

1 Even though some work with many more senses, here it should be sufficient to adhere to the principle of five basic human senses – often traced back to Aristotle's *De Anima* (*On the Soul*).

Appendix 1
Summary of methodology

The methodology used for the thesis work that this monograph is built upon (Vindeløv-Lidzélius, 2018) was a combination of a quantitative and a qualitative approach. It took a starting point in social constructionism (Gergen and Gergen, 2004; Gergen, 2009; McNamee, 2010). Relational constructionism is a meta-theory or discourse of (human) science (McNamee and Hosking, 2012). Hosking (2011) portrays relational constructionism as a number of considerations (or understandings) that are practical, and that suppose research to be a participatory relational process that co-constructs worlds of communication and (social) engagement. Methods are then considered a form of practice (McNamee and Hosking, 2012). The relational – the relationship – as the core principal construct provides an orientation that includes essentially all human activities. It implies that one could use virtually any method, even if, for instance, it might be considered part of a different tradition (e.g. statistics, surveys, etc.).

In the thesis, grounded theory was used as an overall approach to the conduct of research. There was a starting point and some general assumptions on behalf of the researcher, and there was an idea of what the thesis should offer – but the researcher remained open to the findings and did not try to fit those in with his own worldview. The actual outcome of the thesis could point in many different directions.

The thesis used a mixed methods research. Mixed methods can be conceptualised from epistemological debates between advocates of quantitative methods and those of qualitative methods (Pluye and Hong, 2013). A normal classification of mixed methods (Fetters et al., 2013; Pluye and Hong, 2013) describes three types of research design where each represents one type of integration of quantitative and qualitative methods. Here the second approach was used: that is, integration through data transformation. By developing a coding scheme and conducting a thematic analysis, frequencies let themes emerge from the corpus.

The goal of the research was to obtain knowledge about how organisations go about making innovation happen. First, we needed to ask the question: what is the nature of the problem? Second, we needed to ask: through which methodology can this kind of problem be examined? Following the argument of Darsø (2001), the complexity of the problem justifies the approach of a case study. A case study is not a methodological choice, but a choice of object to be studied (Stake, 1994). In a case study framework, both qualitative and quantitative data are collected to build a comprehensive understanding of a case, which is the focus of the study (Yin, 2003). As a research strategy, the case study focuses on understanding the dynamics present within a single setting (Eisenhardt, 1989). According to Yin (2003), case studies are preferred as research strategies when "how" or "why" questions are being posed, when the investigator has little control over events, and/or when the focus is on contemporary phenomena within some real-life context. The research methodology chosen was a single holistic case design. The methodology was multiple since the empirical material was collected using more than one method, and it was not embedded since the study took on the case in its totality.

Internal validity is key for data analysis in case studies that are explanatory or casual, but not for descriptive or exploratory studies (Yin, 1994: 33). This is because when dealing with complex problems some inferences and explanation will be attempted, but casual relationships will hardly be the outcome (Darsø, 2001).

The thesis pursued a wealth of multiple perspectives. This "wealth" is the hallmark of the relational constructionist approach to research, and the study uses a triangulation of data, methods, and researcher perspectives in order to create "thick textured descriptions" (McNamee and Hosking, 2012: 47). Even if we cannot claim theories on the basis of single cases, it is not true that they hold no value outside the particular. Leung (2015: 326) points out that "with rising trend of knowledge synthesis from qualitative research via meta-synthesis, meta-narrative or meta-ethnography, evaluation of generalisability becomes pertinent."

Based on Guba's (1981), Guba and Lincoln's (2005), and Shenton's (2004) criteria for qualitative researchers, this research has striven for authenticity (Morrow, 2005) and transparency.

A thematic analysis (Fox, 2004; Creswell, 2009) was applied; following Kvale (1996) and Kvale and Brinkman (2008), condensation, coding, and interpretation were pursued in the analysis and main discussion in the thesis.

As this exploratory research was rooted in grounded theory (Glaser and Strauss, 1967; Strauss and Corbin, 1990; Glaser, 1992; Seldén, 2005, used a mixed methods approach (Fetters et al., 2013; Pluye and Hong, 2013), and made use of convergent design for the analysis, there was a need to choose how to bring these approaches together. Here the choices were made in line with a constructionist approach (McNamee, 2004, 2010) to make it context relevant, in particular securing authenticity (Guba and Lincoln, 1989; Morrow, 2005) and transferability (Guba, 1981).

Table A.1 follows an overview of the research design and methodology.

188   *Summary of methodology*

Table A.1 Overview of the research design and methodology

Research question	How do organisations go about developing capacity to bring about innovation in complex systems?
Purpose of research	Explore new territory, test existing theory, and co-construct insights and emerging questions
Research design	A grounded theory approach Mixed methods – quantitative and qualitative Case study research – single case holistic design Expert interviews and co-creation Thematic analysis and data conversion
Units of analysis	Lenses (issues, matters, questions) that emerged through the research process
Case criteria (Qualitative)	Big company. Technology rooted, and product and service development.
Case criteria (Quantitative)	Subject matter experts (SMEs). Part of relevant networks. Expressed interest in questions around innovation. Representing an organisation
Data collection	Online survey Qualitative and semi-structures interviews Workshops Focus group Secondary sources
Form of reasoning	Inductive – some abductive and deductive processes
Theory of science	Social constructionism Complexity theory
Form of analysis	Segmenting and cross-referencing of online responses Condensation and categorisation of meaning, narrative structuring, meaning interpretation, and ad hoc methods

Appendix 2

Summary of research

The research process began with an action research phase in which the researcher was contracted as a consultant by the Research and Development Department (PDI) of Telefónica Digital in Barcelona, working with them for around 18 months. This phase also included 13 interviews that were conducted with the management team. As a supplement, a quantitative research phase occurred in which 103 subject matter experts were invited to offer their perspectives on innovation.

As the PDI – indeed the whole division of Telefónica Digital – was dissolved and/or transformed approximately three years later, five interviews were conducted to offer insight into what had emerged instead and how a particular unit (Alpha) served as one answer to the question of how to bring about innovation in complex systems. Finally, the findings and emerging questions were brought into a focus group with five other subject matter experts for further discussion, reflection, and co-construction.

Although the researcher had never worked before at Telefónica, he was contracted to work for them between 2013 and 2014 on a consultancy basis in the form of action research. This work was the starting point for this thesis' fieldwork. After the contracted work was completed, and as the thesis progressed, the researcher maintained a relatively close relationship with some of the individuals involved in the work (primarily the leader of the unit and later the founder and leader of Alpha). As such, the start of the relationship can be seen as a combination of a client–consultant relationship (Schein, 1986, 1988a, 1999, 2009b, 2010; 2013) and that of an interviewee–researcher relationship (Kvale and Brinkmann, 2008), following the social constructionist approach (McNamee, 2010; McNamee and Hosking, 2012). After 2014, the relationship did not extend beyond that of Telefónica being the case study for the PhD; however, this included interviews and further talks and advice on my behalf.

The research process did not follow a straight line. It can even be argued that it began in a somewhat unorthodox fashion. Because the consultancy work was already underway, the research question was developed in the same time period. As indicated, it was not fully decided at the time that the work with Telefónica would become the case study for this thesis. This was something that crystallised as the PhD work became clear.

190 *Summary of research*

There is much written about the subject as such, but little that responds to the actual research question. The literature review needed to be relatively extensive to consider the different aspects of the subject matter (innovation). The subject offers – even when contextualising it in complex systems – many discourses, which required a discussion of their inter-relationships. The initial findings here served as a backdrop and platform for developing the qualitative and quantitative research.

The next step was to unfold the research question and its supporting questions by conducting a more quantitative research study. A survey was developed and posted in different online forums, inviting different subject matter experts (SMEs). It also helped to unpack the work done at Telefónica.

Table A.2 Overview of the research process

2012	
Q4	Started the application process for the PhD at Tao/Tilburg
2013	
Q1	Contract with Telefónica in place
Q2	Acceptance onto the PhD programme
Q3	First round of interviews with Telefónica
Q4	Reconfiguration of research question and strategy
2014	
Q1	Social constructionism course done
Q2	Quantitative research done
Q3	Analysis of quantitative research done
Q4	First draft and outline of chapter on innovation
2015	
Q1	Chapter on complex systems begun
Q2	Chapter on social constructionism begun
Q3	Chapter on innovation begun
Q4	Chapter on methodology begun
2016	
Q1	Bringing together of innovation, complexity, and social constructionism
Q2	Chapter on methodology revisited
Q3	Reconfiguration of the thesis outline, structure, and content
Q4	Finalisation of methodology chapter and case review
2017	
Q1	Final interviews with Telefónica conducted and analysed
Q2	Discussion chapter written
Q3	Conclusion chapter written and first submission of thesis
Q4	Editing structure of the thesis
2018	
Q1	Editing structure and content of the thesis and new submission
Q4	Defence of thesis

The qualitative study was organised around a total of 18 interviews: three with the leaders of Alpha, 13 with the leadership of the former R&D unit (PDI), 1 with another leader of innovation at the company (he was also 1 of the 13), and 1 with a former employee with much insight into Telefónica (he was also the one who helped out with the consultancy work). The interviews were supplemented with public records such as annual reports and newspaper articles. The preliminary findings from quantitative and qualitative research were explored and extrapolated in a focus group, consisting of five other SMEs and the researcher.

The different findings from the qualitative research were contrasted and compared with the quantitative research and the literature review. Eight parameters that were developed during the research to progress the research question further were used in a conversion phase to discuss the different findings. Finally, in the conclusion, the findings were turned directly towards the research question and mirrored against the researcher's own experiences and reflections. The researcher worked very much with emerging questions and views throughout the process as opposed to hypotheses. This is reflected in the thesis as well, offering an exploratory orientation to the work.

Table A.2 follows a timeline of the research process and a description.

References

Aasen, T. M. B. and Johannessen, S. (2009). Managing innovation as communicative processes: A case of subsea technology R&D. *International Journal of Business Science and Applied Management*, 4(3): 22–33.

Abernathy, W. J. and Clark, K. B. (1985). Innovation: Mapping the Winds of Creative Destruction. *Research Policy* 14(1): 3–22.

Aboelmaged, M. and Hashem, G. (2019). Absorptive capacity and green innovation adoption in SMEs: The mediating effects of sustainable organisational capabilities. *Journal of Cleaner Production*, 220: 853–863.

Ackoff, R. L. (1981). *Creating the Corporate Future*. New York: John Wiley & Sons.

Adler, N. (2007). Organizational metaphysics: Global wisdom and the audacity of hope. In Eric H. Kessler and James R. Bailey (eds.), *Handbook of Organizational and Managerial Wisdom*. Thousand Oaks, CA: Sage Publications, pp. 423–258.

Adriansen, H. K. (2010). How criticality affects students' creativity. In C. Nyggard, N. Courtney and C. Holtham (eds.), *Teaching Creativity – Creativity in Teaching*. Faringdon: Libri Publishing, 65–84.

Afuah, A. N. and Bahram, N. (1995). The hypercube of innovation. *Research Policy*, 24(1): 51–76.

Altshuller, G. S. and Shapiro, R. B. (1956). О Психологии изобретательского творчества [On the psychology of inventive creation]. *Вопросы Психологии* [*The Psychological Issues*], 6: 37–39. Available at http://www.altshuller.ru/world/eng/index.asp, accessed 2015.

Amabile, T. M. (1983). The social psychology of creativity. A componential conceptualization. *Journal of Personality and Social Psychology*, 45(2): 357–376.

Amabile, T. M. (September–October, 1998). How to kill creativity. *Harvard Business Review*, 76(5): 76–87.

Amabile, T. M., Hadley, C. N. and Kramer, S. J. (2002). Creativity under the gun. *Harvard Business Review*, August.

Ambrose, S. A., Bridges, M. W., DiPietro, M., Lovett, M. C. and Norman, M. K. (2010). *How Learning Works: Seven Research-Based Principles for Smart Teaching*, First edition. CA: Jossey-Bass.

Anderson, P. (1999). Complexity and organizational science. *Organizational Science*, 10(3): 216–232.

Andriani, P. (2011). Complexity and innovation. In Peter Allen, Steve Maguire and Bill McKelvey (eds.), *The Sage Handbook of Complexity and Management*. Boston, MA: Sage, 454.

Aragón, A. O. (2012). Shifting identity from within the conversational flow of organisational complexity. *IDS Bulletin*, 43(3): 27–44.

Argote, L. (2011). Organizational learning research: Past, present and future. *Management Learning*, 42(4): 439–446.

Argote, L. (2013). *Organizational Learning: Creating, Retaining and Transferring Knowledge*. New York: Springer.

Argyris, C. (1982). *Reasoning, Learning, and Action: Individual and Organisational*. San Francisco, CA: Jossey Bass.

Argyris, C. and Schön, D. (1974). *Theory in Practice. Increasing Professional Effectiveness*. San Francisco, CA: Jossey-Bass.

Argyris, C. and Schön, D. (1978). *Organizational Learning: A Theory of Action Perspective*. Reading, MD: Addison Wesley.

Argyris, C. and Schön, D. (1995). *Organizational Learning: Theory, Method and Practice*. Englewood Cliffs, NJ: Prentice-Hall.

Arthur, W. B. (1999). Complexity and the economy. *Science*, 284(5411): 107–109.

Artto, K., Kujala, J., Dietrich, P. and Martinsuo, M. (2008). What is project strategy? *International Journal of Project Management*, 26(1): 4–12.

Austin, R. D. and Darsø, L. (2009). Innovation processes and closure. In Niina Koivunen and Ald Rehn (eds.), *Creativity and the Contemporary Economy*. Copenhagen: Copenhagen Business School Press, 55–81.

Baregheh, A., Rowley, J. and Sambrook, S. (2009). Towards a multidisciplinary definition of Innovation. *Management Decision*, 47(8): 1323–1339.

Barney, Jay. (1991). Firm resources and sustained competitive advantage. *Journal of Management*, 17(1): 99–120.

Bar-Yam, Y. (1997). *Dynamics of Complex Systems*. Boulder, CO: Westview Press.

Bar-Yam, Y. (2002). General features of complex systems. In *Encyclopedia of Life Support Systems*. Oxford: EOLSS UNESCO Publishers.

Basalla, G. (1998). *The Evolution of Technology*. Cambridge: Cambridge University Press.

Bason, C. (2010). *Leading Public Sector Innovation: Co-creating for a Better Society*. Bristol: Policy Press.

Beinhocker, E. D. (2006). *Origin of Wealth: Evolution, Complexity, and the Radical Remaking of Economics*. Boston, MA: Harvard Business Review Press.

Bennis, W. G. and Nanus, B. (1985). *Leaders: The Strategies for Taking Charge*. New York: Harper & Row.

Bens, I. (2006). *Facilitating to Lead! Leadership Strategies for a Networked World*. San Francisco, CA: Jossey-Bass, 1–33.

Berkhout, A. J., Hartmann, D., van der Duin, P. and Ortt, R. (2006). Innovating the innovation process. *International Journal of Technology Management*, 34(3–4): 390–404.

Birkinshaw, J., Hamel, G. and Mol, J. (2008). Management innovation. *Academy of Management Review*, 33(4): 825–845.

Bizikova, L., Swanson, D. and Roy, D. (2011:3), *Evaluation of Integrated Management Initiatives*. Winnipeg, Manitoba: International Institute for Sustainable Development.

Boden, M. A. (1991). *The Creative Mind: Myths and Mechanisms*. London: Basic Books.

Booz, Allen, & Hamilton. (1982). *New Product Management for the 1980's*. New York: Booz, Allen & Hamilton, Inc.

Bornstein, D. (2004). *How to Change the World: Social Entrepreneurs and the Power of New Ideas*. Oxford: Oxford University Press.

194   *References*

Borum, F. and Christiansen, J. K. (1993). Actors and structures in IS projects: What makes implementation happen? *Scandinavian Journal of Management*, 9(1): 5–28.

Boyer, N. A. (2004). *Finding the Future: Why "Learning Journeys" Give An Adaptive Edge* (Draft, obtained from a compendium for a Masters programme on Leadership and Innovation in Complex System), 1–13.

Brown, J. and Isaacs, D. (2005). *World Café: Shaping Our Futures through Conversations That Matter*. San Francisco, CA: Berrett-Koehler Publisher.

Brown, J. S. and Duguid, P. (1991). Organizational learning and communities-of-practice: Toward a unified view of working, learning, and innovation. *Organization Science*, 2(1): 40–57.

Brynjolfsson, E. and Mcafee, A. (2016). *The Second Machine Age: Work, Progress, and Prosperity in a Time of Brilliant Technologies*. New York: W. W. Norton & Company.

Buckley, W. (1968). Society as a complex adaptive system. In W. Buckley (ed.), *Modern Systems Research for the Behavioral Scientist*. Chicago, IL: Aldine Publishing Company, 490–513.

Buur, J. and Larsen, H. (2010). The quality of conversations in participatory innovation. *CoDesign: International Journal of CoCreation in Design and the Arts*, 6(3): 121–138.

Buur, J. and Matthews, B. (2008). Participatory innovation. *International Journal of Innovation Management*, 12(3): 255–273.

Buur, J. and Mitchell, R. (2011). *The Business Modeling Lab, Track 4: Designing Innovative Business Models*. Paper presented at the Participatory Innovation Conference 2011 Proceedings, 368–373. Available at https://findresearcher.sdu.dk:8443/ws/files/123505278/Buur_J_Mitchell_R_2011_The_Business_Modeling_Lab.pdf

Buur, J. and Sitorus, L. (2007). *Ethnography as Design Provocation*. Paper presented at the Ethnographic Praxis in Industry Conference/EPIC 2007. Colorado: Keystone, 1–11.

Byrne, D. (1988). *Complexity Theory and the Social Sciences: An Introduction*. New York: Routledge.

Büschgens, T., Bausch, A. and Balkin, D. B. (2013). Organizational culture and innovation: A meta-analytic review. *Journal of Product Innovation Management*, 30: 763–781.

Büyüközkan, G. and Feyzioglu, O. (2004). A fussy-logic-based decision-making approach for new product development. *International Journal of Production Economics*, 90: 27–45.

Cameron, K. S. and Quinn, R. E. (2006). *Diagnosing and Changing Organizational Culture: Based on the Competing Values Framework*, Revised edition. San Francisco, CA: Jossey-Bass.

Campbell, J. (1993). *The Hero with a Thousand Faces*. London: Fontana Press.

Campos, E. B. and de Pablos, P. O. (2004). Innovation and learning in the knowledge-based economy: Challenges for the firm. *International Journal of Innovation and Technology Management*, 27(6/7).

Capra, F. (1996). *The Web of Life*. London: HarperCollins.

Casadevall, A. and Fang, F. C. (2016). Moonshot science: Risks and benefits. *mBio*, 7(4): e01381-16. doi: 10.1128/mBio.01381-16.

Castells, M. (1997). An introduction to the information age. *City*, 2(7): 6–16.

Cavé, A. (1994). *Managing Change in the Workplace*. London: Kogan Page.

Chesbrough, H. W. (2003a). The era of open innovation. *MIT Sloan Management Review*, 44(3): 35–41.

Chesbrough, H. (2003b). *Open Innovation: The New Imperative for Creating and Profiting, from Technology*. Boston, MA: Harvard Business School Press.

Chesbrough, H. (2005). Open innovation: A new paradigm for understanding industrial innovation. In H. Chesbrough, W. Vanhaverbeke, and J. West (eds.), *Open Innovation: Researching a New Paradigm*. Oxford: Oxford University Press, 1–25.

Chesbrough, H. (2006). *Open Business Models: How to Thrive in the New Innovation Landscape*. Boston, MA: Harvard Business School Press.

Christensen, C. M. (1997). *The Innovator's Dilemma: When New Technologies Cause Great Firms to Fail*. Boston, MA: Harvard Business Review Press.

Christensen, C. M. and Bower, J. L. (1995). Disruptive technologies: Catching the wave. *Harvard Business Review*, January–February: 43–53.

Christensen, C. M. and Raynor, M. E. (2013). *The Innovator's Solution: Creating and Sustaining Successful Growth*. Boston, MA: Harvard Business Review Press.

Christiansen, U., Kjærgaard, A. and Hartmann, R. K. (2012). Working in the shadows: Understanding ERP usage as complex responsive processes of conversations in the daily practices of a special operations force. *Scandinavian Journal of Management*, 28: 173–184.

Chu, D. (2011). Complexity: Against systems, *Theory in Biosciences*, 130(3): 229–245.

Cilliers, P. (1998). *Complexity and Postmodernism: Understanding Complex Systems*. London: Routledge.

Coccia, M. (2006). *Classifications of Innovations Survey and Future Directions*. Working Paper CERIS-CNR, 8(2).

Cohen, I. B. (1976). The eighteenth-century origins of the concept of scientific revolution. *Journal of the History of Ideas*, 37(2): 257–288.

Cohen, W. M. and Levinthal, D. A. (1989). Innovation and learning: The two faces of R&D. *The Economic Journal*, 99: 569–596.

Cohen, W. M. and Levinthal, D. A. (1990). Absorptive capacity: A new perspective on learning and innovation. *Administrative Science Quarterly*, 35(1): 128–152.

Collins, J. (2001). *Good to Great*. New York: HarperBusiness.

Collins, J. and Porras, J. (1994). *Built to Last*. New York: Harper Business.

Collins, J. and Hansen, M. T. (2011). *Great by Choice: Uncertainty, Chaos, and Luck: Why Some Thrive Despite Them All*. New York: HarperBusiness.

Collins, L. (2006). Opening up the innovation process. *Engineering Management*, 16(1): 14–17.

Cooke, P., Etxebbaria, G. and Uranage, M. G. (1997). Regional innovation systems: Institutional and organizational dimensions. *Research Policy*, 26: 475–491.

Cooper, R. G. (1998). Predevelopment activities determine new product success. *Industrial Marketing Management*, 17(3): 237–247.

Cooper, R. G. (2008). Perspective: The stage-gate idea-to-launch process-update, what's new, and nextGen systems. *Journal of Product Innovation Management*, 25(3): 213–232.

Cooper, R. G. (2009). How companies are reinventing their idea-to-launch methodologies. *Research Technology Management*, 52(2): 47–57.

Cooperrider, D. L. and Srivastva, S. (1987). Appreciative inquiry in organizational life. In R. W. Woodman and W. A. Pasmore (eds.), *Research in Organizational Change and Development*. Stamford, CT: JAI Press, Vol. 1, 129–169.

Cooperrider, D. L., Barrett, F. and Srivastva, S. (1995). Social construction and appreciative inquiry: A journey in organizational theory. In D. Hosking, P. Dachler

196   *References*

and K. Gergen (eds.), *Management and Organization: Relational Alternatives to Individualism*. Aldershot, UK: Avebury, 157–200.

Cooperrider, D. L., Sorensen, P. F., Jr, Whitney, D. and Yaeger, T. F. (2000). *Appreciative Inquiry: Rethinking Human Organization toward a Positive Theory of Change*. Champaign, IL: Stipes Publishing.

Cooperrider, D. L. and Whitney, D. (2001). A positive revolution in change. In D. L. Cooperrider, P. Sorenson, D. Whitney and T. Yeager (eds.), *Appreciative Inquiry: An Emerging Direction for Organization Development*. Champaign, IL: Stipes, 9–29. Available at http://www.tapin.in/Documents/2/Appreciative%20Inquiry%20-%20Positive%20Revolution%20in%20Change.pdf, accessed 2 October 2016.

Cortes Robles, G., Negny, S. and Le Lann, J. M. (2009). Case based reasoning and TRIZ: A coupling for innovative conception in chemical engineering. *Chemical Engineering and Processing*, 48(1): 239–249.

Creswell, J. (2009). *Research Design: Qualitative, Quantitative, and Mixed Methods Approaches*, Third edition. Thousand Oaks, CA: Sage.

Crisp, B. R., Swerissen, H. and Duckett, S. J. (2000). Four approaches to capacity building in health: Consequences for measurement and accountability. *Health Promotion International*, 15(2): 99–107.

Crossan, M. M., Lane, H. W. and White, R. E. (1999). An organizational learning framework: From intuition to institution. *Academy of Management Review*, 24(3): 522–537.

Csíkszentmihályi, M. (1997). *Creativity: Flow and the Psychology of Discovery and Invention*. New York: HarperPerennial.

Cummings, T. and Huse, E. (1989). *Organization Development and Change*. St Paul, MN: West Publishing Company.

Cummings, T. G. and Worley, C. G. (2005). *Organization Development and Change*, Eighth edition. Mason, OH: Thomson South-Western.

Czarniawska-Joerges, B. (1992). *Exploring Complex Organizations: A Cultural Perspective*. Newbury Park, CA: Sage Publications.

Dalkir, K. (2011). *Knowledge Management in Theory and Practice*, Second edition. Cambridge: MIT Press.

Dalling, I. (2007). *Integrated Management Definition*. Chartered Quality Institute Integrated Management Special Interest Group, Issue 2.1, 3.

Damanpour, F. and Schneider, M. (2006). Phases of the adoption of innovation in organizations: Effects of environment, organization and top managers. *British Journal of Management*, 17(3): 215–236.

Danforth, C. M. (2013). Chaos in an atmosphere hanging on a wall. *Mathematics of Planet Earth*. Available at http://mpe2013.org/2013/03/17/chaos-in-an-atmosphere-hanging-on-a-wall/, accessed April 2015.

Darsø, L. (2001): *Innovation in the making*. Samfundslitteratur.

Darsø, L. (2003). Is there a formula for innovation? Translated from Danish: "En formel for innovation", Børsens Ledelseshåndbøger.

Davenport, T. H. (1992). *Process Innovation: Reengineering Work through Information Technology*. Boston, MA: Harvard Business Review Press.

Davila, T., Epstein, M. J. and Shelton, R. (2006). *Making Innovation Work: How to Manage IT, Measure IT and Profit from IT*. Upper Saddle River, NJ: Wharton School Publishing.

De Bono, E. (1971). *Lateral Thinking for Management*. London: Penguin.

Desautels Centre. (2019). Rotman. http://www.rotman.utoronto.ca/FacultyAndResearch/ResearchCentres/DesautelsCentre/Integrative%20Thinking.aspx

Dhanaraj, C. and Parkhe, A. (2006). Orchestrating innovation networks. *Academy of Management Review*, 31(3): 659–669.

Diacu, F. and Holmes, P. (1996). *Celestial Encounters: The Origins of Chaos and Stability*. Princeton, NJ: Princeton University Press.

Dodgson, M. (1993). Organizational learning: A review of some literatures. *Organization Studies*, 14: 375–394.

Dooley, K. J. (1997). A complex adaptive systems model of organization change. *Nonlinear Dynamics Psychology and Life Sciences*, 1(1): 69–97.

Dooley, K. & Van De Ven, A. H. (1999). Explaining complex organizational dynamics. *Organization Science*, 10(3): 358–372. https://doi.org/10.1287/orsc.10.3.358.

Dowling, G. R. and Staelin, R. (1994). A model of perceived risk and intended risk-handling activity. *Journal of Consumer Research*, 21: 119–134.

Downes, L. and Nunes, P. F. (2013). Big bang disruption. *Harvard Business Review*.

Downes, L. and Nunes, P. F. (2014). What's up with WhatsApp? The price of a big bang disruptor. *Forbes*, March. Available at http://www.forbes.com/sites/bigbangdisruption/2014/03/03/whats-up-with-whatsapp-the-price-of-a-big-bang-disruptor/

Drucker, P. F. (1967). *The Effective Executive*. New York: Harper & Row.

Drucker, P. F. (1969). *The Age of Discontinuity: Guidelines to Our Changing Society*. New York: Harper & Row.

Drucker, P. F. (1985). *Innovation and Entrepreneurship*. London: Pan Books.

Drucker, P. F. (1992). New society of organizations. *Harvard Business Review*, 70(5): 95–104.

Drucker, P. F. (1993). *Post-capitalist Society*, Reprint edition. HarperBusiness.

Drucker, P. F. (2006). *Innovation and Entrepreneurship*. New York: Harper Business.

Duncan, R. (1976). The ambidextrous organization: Designing dual structures for innovation. R. H. Killman, L. R. Pondy and D. Sleven (eds.), *The Management of Organization*. New York: North Holland, 167–188.

Du Preez, N. D., Louw, L. and Essmann, H. (2006). An innovation process model for improving innovation capability. *Journal of High Technology Management Research*, 1–24. http://www.indutech.co.za/attachments/188_LouwEssmannDu%20Preez%20-%20An%20Innovation%20Process%20Model%20for%20Improving%20Innovation%20Capability.pdf

Easterby-Smith, M., Crossan, M. and Niccolini, D. (2000). Organizational learning: Debates past, present and future. *Journal of Management Studies*, 37(6): 783–796.

Edison, H., Ali, N. B. and Torkar, R. (2013). Towards innovation measurement in the software industry. *Journal of Systems and Software*, 86(5): 1390–1407.

Edquist, C. (1997). Systems of innovation approaches: Their emergence and characteristics. In C. Edquist (ed.), *Systems of Innovation: Technologies, Institutions and Organizations*. London: Pinter, 1–35.

Edquist, C. (2001). *The Systems of Innovation Approach and Innovation Policy: An Account of the State of the Art*. Lead paper presented at the DRUID Conference, Aalborg, June 12–15.

Eisenhardt, K. M. (1989). Building case study from case study research. *Academy of Management Review*, 14(4): 532–550.

Eisenhardt, K. M. and Martin, J. A. (2000). Dynamic capabilities: What are they? *Strategic Management Journal*, 21(10–11): 1105–1121.

Elias, N. (1939/1991). *The Society of Individuals*. Oxford: Blackwell.

Elias, N. (1939/2000). *The Civilising Process*. Oxford: Blackwell.

198   *References*

Elwell, F. W. (2013). *The Sociology of Norbert Elias.* Available at http://www.faculty.rsu.edu/~felwell/Theorists/Essays/Elias1.htm, accessed 12 December 2014.

Engel, J., Kollat, D. and Blackwell, R. (1978). *Consumer Behaviour.* New York: Dryden Press.

Fagerberg, J., Mowery, D. C. and Nelson, R. R. (2006). *The Oxford Handbook of Innovation.* New York: Oxford University Press.

Fagerberg, J. and Verspagen, B. (2009). Innovation studies: The emerging structure of a new scientific field. *Research Policy,* 38: 218–233.

Fetters, M. D., Curry, L. A. and Creswell, J. W. (2013). Achieving integration in mixed methods designs-principles and practices. *Health Services Research,* 48: 2134–2156.

Fiol, C. M. and Lyles, M. (1985). Organizational learning. *Academy of Management Review,* 10: 803–813.

Fischer, M. M. (2001). Innovation, knowledge creation and systems of innovation. *The Annals of Regional Science,* 35(2): 199–216.

Fishbein, M. and Ajzen, I. (1975). *Belief, Attitude, Intention And Behavior.: An Introduction to Theory and Research.* Reading, MA: Addison-Wesley. Available at http://people.umass.edu/aizen/f&a1975.html

Flaherty, J. (1999). *Coaching: Evoking Excellence in Others.* Woburn, MA: Butterworth-Heinemann.

Florea, D.-L. (2015). The relationship between branding and diffusion of innovation: A systematic review. *Procedia Economics and Finance,* 23: 1527–1534. From Science Direct.

Florida, R. (2002). *The Rise of the Creative Class.* New York: Basic Books.

Fonseca, J. (2002). *Complexity and Innovation in Organizations.* New York: Routledge.

Fox, N. J. (2004). *Qualitative Data Analysis: HAR6010.* (Taught unit from MSc in Health and Social Care Research). Sheffield: University of Sheffield. Available at https://www.researchgate.net/post/What_is_the_difference_between_content_analysis_and_thematic_analysis_as_methods_used_in_qualitative_data_analysis, accessed 26 February 2017.

Frascati Manual. (2015). *The Measurement of Scientific, Technological and Innovation Activities.* Guidelines for Collecting and Reporting Data on Research and Experimental Development. Paris: OECD Publishing.

Fraser, S. W. and Greenhalgh, T. (2001). Coping with complexity: educating for capability. *BMJ,* 323(15): 799–803.

Freeman, C., Clark, J. and Soete, L. (1982). *Un-employment and Technical Innovation: A Study of Long Waves and Economic Development.* London: Frances Printer.

Freeman, J. and Engel, J. S. (2007). Models of innovation: Startups and mature corporations. *California Review Management,* 50(1): 94–119.

French, S. (2013). Cynefin, statistics and decision analysis. *Journal of the Operational Research Society,* 64: 547–561.

French, S. (2015). Cynefin: Uncertainty, small worlds and scenarios. *Journal of the Operational Research Society,* 66: 1635–1645.

Frenken, K. (2005). Technological innovation and complexity theory. *Economics of Innovation and New Technology,* 15(2): 137–155.

Friedman, T. L. (2006). *The World Is Flat. A Brief History of the Twenty-first Century,* Updated and expanded edition. New York: Farr, Straus and Giroux.

Galanakis, K. (2006). Innovation process: Make sense using systems thinking. *Technovation,* 26: 1222–1232.

Garcia, R. and Calantone, R. (2001). A critical look at technological innovation typology and innovativeness terminology: A literature review. *The Journal of Product Innovation Management,* 19: 110–132.

Gardner, H. (1983). *Frames of Mind: the Theory of Multiple Intelligences.* New York: Basic Books.

Gassmann, O. (2006). Opening up the innovation process: Towards an agenda. *R&D Management,* 36(3): 223–228.

Gell-Mann, M. (1995). *The Quark and the Jaguar: Adventures in the Simple and the Complex.* London: Abacus.

Gell-Mann, M. (1995/1996). What is complexity? Remarks on simplicity and complexity by the Nobel Prize-winning author of The Quark and the Jaguar. *Complexity,* 1(1): 16–19.

Gergen, K. J. and Gergen, M. (2004). *Social Construction: Entering the Dialogue.* Chagrin Falls, OH: Taos Institute.

Gergen, K. J. (2009). *Relational Being: Beyond Self and Community.* New York: Oxford University Press.

Gertner, J. (2014). The truth about Google X: An exclusive look behind the secretive lab's closed doors. *Fast Company.* Available at https://www.fastcompany.com/3028156/united-states-of-innovation/the-google-x-factor, accessed 13 September 2016.

Ghais, S. (2005). *Extreme Facilitation: Guiding Groups through Controversy and Complexity.* San Francisco, CA: Jossey-Bass, 1–46.

Glaser, B. G. (1992). *Basics of Grounded Theory Analysis: Emergence vs Forcing.* Mill Valley, CA: Sociology Press.

Glaser, B. G. and Strauss, A. L. (1967). *The Discovery of Grounded Theory: Strategies for Qualitative Research.* New York: Aldine, Hawthorne.

Gleick, J. (1987). *Chaos: Making a New Science.* New York: Penguin Books.

Godin, B. (2002). The rise of innovation surveys: Measuring a fuzzy concept. Project on the history and sociology of S&T statistics, Working Paper No. 16. Montreal: CSIIC.

Godin, B. (2006). The linear model of innovation: The historical construction of an analytical framework. *Science, Technology and Human Values,* 31(6): 639–667.

Godin, B. (2008). In the shadow of Schumpeter: W. Rupert Maclaurin and the study of technological innovation. Project on the Intellectual History of Innovation. Working Paper No. 2. Montréal: INRS.

Godin, B. (2009). The linear model of innovation (II): Maurice Holland and research cycle. Project on the Intellectual History of Innovation. Working Paper No. 3. Montréal: INRS.

Godin, B. (2010a). Innovation without the word: William F. Ogburn's contribution to technological innovation studies. Project on the Intellectual History of Innovation. Working Paper No. 5. Montreal: INRS.

Godin, B. (2010b). "Meddle not with them that are given to change": Innovation as evil, project on the intellectual history of innovation. Working Paper No. 6. Montreal: INRS.

Godin, B. (2011). Καινοτομία: An old word for a new world; or, The de-contestation of a political and contested concept. Project on the Intellectual History of Innovation. Working Paper No. 9. Montreal: INRS.

Godin, B. (2012a). καινοτομία: An old word for a new world; or, The de-contestation of a political and contested concept. In Karl-Erik Sveiby, Pemilla Gripenberg and

200 References

Beata Segercrantz (eds.), *Challenging the Innovation Paradigm*. London: Routledge, 37–60.

Godin, B. (2012b). Innovation studies: The invention of a specialty. *Minerva*, 50(4): 397–421.

Godin, B. (2012c). Social innovation: Utopias of innovation from c. 1830 to the present. Project on the Intellectual History of Innovation. Working Paper No. 11. Montreal: INRS.

Godin, B. (2013a). Innovation after the French Revolution, or, innovation transformed: From word to concept. Project on the Intellectual History of Innovation. Working Paper No. 14. Montreal: INRS.

Godin, B. (2013b). Invention, diffusion and linear models of innovation. Project on the Intellectual History of Innovation. Working Paper No. 15. Montreal: INRS.

Godin, B. (2014a). Innovation and science: When science had nothing to do with innovation, and vice-versa. Project on the Intellectual History of Innovation. Working Paper No. 16. Montreal: INRS.

Godin, B. (2014b). Innovation and creativity: A slogan, nothing but a slogan. Project on the Intellectual History of Innovation. Working Paper No. 17. Montreal: INRS.

Goodwin, T. (2015). In the age of disintermediation the battle is all for the consumer interface. *TechCruch*. Available at https://techcrunch.com/2015/03/03/in-the-age-of-disintermediation-the-battle-is-all-for-the-customer-interface/

Gorze-Mitka, I. and Okreglicka, M. (2014). Improving decision making in complexity environment. *Procedia Economics and Finance*, 16: 402–409.

Grant, R. M. (2001). The resource-based theory of competitive advantage: Implications forstrategy formulation. *California Management Review*, Spring, 114–135.

Grantham, C. E. and Nichols, L. D. 1993. *The Digital Workplace: Designing Groupware Platforms*. New York: Van Nostrand Reinhold.

Greenhalgh, T., Robert, G., Macfarlane, F., Bate, P., Kyriakidou, O. and Peacock, R. (2005). Storylines of research in diffusion of innovation: A meta-narrative approach to systematic review. *Social Science & Medicine*, 61(2): 417–430.

Griffin, D. (2002). *The Emergence of Leadership: Linking Self-organisation and Ethics*. Routledge: London.

Griffin, R. W., Sawyer, J. E. and Woodman, R. W. (1993). Toward a theory of organizational creativity. *Academy Management Review*, 18(2): 293–321.

Grint, K. (2005). Problems, problems, problems: The social construction of 'leadership'. *Human Relations*, 58(11): 1467–1494.

Grint, K. (2011). A history of leadership. In A. Bryman, D. Collinson, K. Grint, B. Jackson and M. Uhl-Bien (eds.), *The Sage Handbook of Leadership*. Los Angeles, CA: Sage Publications, 3–15.

Guba, E. G. (1981). Criteria for assessing the trustworthiness of naturalistic inquiries. *Educational Communication and Technology Journal*, 29: 75–91.

Guba, E. G. and Lincoln, Y. S. (2005). Paradigmatic controversies, contradictions, and emerging confluences. In N. K. Denzin and Y. S. Lincoln (eds.), *The Sage Handbook of Qualitative Research*, Third edition. Thousand Oaks, CA: Sage, 191–215.

Habermas, J. (1987 [1981]). *Theory of Communicative Action, Volume Two: Lifeworld and System: A Critique of Functionalist Reason* (Book). Translated by Thomas A. McCarthy. Boston, MA: Beacon Press. ISBN 0–8070-1401-X.

Hamel, G. (2006). *The Why, What, and How of Management Innovation*. Boston, MA: Harvard Business Review.

Hamel, G. (2009). Moon shots for management. *Harvard Business Review*, February.

Hamel, G. and Prahalad, C. K. (1994). *Competing for the Future*. Boston, MA: Harvard Business School Press.

Hargrave, T. and van de Ven, A. H. (2006). A collective action model of institutional innovation. *Academy of Management Review*, 31: 864–888.

Harkema, S. (2003). A complex adaptive perspective on learning within innovation projects. *The Learning Organization*, 10(6): 340–346.

Harrison, O. (2008). *Open Space Technology: A User's Guide*, Third edition. San Francisco, CA: Berrett-Koehler.

Hartley, R. (1994). *Mistakes and Success*. New York: John Wiley.

Hartmann, D. and Trott, P. (2009). Why "open innovation" is old wine in new bottles. *International Journal of Innovation Management*, 13(4): 715–736.

Harvard Business Essentials. (2003). *Managing Creativity and Innovation*. Boston, MA: Harvard Business Review Press.

Hayles, N. K. (1991). *Chaos Bound: Orderly Disorder in Contemporary Literature and Science*. Ithaca, NY: Cornell University Press.

Henry, J. and Mayle, D. (ed.). (2002). *Managing Innovation and Change*, Second revised edition. London: SAGE Publications Inc; Accessed from Google Books.

Heslop, V. R. (2010). Sustainable capacity: building institutional capacity for sustainable development. Diss. ResearchSpace@ Auckland.

Herzberg, F. (1966). *Work and the Nature of Man*. Cleveland, OH: World Publishing.

Hislop, D., Newell, S., Scarbrough, H. and Swan, J. (2000). Networks, knowledge, power: Decision making, politics and the process of innovation. *Technology Analysis & Strategic Management*, 12(3): 399–411.

Hjorth, D. (2005). Organizational entrepreneurship: With de Certeau on creating heterotopias (or space for play). *Journal of Management Inquiry*, 14(4): 386–398.

Hjorth, D., Austin, R. and O'Donnell, S. (2011). Learning to lead collective creativity from Miles Davies, I–III. The Department of Management, Politics and Philosophy, Copenhagen Business School.

Hock, D. W. (1999). *The Birth of the Chaordic Age*. San Francisco, CA: Berrett-Koehler.

Holland, J. H. (1992). *Adaptation in Natural and Artificial Systems: An Introductory Analysis with Applications to Biology, Control, and Artificial Intelligence*. Cambridge, MA: MIT Press.

Holland, J. H. (1993). Echoing Emergence. Santa Fe Institute Working Paper No. 1993–04–023.

Holland, J. H. (1996). *Hidden Order: How Adaptation Builds Complexity*. Reading, MA: Perseus Books.

Holland, J. H. (1999). *Emergence: From Chaos to Order*. Reading, MA: Perseus Books.

Holland, J. H. (2006). Studying complex adaptive systems. *Journal of Systems Science & Complexity*, 19: 1–8.

Horgan, J. (1995). From complexity to perplexity: Trends in complexity studies. *Scientific American*, 272: 74–79.

Hosking, D. M. (2011). Telling tales of relations: Appreciating relational constructionism. *Organization Studies*, 31(1): 47–65.

Huber, G. P. (1991). Organizational learning: The contributing processes and the literatures. *Organization Science*, 2(1): 88–115.

202 *References*

Humbert, M. (2007). Technology and workforce: Comparison between the information revolution and the industrial revolution. University of California, Berkeley School of Information. Available at https://infoscience.epfl.ch/record/146804/files/InformationSchool.pdf, accessed 8 October 2016.

Husserl, E. (1936). *The Crisis of European Sciences and Transcendental Phenomenology.* Translated by David Carr. Evanston, IL: Northwestern University Press, 1970. Available at https://d1wqtxts1xzle7.cloudfront.net/34337886/Husserlcrisis.pdf?1406885508=&response-content-disposition=inline%3B+filename%3DThe_Crisis_of_European_Sciences_and_Tran.pdf&Expires=1591879720&Signature=GZ6rdbrkozSicRTIpZTirfz1fqBRhPEHdoCPSczl46iqVBpagDjh~2wo3UUhvOjNw6Oljy30pIxJgyePohNpMaFLdvntQOy-kqTFLCo7aqxw9pICX-5noSNTx0xvkjizrwiPVxl2v-5yhRctxNeklas3NnwO2t6t4SUEFlTEcUWcMOFCIAz0r11qugPJIOHL~AruOZITMnupUbjUBdHyjnepyHzj6N9m4g6sW7xt8~J22KI6i6ZwGT73HB7hM8~9Lp6MDh1OaxgHkllYFNtuXEMD2cLfBHn89uW8s8YIf0k4obXego~nG7gLD~u~QNassjYg~gHSs~gb6BxQRfaWjA__&Key-Pair-Id=APKAJLOHF5GGSLRBV4ZA

Jaafari, A. (2001). Management of risks, uncertainties and opportunities on projects: Time for a fundamental shift. *International Journal of Project Management*, 19(2): 89–101.

Jackson, M. (2000). *Systems Approaches to Management.* New York: Kluwer Academic.

Jackson, M. C. (2003). *Systems Thinking: Creative Holism for Managers.* New York: John Wiley & Sons.

Jackson, M. C. (2010). Reflections on the development and contribution of critical systems thinking and practice. *Systems Research and Behavioral Science*, 27: 133–139.

Jacobs, Jane. (1961). *The Death and Life of Great American Cities.* New York: Random House.

Jarvis, C., Gulati, A., McCririck, V. and Simpson, P. (2013). Leadership matters: Tensions in evaluating leadership development. *Advances in Developing Human Resources*, 15(1): 27–45.

Jimenez-Jimenez, D. and Sanz-Valle, R. (2005). Innovation and human resource management fit: an empirical study. *International Journal of Manpower*, 26(4): 364–381.

Jimenez-Jimenez, D. and Sanz-Valle, R. (2011). Innovation, organizational learning, and performance. *Journal of Business Research*, 64(4): 408–417.

Johansson, F. (2004). *The Medici Effect, Breakthrough Insights at the Intersection of Ideas, Concepts and Culture.* Boston, MA: Harvard Business School Press.

Johnson, N. F. (2009). *Two's Company, Three is Complexity.* Richmond, VA: Oneworld Publications.

Kaine, G. (2004). Consumer behaviour as a theory of innovation adoption in agriculture. Social Research Working Paper No. 01/04, Social Research Group, AgResearch.

Kanter, R. M. (1988). When a thousand flowers bloom: Structural, collective, and social conditions for innovation in organizations. *Research in Organizational Behavior*, 22: 169–211.

Kaplan, Allan. (August 2000). Capacity building: Shifting the paradigms of practice. *Development in Practice*, 3/4(10th Anniversary Issue): 517–526.

Kaplinksy, R. (2007). The impact of the Asian drivers on innovation and development strategies: Lessons from Sub-Saharan Africa experience. *International Journal of Technological Learning, Innovation and Development*, 1(1): 65–82.

Kaplinksy, R. (2011). Schumacher meets Schumpeter: Appropriate technology below the radar. *Research Policy*, 40: 193–203.

Kaplinksy, R., Chataway, J., Hanlin, R., Clark, M., Kale, D. et al. (2010). Below the radar: What does innovation in emerguing economies have to offer other low income economies? Working Paper Series. Maastricht: United Nations University, 1–34.

Kapsali, M. (2011). Systems thinking in innovation project management: A match that works. *International Journal of Project Management*, 29(4): 396–407.

Kardes, F., Cronley, M. and Cline, T. (2011). *Consumer Behavior*. Mason, OH, South-Western Cengage, 7.

Kauffman, S. A. (1995). *At Home in the Universe: The Search for Laws of Self-Organization and Complexity*. New York: Oxford University Press.

Kauffman, S. A. (2008). *Reinventing the Sacred*. New York: Basic Books.

Keeley, L., Walters, H., Pikkel, R. and Quinn, B. (2013). *Ten Types of Innovation: The Discipline of Building Breakthroughs*. New York: Wiley.

Kellert, S. (1993). *In the Wake of Chaos*. Chicago, IL: Chicago University Press.

Khurana, A. and Rosenthal, S. R. (1998). Towards holistic 'front ends' in new product development. *R&D Management*, 32(4): 269–279.

Khurana, R. (2007). *From Higher Aims to Hired Hands: The Social Transformation of American Business Schools and the Unfulfilled Promise of Management as a Profession*. Princeton, NJ: Princeton University Press.

Kim, W. C. and Mauborgne, R. (2005). *Blue Ocean Strategy: How to Create Uncontested Market Space and Make Competition Irrelevant*. Boston, MA: Harvard Business Press.

Kline, S. and Rosenberg, N. (1986). An overview of innovation. In R. Landau and N. Rosenberg (eds.), *The Positive Sum Strategy: Harnessing Technology for Economic Growth*. Washington, DC: National Academy Press, 275–306.

Koen, P. A. (2007). The fuzzy front end for incremental, platform, and breakthrough products. In K. B. Kahn (ed.), *PDMA Handbook of New Product Development*, Second edition. New York: John Wiley & Sons, Inc. doi: 10.1002/9780470172483.ch6.

Koen, P. A., Ajamian, G., Burkart, R., Clamen, A., Davidson, J., D'Amore, R., Elkins, C., Herald, K., Incorvia, M., Johnson, A., Karol, R., Seibert, R., Slavejkov, A. and Wagner, K. (2001). Providing clarity and common language to the fuzzy front end. *Research Technology Management*, 44: 46–55.

Kolb, D. A. (1984). *Experiential Learning: Experience as the Source of Learning and Development*. Englewood Cliffs, NJ: Prentice-Hall, Vol. 1.

Kotler, P. and Keller, K. L. (2015). *Marketing Management*. Pearson Education Limited.

Kumar, V. (2013). *101 Design Methods: A Structured Approach for Driving Innovation in your Organization*. Hoboken, NJ: John Wiley & Sons.

Kusiak, A. (2007). Innovation of products and services: Bridging world's economies. In J. A. Ceroni (ed.), *19th International Conference on Production Research*. Valparaiso, Chile, August, 1–6.

Kvale, S. (1996). *Interviews: An Introduction to Qualitative Research Interviewing*. Thousand Oaks, CA: Sage Publications.

Kvale, S. and Brinkmann, S. (2008). *InterViews: Learning the Craft of Qualitative Research Interviewing*, Second edition. Thousand Oaks, CA: Sage Publications.

Lachapelle, T. (2018). Urge To Converge: Corporate America's Dealmakers Are Cross-Pollinating. Bloomberg (January 2nd).

Ladyman, J., Lambert, J. and Wiesner, K. (2012). What is a complex system? Available at http://philsci-archive.pitt.edu/9044/4/LLWultimate.pdf, accessed 7 February 2015.

204 *References*

Laloux, F. (2014). *Reinventing Organizations*. Brussels: Nelson Parker.

Lamberg, J.-A. and Parvinen, P. (2003). The river metaphor for strategic management. *European Management Journal*, 21(5): 549–557.

Landry, J. (1992). *Information Characteristics as Constraints to Innovation*. Proceedings of the Twenty-Fifth Hawaii International Conference on System Sciences '92, California: IEEE Press, 482–491.

Lee, J. and Davis, J. (2016). How collective learning improves innovation. *Insead Knowledge*, September 27, 2016. Available at https://knowledge.insead.edu/entrepreneurship/how-collective-learning-improves-innovation-4950

Leonard, D. and Strauss, S. (1997). Putting your company's whole brain to work. *Harvard Business Review*, 75: 110–121.

Lepore, J. (2014). The disruption machine. What the gospel of innovation gets wrong. *The New Yorker*, 23 June, 30–36.

Leung, L. (2015). Validity, reliability, and generalizability in qualitative research. *Journal of Family Medicine and Primary Care*, 4(3): 324–327.

Levitt, T. (1963). Creativity is not enough. *Harvard Business Review*, 80(8): 137–145.

Lewin, K. (1951). *Field Theory in Social Science*. New York: Harper and Row.

Lewin, R. (1992). *Complexity, Life at the Edge of Chaos*. Chicago, IL: University of Chicago Press.

Long, Norton E. (1962). The administrative organization as a political system. In S. Mailick and E. H. Van Ness (eds.), *Concepts and Issues in Administrative Behaviour*. Englewood Cliffs, NJ: Prentice Hall, 110–121.

Lorenz, E. N. (1963). Deterministic non-periodic flow. *Journal of the Atmospheric Sciences*, 20(2): 130–141.

Lorsch, J. W. and McTague, E. (2016). Culture is not the culprit: When Organizations Are in Crisis, It's Usually Because the Business Is Broken. *Harvard Business Review* 94(4): 96–105.

Luhmann, N. (1996). *Social Systems*. Palo Alto, CA: Stanford University Press.

Luoma, J., Hämäläinen, R. P. and Saarinen, E. (2011). Acting with systems intelligence: Integrating complex responsive processes with the systems perspective. *Journal of the Operational Research Society*, 62: 3–11.

Maclaurin, W. R. (1953). The sequence from invention to innovation and its relation to economic growth. *Quarterly Journal of Economics*, 67(1): 97–111.

Magee, J. (2008). The contribution revolution: Letting volunteers build your business. *Harvard Business Review*, October.

Mandelbrot, B. (1967). How long is the coast of Britain? Statistical self-similarity and fractional dimension. *Science*, New Series, 156(3775): 636–638.

March, J. G. (1976). The technology of foolishness. In J. G. March and J. P. Olsen (eds.), *Ambiguity and Choice in Organizations*. Oslo: Universitetsforlaget, 69–81.

March, J. G. (1991). Exploration and exploitation in organizational learning. *Organization Science*, 2(1): 71–87.

March, J. G. and Olesen, J. P. (1976a). Organizational choice under ambiguity. In J. G. March and J. P. Olesen, (eds.), *Ambiguity and Choice in Organizations*. Oslo: Universitetsforlaget, 10–23.

March, J. G. and Olesen, J. P. (1976b). Organizational learning under the ambiguity of the past. In J. G. March J. P. and Olesen (eds.), *Ambiguity and Choice in Organizations*. Oslo: Universitetsforlaget, 54–67.

Maslow, A. H. (1943). A theory of human motivation. *Psychological Review*, 50(4): 370–396.

Maslow, A. H. (1974). *Toward a Psychology of Being.* New York: Van Nostrand Reinhold Company.

Mason, R. M. (1993). *Strategic Information Systems: Use of Information Technology in a Learning Organization.* Proceedings of the Twenty-Sixth Hawaii International Conference on System Sciences '93, California: IEEE Press, 840–849.

Mason, M. (2008). What is complexity theory and what are its implications for educational change? *Educational Philosophy and Theory,* 40(1): 35–49.

Maturana, H. R. and Varela, F. J. (1992). *The Tree of Knowledge: The Biological Roots of Human Understanding.* Shambhala.

May, R. and Oster, G. F. (1973). Bifurcations and dynamic complexity in simple ecological models. *The American Naturalist,* 110(974): 573–599.

McGrath, M. E. (1996). *Setting the PACE in Product Development: A Guide to Product and Cycle-time Excellence.* Butterworth-Heinemann.

McKinley, W. (2010). *A Supplement to A Compilation of the Messages and Papers of the Presidents.* Charleston, SC: Qontro Classic Books.

McLeod, S. A. (2013). Kolb – Learning Styles. Available at www.simplypsychology. org/learning-kolb.html

McLeod, J. and Childs, S. (2013). The Cynefin framework: A tool for analyzing qualitative data in information science? *Library & Information Science Research,* 35(4): 299–309.

McLaughlin, H., McLaughlin, G. and Presiosi, R. C. (2004). The relationship of learning orientation to organizational performance. *Journal of Business and Economics Research,* 2(4): 9–16.

McLoughlin, I. (1999). *Creative Technological Change: The Shaping of Technology and Organisations.* London: Routledge.

McNamee, S. (2004). Relational bridges between constructionism and constructivism. Draft for J. D. Raskin and S. K. Bridges (eds.), Studies in Meaning 2: Bridging the Personal and the Social, 2004. Available at file:///Users/tim/Downloads/McNamee-Relational_Bridges_Between_Constructionism_and_Constructivism.pdf

McNamee, S. (2010). Research as social construction: Transformative inquiry. *Saúde & Transformação Social/Health and Social Change,* 1(1): 9–19.

McNamee, S. and Hosking, D. M. (2012). *Research and social change. A relational constructionist approach.* New York: Routledge.

McQuillan, P. J. (2008). Small-school reform through the lens of complexity theory: It's good to think with. *Teachers College Record,* 110(9): 1772–1801.

Mead, G. H. (1934). *Mind, Self, and Society: The Definitive Edition,* Annotated edition. Chicago, IL: University of Chicago Press.

Merton, R. K. (1938). Science, technology and society in seventeenth century England. *Osiris,* 4(2): 360–632.

Merton, R. K. (1945). Sociology theory. *American Journal of Sociology,* 50(6): 462–473.

Meyerson, D., Weick, K. E. and Kramer, R. M. (1996). Swift trust and temporary groups. In R. M. Kramer and T. R. Tyler (eds.), *Trust in Organizations: Frontiers of Theory and Research.* Thousand Oaks, CA: Sage Publications, 166–195.

Michie, J. and Sheehan, M. (1999). Human resource management practices, R&D expenditure and innovative investment: Evidence for the UK's 1990 workplace industrial relations survey. *Industrial and Corporate Change,* 8(2): 211–234.

Mikulecky, D. C. (2003). Definition of complexity. Available at http://www.vcu.edu/complex/ON%20COMPLEXITY.html, accessed 6 February 2015.

206 References

Miller, C. C. and Bilton, N. (2011). Google's lab of wildest dreams. *New York Times*, 13 November.

Mintzberg, H. (1985). The organization as political arena. *Journal of Management Studies*, 22(2): 133–154.

Mintzberg, H., Ahlstrand, B. and Lampel, J. (1998). *Strategy Safari: A Guided Tour Through the Wilds of Strategic Management*. New York: The Free Press.

Miyazaki, K. (1994). Search, learning and accumulation of technological competencies: The case of optoelectronics. *Industrial and Corporate Change*, 3: 631–654.

Mokyr, J. (2003). *The Second Industrial Revolution, 1870–1914*. Evanston, IL: Northwestern University. Available at https://pdfs.semanticscholar.org/769c/a06c2ea1a b122e0e2a37099be00e3c11dd52.pdf, accessed 8 August 2015.

Mønsted, M. (2006). High-tech, uncertainty and innovation: The opportunity for high-tech entrepreneurship. In M. Bernasconi, S. Harris and M. Mønsted (eds.), *High-tech Entrepreneurship: Managing Innovation, Variety and Uncertainty*. London: Routledge, 15–32.

Morgan, G. (1996). *Images of Organization*. Thousand Oaks, CA: Sage Publications.

Morgan, M., Elbe, J. and Curiel, J. de E. (2009). Has the experience economy arrived? The views of destination managers in three visitor-dependent areas. *International Journal of Tourism Research*, 11: 201–216.

Morrow, S. L. (2005). Quality and trustworthiness in qualitative research in counseling psychology. *Journal of Counseling Psychology*, 52(2): 250–260. Avaiable at http://www.safranlab.net/uploads/7/6/4/6/7646935/quality__trustworthiness_ 2005.pdf, accessed 26 February 2017.

Mowles, C., Stacey, R. and Griffin, D. (2008). What contribution can insights from the complexity sciences make to the theory and practice of development management? *Journal of International Development*, 20: 804–820.

Mowles, C., van der Gaag, A. and Fox, J. (2010). The practice of complexity: Review, change and service improvement in an NHS department. *Journal of Health Organization and Management*, 24(2): 127–144.

Mulgan, G. (2007). *Social Innovation: What It Is, Why It Matters and How It Can Be Accelerated*. Oxford: Said School of Business.

Mullen, B., Johnson, C. and Salas, E. (1991). Productivity loss in brainstorming groups: A meta-analytic integration. *Basic and Applied Social Pshychology*, 12: 3–23.

Mumford, M. D. (2003). Where have we been, where are we going? Taking stock in creativity research. *Creativity Research Journal*, 15: 107–120.

Nambisan, S. and Sawhney, M. (2007). A buyer's guide to the innovation bazaar. *Harvard Business Review*, 85(6): 109–118.

Nevis, E. C., DiBella, A. J. and Gould, J. M. (1995). Understanding organizations as learning systems. *Sloan Management Review*, Winter: 73–85.

Nonaka, I. and Konno, N. (1998). The concept of Ba: Building a foundation for knowledge creation. *California Management Review*, 40(3): 45.

Nonaka, I. and Takeuchi, H. (1995). *The Knowledge Creating Company*. New York: Oxford University Press.

OECD. (1966). *Government and Technical Innovation*. Paris: OECD.

OECD. (2005). *Oslo Manual: Guidelines for Collecting and Interpreting Innovation Data*, Third edition. Paris: OECD.

Ogle, R. (2008). *Smart World: Breakthrough Creativity and the New Science of Ideas*. London: Marshall Cavendish.

References 207

O'Gorman, F. (1973). *Political Thinkers. Volume II, Edmund Burke.* New York: Routledge.

Olson, E. E. and Eoyongi, G. H. (2001). *Facilitating Organisational Change: Lessons from Complexity Sciences.* Chichester, UK: Jossey-Bass.

Olson, E. M., Walker, O. C. and Ruekert, R. W. (1995). Organizing for effective new product development: The moderating role of product innovativeness. *Journal of Marketing,* 59: 48–62.

Olsson, P., Folke, C. and Berkes, F. (2004). Adaptive comanagement for building resilience in social-ecological systems. *Environmental Management,* 34(1): 75–90.

Osterwalder, A. and Pigneur, Y. (2010). *Business Model Generation: A Handbook for Visionaries, Game Changers, and Challengers.* New York: John Wiley & Sons.

Owen, H. (2008). *Open Space Technology: A User's Guide.* Berrett-Koehler Publishers.

Parminter, T. G. and Wilson, J. A. (2003). *Systemic Interventions into Biodiversity Management Based upon the Theory of Reasoned Action.* Proceedings of the 1st Australian Farming Systems Association Conference, 199.

Pascale, R. (1991). *Managing on the Edge: How the Smartest Companies Use Conflict to Stay Ahead.* St Ives: Penguin Books.

Peters, T. and Waterman, R. (1982). *In Search of Excellence.* New York: Harper & Row.

Pfeffer, J. (1992). Understanding power in organizations. *California Management Review,* 34(2): 29–50.

Pine II, J. B. and Gilmore, J. H. (1999). *The Experience Economy. Work IS Theatre and Every Business a Stage.* Boston, MA: Harvard Business School Press.

Pisano, G. P. (2015). You need an innovation strategy. *Harvard Business Review,* June.

Plsek, P. E. and Greenhalgh, T. (2001). The challenge of complexity in health care. *BMJ,* 323: 625–628.

Plsek, P. E. and Wilson, T. (2001). Complexity, leadership, and management in healthcare organisations. *BMJ,* 323: 746–749.

Pluye, P. and Hong, Q. N. (2013). Combining the power of stories and the power of numbers: Mixed methods research and mixed studies reviews. *Annual Review of Public Health,* 35: 29–45.

Poole, D. L. (1997). Building community capacity to promote social and public health: Challenges for universities. *Health and Social Work,* 22: 163–170.

Poole, M. S. and van de Ven, A. H. (2004). *Handbook of Organizational Change and Innovation.* Oxford: Oxford University Press.

Porter, M. E. (1998). *On Competition.* Boston, MA: Harvard Business School.

Porter, M. E. and Kramer, M. R. (2011). Creating shared value: How to reinvent capitalism – And unleash a wave of innovation and growth. *Harvard Business Review,* January–February.

Powell, W. W. and Grodal, S. (2006). Networks of innovators. In J. Fagerberg, D. C. Mowery and R. R. Nelson (eds.), *The Oxford Handbook of Innovation.* Oxford: Oxford University Press, 56–85.

Pourdehnad, G. (2007). Synthetic (integrative) project management, an idea whose time has come. *Business Strategy Series Journal,* 8(6): 426–434.

Prahalad, C. K. (2006). *The Fortune at the Bottom of the Pyramid: Eradicating Poverty through Profits.* Upple Saddle River, NJ: Wharton School Publishing.

Prahalad, C. K. and Hammond, A. (2002). Serving the world's poor, profitably. *Harvard Business Review,* 80: 48–57, 124.

Prahalad, C. K. and Hart, S. L. (2002). The fortune at the bottom of the pyramid. *Strategy & Business,* 26(1): 2–14.

208 *References*

Prahalad, C. and Ramaswamy, V. (2004). Co-creating unique value with customers. *Strategy & Leadership*, 32(3): 4–9.

Prigogine, I. (1984). *Order out of Chaos*. Toronto: Bantam.

Prigogine, I. (1997). *The End of Certainty*. New York: The Free Press.

Prajogo, D. I. and Ahmed, P. K. (2006). Relationships between innovation stimulus, innovation capacity, and innovation performance. *R&D Management*, 36(5): 499–515.

Quinn, J. B., Anderson, P. and Finkelstein, S. (1996). Managing professional intellect: Making the most of the best. *Harvard Business Review*, March–April: 73–75.

Qvist-Sorensen, O. and Baastrup, L. (2019). *Visual Collaboration: A Powerful Toolkit for Improving Meetings, Projects, and Processes*. New Jersey: John Wiley & Sons.

Ranft, A. L. and Lord, M. D. (2002). Acquiring new technologies and capabilities: A grounded model of acquisition implementation. *Organization Science*, 13(4): 420–441.

Ravenell, E. (2018). The Osborn-Parnes creative problem solving procedure, Munich. *GRIN Verlag*, https://www.grin.com/document/428486

Reeves, M., Haanaes, K. and Sinha, J. (2015). *Your Strategy Needs a Strategy: How to Choose and Execute the Right Approach*. Boston, MA: Harvard Business Review Press, 76–83.

Reeves, M., Levin, S. and Ueda, D. (2016). The biology of corporate survival. *Harvard Business Review*, January–February: 46–55.

Reeves, M., Love, C. and Tillmanns, P. (2012). Your strategy needs a strategy. *Harvard Business Review*, September, 76–83.

Rhodes, M. (1961). An analysis of creativity. *Phi Delta Kappan*, 42(7): 306–307.

Ridgeway, C. and Wallace, B. (1994). *Empowering Change: The Role of People Management*. London: Institue of Personnel and Development.

Rifkin, J. (2012). The third industrial revolution: How the internet, green electricity, and 3-D printing are ushering in a sustainable era of distributed capitalism. *The World Financial Review*, March–April. Available at https://www.fona.de/mediathek/gek/vortraege/eroeffnung_rifkin_jeremy_01_presentation_ge2012.pdf, accessed 15 October 2016.

Roe Smith, M. (2003). *Historical Perspectives on Invention and Creativity, 14–16 March*. Massachusetts Institute of Technology. Available at http://web.mit.edu/monicaru/Public/old%20stuff/For%20Dava/Grad%20Library.Data/PDF/history-3289136129/history.pdf, accessed 8 October 2013.

Rogers, C. R. (1995). *On Becoming a Person: A Therapist's View of Psychotherapy*. New York: Houghton Mifflin.

Rogers, E. M. (1995). *Diffusion of Innovations*. New York: Free Press.

Roos, J. and Victor, B. (1998). In search of original strategies: How about some serious play? *IMD Perspectives for Managers*, 56(15).

Rothwell, R. (1992). Successful industrial innovation: Critical factors for the 1990s. *R&D Management*, 22(3): 221–240.

Rothwell, R. (1994). Towards the fifth-generation innovation process. *International Marketing Review*, 11(1): 7–31.

Rowan, D. (2013). Astro Teller of Google[x] wants to improve the world's broken industries. *Wired*, November. Available at: https://www.wired.co.uk/article/destination-moon.

Rumelt, R. (2011). *Good Strategy Bad Strategy: The Difference and Why It Matters*. London: Profile Books LTD.

References 209

Rumyantseva, Maria, Grzegorz Gurgul and Ellen Enkel. (2002). *Knowledge Integration after Mergers & Acquisitions*. University of Mississippi Business Department. University of Mississippi, July.

Röling, N. (1988). *Extension Science: Information Systems in Agricultural Development*. Cambridge, UK: Cambridge University Press.

Saad, M., Cicmil, S. and Greenwood, M. (2002). Technology transfer projects in developing countries: Furthering the project management perspectives. *International Journal of Project Management*, 20: 617–662.

Saatcioglu, A. (2002). Using grounded inquiry to explore idea management for innovativeness. *Academy of Management Proceedings*, C1–C6.

Salancik, G. R. and Pfeffer, J. (1977). Who gets power – And how they hold on to it – A strategic contingency model of power. *Organizational Dynamics*, 5(3): 3–21.

Sardar, Z. and Abrams, I. (2004). *Introducing Chaos*. Duxford, UK: Icon Books.

Savioz, P. and Sannemann, E. (1999). The concept of the integrated innovation process. In D. F. Kocaoglu and T. R. Anderson (eds.), *Technology and Innovation Management*. Portland International Conference on the Management of Engineering and Technology, PICMET'99, Proceedings Vol-1: Book of Summaries (IEEE Cat. No.99CH36310), Portland, OR, 137–143. doi: 10.1109/PICMET.1999.787797.

Scharmer, O. (2009). *Theory U: Leading from the Future as It Emerges*. San Francisco, CA: Berrett-Koehler.

Schein, E. H. (1986). *Process Consultation: Lessons for Managers and Consultants, Volume II*. Reading, MA: Addison-Wesley Publishing.

Schein, E. H. (1988a). *Process Consultation: Its Role in Organization Development, Volume I*, Second edition. Reading, MA: Addison-Wesley Publishing.

Schein, E. H. (1988b). Innovative cultures and organizations. Available at http://dspace. mit.edu/bitstream/handle/1721.1/2214/SWP-2066-21290193.pdf?sequence=1

Schein, E. H. (1999). *Process Consultation Revisited: Building the Helping Relationship*. Reading, MA: Addison Wesley Longman.

Schein, E. H. (2009a). *The Corporate Survival Guide*. San Francisco, CA: Jossey-Bass.

Schein, E. H. (2009b). *Helping: How to Offer, Give, and Receive Help*, Reprint edition. San Francisco, CA: Berrett-Koehler Publishers.

Schein, E. H. (2010). *Organizational Culture and Leadership*, Fourth edition. San Francisco, CA: Jossey-Bass.

Schein, E. H. (2013). *Humble Inquiry: The Gentle Art of Asking Instead of Telling*. San Francisco, CA: Berrett-Koehler Publishers Inc.

Schilling, J. and Kluge, A. (2009). Barriers to organizational learning: An integration of theory and research. *International Journal of Management Reviews*, 11(3): 337–360.

Schumpeter, J. A. (1939). *Business Cycles: A Theoretical, Historical, and Statistical Analysis of the Capitalist Process, Volume 1*. New York: McGraw Hill.

Schumpeter, J. A. (1942). *Capitalism, Socialism and Democracy*. New York: Harper.

Schwab, K. (2017). *The Fourth Industrial Revolution*. World Economic Forum.

Schön, D. A. (1983). *The Reflective Practitioner: How Professionals Think in Action*. New York: Basic Books.

Schön, D. A. (1986). Generative metaphor: A perspective on problem-setting in social policy. In A. Ortony (ed.), *Metaphor and Thought*. Cambridge: Cambridge University Press, 254–283.

Scordialou, M. (2005). *Gathering at the shire: Stewards of the art of hosting story*. Available at http://artofhosting.ning.com/u

210 *References*

Seldén, L. (2005). On grounded theory – With some malice. *Journal of Documentation*, 61(1): 114–129.

Senge, P. (1990). *The Fifth Discipline: The Art and Practice of the Learning Organization*. New York: Doubleday.

Senge, P. (1994). *The Fifth Discipline Fieldbook*. New York: Crown Business.

Sheng, I. L. S. and Kok-Soo, T. (2010). Eco-efficient product design using theory of inventive problem solving (TRIZ) principles. *American Journal of Applied Sciences*, 7(6): 852–858.

Shenton, A. K. (2004). Strategies for ensuring trustworthiness in qualitative research projects. *Education for Information*, 22: 63–75.

Sherman, J. D., Berkowitz, D. and Souder, W. E. (2005). New product development performance and the interaction of cross-functional integration and knowledge management. *Journal of Product Innovation Management*, 22: 399–411.

Sibbet, D. (2009). *A Graphic Facilitation Retrospective*. Available at http://web.archive.org/web/20110813033508/http://www.davidsibbet.com/GF%20Retrospective (Updated).pdf

Simon, H. A. (1962). The architecture of complexity. *Proceedings of the American Philosophical Society*, 106(6): 467–482. Available at https://www.cc.gatech.edu/classes/AY2013/cs7601_spring/papers/Simon-Complexity.pdf

Simon, H. A. (1981). *The Sciences of the Artificial*. Cambridge, MA: MIT Press.

Simon, H. A. (1986). What we know about the creative process. In R. L. Kuhn (ed.), *Frontiers in Creative and Innovative Management*. Cambridge, MA: Ballinger Publishing Company, 3–22.

Simon, H. A. (1991). *Models of My Life*. New York: Basic Books.

Simpson, P. (2007). Organizing in the mist: A case study in leadership and complexity. *Leadership & Organization Development Journal*, 28(5): 465–482.

Simpson, P. (2012). Complexity and change management: Analyzing church leaders' narratives. *Journal of Organizational Change Management*, 25(2): 283–296.

Skinner, Q. (1978). *The Foundations of Modern Political Thought, Volume 1, The Renaissance*. Cambridge: Cambridge University Press.

Skyttner, L. (2006). *General Systems Theory: Problems, Perspectives, Practice*, Second edition. Singapore: Wspc.

Smith, A., Courvisanos, J., Tuck, J. and McEachern, S. (2011). Building innovation capacity: The role of human capital formation in enterprises. *NCVER*.

Snowden, D. J. (2002). Complex acts of knowing: Paradox and descriptive self-awareness. *Journal of Knowledge Management*, 6(2): 100–111.

Snowden, D. J. and Boone, M. E. (2007). A leader's framework for decision making. *Harvard Business Review*, November.

Snowden, D. J. (2012). The origins of Cynefin: Part 1. Available at http://cognitive-edge.com/blog/entry/3451/part-seven-origins-of-cynefin

Spanos, A. (2010). To every innovation, anathema(?) Some preliminary thoughts on the study of Byzantine innovation. In H. Knudsen, J. Falkenberg, K. Grønhaug and Å. Garnes (eds.), *Mysterion, strategike og kainotomia. Et festskrift til ære for Jonny Holbek*. Oslo: Novus Forlag, 51–59.

Spanos, A. (2014). Was innovation unwanted in Byzantium? In I. Nilsson and P. Stephenson (eds.), *Wanted, Byzantium: The Desire for a Lost Empire*. Uppsala: Uppsala University, 43–56.

Stake, R. (1994). Case studies. In N. K. Denzin and Y. S. Lincon (eds.), *Handbook of Qualitative Research*. Thousand Oaks, CA: Sage Publications.

References 211

Stata, R. (1989). Organizational learning – The key to management innovation. *Sloan Management Review*, Spring: 63–74.

Stacey, R. D. (1995). The science of complexity: An alternative perspective for strategic change processes. *Strategic Management Journal*, 16(6): 477–495.

Stacey, R. D. (2001). *Complex Responsive Processes in Organizations: Learning and Knowledge Creation*. Routledge.

Stacey, R. D. (2007). The challenge of human interdependence: Consequences for thinking about the day to day practice of management in organizations. *European Business Review*, 19(4): 292–302.

Stacey, R. D. (2011). *Strategic Management and Organizational Dynamics*. Sixth edition. Harlow: Prentice-Hall.

Stacey, R. D., Griffin, D. and Shaw, P. (2000). *Complexity and Management: Fad or Radical Challenge to Systems Thinking?* Routledge: London.

Stavros, J. and Hinrichs, G. (2009). *The Thin Book of SOAR: Building Strength-based Strategy*. Bend, OR: Thin Book Publishing.

Stern, H. (1962). The significance of impulse buying today. *Journal of Marketing*, April: 59–62.

Sternberg, R. J. (1986). *Beyond IQ: Triarchic Theory of Human Intelligence*. New York: Cambridge University Press.

Stichweh, R. (2011). Systems theory. In Bertrand Badie et al. (eds.), *International Encyclopedia of Political Science*. New York: Sage, Vol. 8, 2579–2582.

Straub, Thomas. (2007). *Reasons for Frequent Failure in Mergers and Acquisitions: A Comprehensive Analysis*. Wiesbaden: Deutscher Universitäts-Verlag (DUV), Gabler Edition Wissenschaft.

Strauss, A. and Corbin, J. (1990). *Basics of Qualitative Research: Grounded Theory Procedures and Techniques*. Newbury Park, CA: Sage.

Sutton, R. (2002). Fresh start 2002: Weird ideas that work. *Fast Company*, 54: 68–74.

Svyantek, D. J. and DeShon, R. P. (1993). Organizational attractors: A chaos theory explanation of why cultural change efforts often fail. *Public Administration Quarterly*, 17(3), 339–355.

Tabak, R. G., Khoong, E. C., Chambers, D. A. and Brownson, R. C. (2012). Bridging research and practice: Models for dissemination and implementation research. *American Journal of Preventive Medicine*, 43(3): 337–350.

Takeuchi, H. and Nonaka, I. (1986). The New New Product Development Game. *Harvard Business Review*, 64: 137–146.

Tamm, M. (1987). *Psykologi*. Gothenburg: Esselte Studium AB.

Tanner, D. and Reisman, F. (2014). *Creativity as a Bridge between Education and Industry Fostering New Innovations*. CreateSpace Independent Publishing Platform.

Tatikonda, M. V. and Rosenthal, S. R. (2000). Successful execution of product development projects: Blancing firmness and flexibility in the innovation process. *Journal of Operations Management*, 18: 401–425.

Teece, D., Pisano, G. and Shuen, A. (1997). Dynamic capabilities and strategic management. *Strategic Management Journal*, 18(7): 509–533.

The Cox Review of Creativity in Business: Building on the UK's Strengths. (2005). UK: HM Treasury. Available at http://webarchive.nationalarchives.gov.uk/+/http://www.hm-treasury.gov.uk/coxreview_index.htm

The Health Foundation. (2010). *Complex Adaptive Systems*. Available at https://www.health.org.uk/sites/default/files/ComplexAdaptiveSystems.pdf

212 References

The President's Emergency Plan for AIDS Relief (PEPFAR). Capacity Building and Strengthening Framework (2012). https://www.pepfar.gov/documents/organization/197182.pdf

Theodossiou, E., Kalachanis, K., Manimanis, B. N. and Dimitrijevic, M. S. (2012). The notion of chaos: From the cosmogonical chaos of Ancient Greek philosophical thought to the chaos theory of modern physics. *Facta Universitatis*. Series: Philosophy, Sociology, Psychology and History, 11(2): 211–221.

Thomke, S. and Hippel, E. V. (2002). Customers as innovators: A new way to create value. *Harvard Business Review*, April: 74–81.

Thompson, T. A. and Purdy, J. M. (2009). When a good idea isn't enough: Curricular innovation as a political process. *Academy of Management Learning and Education*, 8(2): 188–207.

Tidd, J. (2001). Innovation management in context: Environment, organization and performance. *International Journal of Management Reviews*, 3(3): 169–183.

Tidd, J., Bessant, J. and Pavitt, K. (2005). *Managing Innovation: Integrating Technological, Market and Organizational Change*, Third edition. Chichester: John Wiley & Sons.

Torelli, C. J. and Rodas, M. (2017). Globalization, branding and multicultural consumer behavior. In Cathrine V. Jansson-Boyd and Magdalena J. Zawisza (eds.), *Routledge International Handbook of Consumer Psychology*. Abingdon: Routledge, 41–58.

Torrance, E. P. (1966). *The Torrance Tests of Creative Thinking Norms – Technical Manual Research Edition – Verbal Test, Forms A and B – Figural Tests, Forms A and B*. Princeton, NJ: Person Press.

Trott, P. (2005). Innovation Management and New Product Development. 3rd edition. Harlow, England: Pearson Education Limited.

Tushman, M. L. and Anderson, P. (1986). Technological Discontinuities and Organizational Environments. *Administrative Science Quarterly*, 31(3): 439–465.

Tushman, M., Newman, W. and Romanelli, R. (1986). Convergence and upheaval: Managing the unsteady pace of organizational evolution. *California Management Review*, 29(1): 29–44.

Uhl-Bien, M., Marion, R. and McKelvey, B. (2007). Complexity leadership theory: Shifting leadership from the industrial age to the knowledge era. *The Leadership Quarterly* 18(4): 298–318; Special Issue on Leadership and Complexity; doi: 10.1016/j.leaqua.2007.04.002. Downloaded from: Leadership Institute Faculty Publications. Paper 18. Available at http://digitalcommons.unl.edu/leadershipfacpub/18

Ulwick, A. (2002). Turn customer input into innovation. *Harvard Business Review*, 80(1): 91–97.

United Nations Development Programme (UNDP). Supporting capacity building the UNDP approach. Archived from the original on 30 June 2011. Retrieved 23 April 2011.

Utterback, J. M. (1996). *Mastering the Dynamics of Innovation*. Boston, MA: Harvard Business School Press.

Utterback, J. M. and Abernathy, W. J. (1975). A dynamic model of process and product innovation. *Omega, The International Journal of Management Science*, 3(6): 639–656.

Valente, T. and Rogers, E. (1995). The origins and development of the diffusion of innovations paradigm as an example of scientific growth. *Science Communication*, 16(3): 242–273.

References 213

Vandenbosch, B., Saatcioglu, A. and Fay, S. (2006). Idea management: A systemic view. *Journal of Management Studies*, 43(2): 259–288.

van Beurden, E. K., Kia, A. M., Zask, A., Dietrich, U. and Rose, L. (2013). Making sense in a complex landscape: How the Cynefin framework from complex adaptive systems theory can inform health promotion practice. *Health Promotion International*, 28(1): 73–83.

van de Ven, A. H. (1986). Central problems in the management of innovation. *Management Science*, 32: 590–607.

van de Ven, A. H., Angle, H. L. and Poole, M. S. (1989). *Research on the Management of Innovation: The Minnesota Studies*. New York: Harper & Row, 3–30.

van de Ven, A. H., Polley, D., Garud, R. and Venkataraman, S. (2008). *The Innovation Journey*. Oxford: Oxford University Press.

van de Ven, A. H. and Poole, M. S. (1995). Explaining development and change in organizations. *Academy of Management Review*, 20: 510–540.

van Dijk, G. M. and Peters, F. (2011). Organisaties als levende systemen. *HRM Handboek*, 56(2/9–1.2): 1–22.

van Loon, R. and van Dijk, G. M. (2015). Dialogical leadership: Dialogue as condition zero. *Journal of Leadership, Accountability and Ethics*, 12(3): 62–75.

Van de Ven, A. H., Polley, D., Garud, R. and Venkataraman, S. (1999). *The Innovation Journey*. New York: Oxford University Press.

Ven, A.H. (1986). Central problems in the management of innovation. *Management Science*, 32, 590–607.

Vincent, J. F. V. (2001). Stealing ideas from nature. In S. Pellegrino (ed.), *Deployable Structures*. Vienna: Springer, 51–58. Available at http://www.researchgate.net/profile/Julian_Vincent/publication/242173807_STEALING_IDEAS_FROM_NATURE/links/00b495304a989daca7000000.pdf, accessed 16 October 2014.

Vindeløv-Lidzélius, C. (2018). *Innovation in Complex Systems: An Exploration in Strategy, Leadership and Organization*. Tilburg University.

Visser, M. (2003). Gregory Bateson on deutero-learning and double bind: A brief conceptual history. *Journal of the History of the Behavioral Sciences*, 39: 269–278. doi: 10.1002/jhbs.10112

Visser, M. (2007). Deutero-learning in organizations: A review and a reformulation. *The Academy of Management Review*, 32(2): 659–667.

Vogt, E. E., Brown, J. and Isaacs, D. (2003). *The Art of Powerful Questions: Catalyzing Insight, Innovation and Action*. Mill Valley, CA: Whole Systems Associates, 1–14.

von Hippel, E. (1986). Lead users: A source of novel product concepts. *Management Science*, 32(7): 791–805.

von Hippel, E. (2005). *Democratizing Innovation*. Cambridge, MA: MIT Press.

von Hippel, E. (2007). Horizontal innovation networks: By and for users. *Industrial and Corporate Change*, 16(2): 293–315.

Waldrop, M. (1992). *Complexity: The Emerging Science at the Edge of Order and Chaos*. New York: Simon & Schuster.

Wallas, G. (1926). *The Art of Thought*. New York: Harcourt, Brace & Company. Re-issued by Solis Press 2014.

Watkins, M. D. (2013). What is organizational culture? And why should we care? *Harvard Business Review*, May. Available at https://hbr.org/2013/05/what-is-organizational-culture

Watzlawick, P., Weakland, J. and Fisch, R. (1974). *Change: Principles, Problem Formulation and Problem Resolution*. New York: Norton.

214 *References*

Weaver, W. (1948). Science and complexity. *American Scientist*, 36(4): 536–544.

Webb, J. W., Kistruck, G. M., Ireland, R. D. and Ketchen, D. J., Jr. (2009). The entrepreneurship process in the base of the pyramid markets: The case of multinational enterprise/nongovernment organization alliances. *Entrepreneurship Theory and Practice*, 34(3): 555–581.

Weick, K. E. (1995). *Sensemaking in Organizations (Foundations for Organizational Science)*. Thousand Oaks, CA: Sage Publications.

Weiner, B. J. (2009). A theory of organizational readiness to change. *Implementation Science*, 4(67). doi: 10.1186/1748-5908-4-67.

Weick, K. E. and Sutcliffe, K. (2001). *Managing the Unexpected: Assuring High Performance in an Age of Complexity*. London: Jossey-Bass.

Weiner, B. J., Amick, H. and Lee, S. Y. (2008). Review: Conceptualization and measurement of organizational readiness for change: A review of the literature in health services research and other fields. *Medical Care Research and Review*, 65(4): 379–436.

Wheatley, M. J. (1992). *Leadership and the New Science*. San Francisco, CA: Berrett-Koehler Publishers.

Wheatley, M. J. and Kellner-Rogers, M. (1998). *A Simpler Way*. San Francisco, CA: Berrett-Koehler Publishers.

Whitehead, A. N. (1961). *Adventures of Ideas*. New York:The Free Press (referenced in the Vandenbosch, B., Saatcioglu, A. and Fay, S. (2006). Idea management: A systemic view. *Journal of Management Studies*, 43(2): 259–288).

Wilson, T. and Holt, T. (2001). Complexity and clinical care. *BMJ*, 323: 685–688.

Wisdom, J. P., Chor, K. H. B., Hoagwood, K. E. and Horwitz, S. M. (2014). Innovation adoption: A review of theories and constructs. *Administration and Policy in Mental Health*, 41(4): 480–502.

Yin, R. K. (1994). *Case Study Research Design and Methods: Applied Social Research and Methods Series*, Second edition. Thousand Oaks, CA: Sage Publications Inc.

Yin, R. K. (2003). *Case Study Research: Design and Methods*. Thousand Oaks, CA: Sage Publications.

Yukl, G. (1994). *Leadership in Organizations*. Englewood Cliffs, NJ: Prentice-Hall.

Yunus, M. (2007). *Creating a World Without Poverty: Social Business and the Future of Capitalism*. New York: Public Affairs.

Zahra, S. A. and George, G. (2002). Absorptive capacity: A review, reconceptualization, and extension. *Academy of Management Review*, 27(2): 185–203.

Zgrzywa-Ziemak, A. (2015). The impact of organisational learning on organisational performance. *Management and Business Administration. Central Europe*, 23(4): 98–112.

Zhu, Z. (2007). Complexity science, systems thinking and pragmatic sensibility. *Systems Research and Behavioral Science*, 24: 445–464.

Zou, T., Ertug, G. and George, G. (2018). The capacity to innovate: A meta-analysis of absorptive capacity. *Innovation*, 20: 87–121.doi: 10.1080/14479338.2018.1428105

Index

Note: **Bold** page numbers refer to tables; *Italic* page numbers refer to figures and page numbers followed by "n" denote endnotes.

Aasen, T. M. B. 63–64, 128, 164, 168
Abernathy, W. J. 23, 91
absorptive capacity 5, 73–74
Ackoff, R. L. 175, 183
acquisitions 147–148
Adler, N. 93
adoption process, of innovation 66–67
Adriansen, H. K. 159
Afuah, A. N. 24
"the age of discontinuity" 97–98
Age of Enlightenment 14
Age of Reason 14
Ahmed, P. K. 7, 136–137
Airbnb 18, 91, 184
Ajzen, Icek 70
Alibaba 18
Alphabet 171
Altshuller, Genrich 54, **55**
Amabile, T. M. 37, 41, 47–48, 170
American Marketing Association 72
Anderson, P. 23–24, 119
Andriani, P. 122
aperiodic behaviour 105
Argyris, Chris 77, 80, 124
The Art of Hosting 157–158
The Art of Thought (Wallas) 40
Austin, R. D. 62

Bacon, Francis 14
Bahram, N. 24
Bar-Yam, Y. 107
Beinhocker, E. D. 90
Bennis, W. G. 169
Bens, I. 152
Berkhout, A. J. 10, 57, 58
Bessant, J. 5

Better Homes and Gardens 12
"Big Bang Disruption" 26
Birkinshaw, J. 64
Bloomberg 26
Boden, M. A. 30, 37, 39–40
Boone, M. E. 129–130, 132, 146
Borum, F. 165–166
The Boston Consulting Group 26, 27
bounded rationality 4, 69–70
Bower, Joseph L. 25
brainstorming 41
brand, defined 72
branding, and innovation 72–73
Brown, Juanita 157
Brynjolfsson, E. 18
Buckley, Walter 111
Built to Last (Collins and Porras) 167
Burke, Edmund 11
Business Dictionary 107
business models 94–96
Buur, J. 158–159
Büyüközkan, G. 44–45

Calantone, R. 25
Campos, E. B. 81
Cavé, A. 100
Chain-Linked Model 57, *57*
change, and innovation 30, 97–100
"change readiness" 98–99
Chaordic model: concept 131; dimensions of 131–132; and innovation 130–132; people 131; practice 131; principles 131; purpose 131; structure 131
Chaos: Making a New Science (Gleick) 105
chaos theory 104–105, 119n1

216   *Index*

Chesbrough, H. 59, 95
Christensen, Clayton 25–26, 92;
    predicaments for businesses 93
Christiansen, J. K. 165–166
Chu, D. 107
Cilliers, P. 110
"civilisation process" 134n3
Clark, K. B. 23
classical antiquity: described 12; and
    innovation 12–13
classical motivation-hygiene theory 96
co-creation 95
Cohen, I. B. 5
Cohen, W. M. 73
Collins, Jim 55, 144, 152, 168, 184
competition: and innovation 91–92
complex adaptive systems (CAS) 104,
    111–113; chaos theory 104–105;
    co-evolution 113; complexity theory
    106–107; complex systems 107–110;
    connectivity 113; edge of chaos 113;
    emergence 113; innovation as 113–
    119; and innovation characteristics
    114–117; iteration 113; nested systems
    113; overview 102–104; properties
    of 113; requisite variety 113; self-
    organisation 113; simple rules 113;
    sub-optimal 113; systems 105–106
Complexity, Life at the Edge of Chaos
    (Lewin) 106
"Complexity Science" 111
*Complexity: The Emerging Science at the
    Edge of Order and Chaos* (Waldrop) 106
complexity theory 106–107
complex systems 107–110; leading
    innovation in 156–161
consumer behaviour theories 4, 71–72
Cooper, R. G. 45
Cooperrider, D. L. 146
creativity: defined 4, 30, 37–40, 50; and
    ideas 35–36; and innovation 3–4, 30,
    36–37; management and nurturing
    47–48; overview 35–36; theories
    relevant to innovation 40–42; *see also*
    ideas; innovation
*Creativity as A Bridge Between Education
    and Industry Fostering New Innovations*
    (Tanner and Reisman) 40
Crossan, M. M. 84
CRPs and innovation 125–128
Csíkszentmihályi, M. 37, 41
Cummings, T. G. 153, 167, 168
Cynefin, and innovation 128–130
Czarniawska-Joerges, B. 162

Dalling, I. 180
Danske Bank 172
Darsø, L. 45, 62, 187
Davila, T. 170
Davis, J. 85–87
De Bono, Edward 38
de Pablos, P. O. 81
Deutero-learning 80
Dhanaraj, C. 165
Diffusion on Innovations (Rogers) 67
Diffusion Theory 4, 67–69
disruption 25–26
Dodgson, M. 77, 81, 86
"dominant design" 91
Dooley, K. J. 62
Double Diamond Model 43, *44*
double-loop learning 80
Downes, Larry 26
Drucker, Peter F. 3, 10, 51–53, 95, 97–98,
    152, 183
Du Preez, N. D. 59

economic growth, and innovation 89
Edison, H. 32
Edquist, C. 19
Einstein, Albert 102
EKB model 70–71
Elias, Norbert 126, 127, 134n3
Engel, J. S. 33
Engel Kollat Blackwell Model of
    Consumer Behaviour 71
enterprise resource planning (ERP) 22
entrepreneurship 152, 159
Etymology Dictionary 12
experience design (XD) 21
Experiential Learning Cycle 79
Extension Theory 4

Facebook 18, 171
Fagerberg, J. 3
Fast Company 26
Feyzioglu, O. 44–45
The Fifth Discipline (Senge) 82
Fiol, C. M. 86
First Industrial Revolution 14–15
Fishbein, Martin 70
Five Forces Framework 91
Florea, D.-L. 72
Florida, 10
Fonseca, J. 170
Forbes 12, 26, 27
"force field model" 98
Fourth Industrial Revolution 17–18
Freeman, C. 33, 54

Index 217

French Revolution 14–15, 18
Frenken, K. 114, 118
Friedman, T. L. 92
"front-end of innovation" 45–46, *46*

Galanakis, K. 124
Garcia, R. 24, 25
Gardner, Howard 42
Gell-Mann, Murray 111
General Systems Theory 106
George, G. 73
Gilmore, J. H. 19, 21
Gleick, James 105
Global Innovation Index 26
globalisation 89; and innovation
92–93
Godin, Benoît 12, 15, 16–17, 27–28, 54,
55, 88, 100, 173
Good to Great (Collins) 167–168
Goodwin, T. 18
Google 171–172, 184
Google Glass 171
Google Wings 171
Google X 171
gradualism 122
Grantham, C. E. 77–78
Graphic Facilitation 157
Griffin, D. 30, 37–39, 126
Grint, K. 154
Grodal, S. 165
Grove Consultants 157
Guba, E. G. 187

Habermas, Jürgen 181
Hamel, G. 83
Hammond, A. 93
Harkema, Saskia 84
Hart, S. L. 93
Hartley, R. 98
Hartman, D. 59
Harvard Business Essentials 143, 175
Harvard Business Review 25
Hawkins Stern Impulse Buying
Theory 71
Henry, J. 57
Herzberg, F. 96
Heslop, V. R. 150
Hierarchy of Human Needs 42, 96–97
Hinrichs, G. 143, 146
Hislop, D. 165
Hjorth, D. 95, 153
Hock, Dee 130, 132, 152, 157
Holland, J. H. 111–112, 125
Holland, Maurice 16

"How Long is the Coast of Britain?
Statistical and Self-Similarity
and Fractional Dimension"
(Mandelbrot) 105
Huber, G. P. 77
Hugo, Victor 43
human resource development 150
Humbert, M. 183
Husserl, Edmund 181

ideas: and creativity 35–36; defined 4;
evaluation and selection of 43–45, *44*;
and ideation 42–43; and innovation
3–4; management and nurturing
47–48; overview 35–36; *see also*
creativity; innovation
ideation 42–43
impluse buying 71–72
incremental innovation 23
individual innovativeness theory 68
Industrial Age 183
Industrial Revolution 14–15
Information Age 16, 183
information sharing 82
innovation: categorising 19–22; Chaordic
and 130–132; as a complex adaptive
system 113–119; and complexity 2;
creating/making 50–65; creating space
for 164–166; CRPs and 125–128;
Cynefin and 128–130; definitions/
meaning 3, 10, 28–34; drivers of
88–100; *vs.* invention 17, 31; kernel of
175–178; as learning 85–87; lifeworld
of 180–182; making of 4; measuring
26–28; models of 54–62, **60–61**; need
for 89–90; OECD typology of **25**;
overview 1, 28–29, 121–123; processes
62–63; and R&D 31–32; retrospective
view of idea of 11–19; sources 51–53;
synonyms 29–30; systems thinking
and 123–125; taxonomy of 19, *20*;
theortical challenges 2–3; towards
theoretical foundation of 132–134
Innovation and Entrepreneurship (Drucker)
51–52
innovation capacity: beyond the
organisation 178–179; future areas
of research 182; integrative approach
179–180; kernel of innovation
175–178; lifeworld of innovation
180–182; overview 174–175
innovation capacity building: described
1; for innovation, challenges 3–5;
meaning of 136–137; measuring

218 *Index*

capacity building 141; and organisation 6–7; overview 135–136; 6P model 138–141; two challenges and opportunities with 137–138
innovation-decision process theory 68
"innovation economy" 10
innovation strategy 144–145; crafting 145–146
The Innovator's Solution (Christensen) 25–26
In Search of Excellence (Peters and Waterman) 167
integrated model of innovation 58
"integrative thinking" 180
intended desirable learning 78
internal development 149–150; and innovation 53
invention: defined 31; *vs.* innovation 17, 31
Isaacs, David 157

Jackson, M. 123, 124, 125, 132
Jimenez-Jimenez, D. 7, 85
Johannessen, S. 63–64, 128, 164
Johnson, N. F. 106
just-in-time (JIT) 22

Kanter, R. M. 170
Kaplan, Allan 138
Kaplinksy, R. 64, 94
Kapsali, M. 125
Kauffman, S. A. 118, 125
Kellert, S. 105
Khoong, E. C. 67
Khurana, A. 45
Kim, W. C. 92, 170
Kline, S. 57
Kluge, A. 84
knowledge: creation 81–82; management 81–82; retention 81–82; transfer 81–82; *see also* learning
Knowledge Economy 16
Koen, P. A. 45
Kolb, D. A. 79
Kramer, M. R. 94
Kusiak, A. 62

Ladyman, J. 103, 108–109
leadership: bridging creative tensions 161; building relations 160; configurating to current reality 161; crafting cross-boundary spanning 160; creating conditions 160; direction, setting 160; enhancing motivation 160;

facilitates learning 160; framing the challenge and opportunity 160; generating meaning 160; leading innovation in complex systems 156–161; methodologies and tools 156–159; overview 152–153; role and responsibility of 153–155; skills and style 155–156
LEAN 22
learning: as innovation 85–87; innovation as 85–87; loops of 79–81; *see also* knowledge; organisational learning (OL)
learning curve 79
learning organisation (LO) 77, 82–84
le Carré, John 92
Lee, J. 85–87
legislation, and innovation 53
Lego Serious Play 159
Leonard, D. 37, 39, 47–48, 163
Lepore, Jill 11, 26, 29, 89
Levinthal, D. A. 5, 73
Levitt, Ted 47–48
Lewin, K. 98
Lewin, Roger 106
Li, Tien Yien 105
Lincoln, Y. S. 187
linear technology model 55–56
Long, Norton 164
Lord, M. D. 147
Lorenz, Edward 104, 105
Luoma, J. 124, 132
Lyles, M. 86

Machiavelli, Niccolò 14
Maclaurin, W. Rupert 17
management, innovation 63–64
Mandelbrot, Benoît 105
March, J. G. 39, 62, 163, 165
marketing: 4Ps of 73; and innovation 72–73; and R&D 57, 57
market pull model 56
Martin, J. A. 150
Martin, Luther 13
Maslow, Abraham 42, 71, 96–97
Mason, R. M. 81
Matthews, B. 158
Maturana, H. R. 121
Mauborgne, R. 92
May, Robert 104
Mayle, D. 57
McAfee, A. 18
McKinley, William 11
Mead, George Herbert 126, 127

Index 219

measuring capacity building 141
mergers, defined 147
mergers and acquisitions 147–148
Merton, R. K. 17
Michie, J. 5
Microsoft 171
Middle Ages, and innovation 13
Mikulecky, D. C. 103, 106
Mintzberg, H. 146, 164, 165
Mitchell, R. 158–159
Miyazaki, K. 99
models of innovation 54–62, **60–61**;
   coupling of R&D and marketing
   57, *57*; integrated model 58; linear
   technology model 55–56; market pull
   model 56; systems integration and
   networking model 58–62
Mokyr, J. 15
Møller, Toke 157
Moonshot Factory 163, 170–173
Mowles, C. 125
Mumford, Michael 38

Nanus, B. 169
"negative feedback" 104
Nelson, Richard 90
networking model 58–62
Newtonian mechanics 102
Newtonian Paradigm 106
The New Yorker 12
NGOs 135–136
Nichols, L. D. 77–78
Nonaka, Ikujiro 16, 47, 81, 85
non-intended, desirable learning 78
Nunes, Paul F. 26

OECD countries 27–28
OECD typology of innovation **25**
Ogburn, William F. 17
Ogle, Richard 38, 39
Olesen, J. P. 165
Olson, E. E. 24
Open Space Technology 157
organisation: creating space for
   innovation 164–166; moonshot
   factories 170–173; organisational
   culture 166–170; overview
   162–163
organisational creativity 37
organisational culture 166–170
organisational learning (OL): barriers
   to 84–85; defined 77; goal and
   measurement 77–79; loops of 79–81;
   overview 76–77

organisational theory 4–5
Osterwalder's Business Model Canvas 159

Parkhe, A. 165
partnerships 148–149
Pavitt, K. 5
Peters, T. 98, 99
Pfeffer, J. 164, 165
Pine II, J. B. 19, 21
Pisano, G. P. 145
Poincaré, Henri 104
Porras, J. 168
Porter, M. E. 94
Porter, Michael 91
Powell, W. W. 165
Prahalad, C. K. 83, 93, 94–95
Prajogo, D. I. 7, 136–137
President's Emergency Plan for AIDS
   Relief 135
Prigogine, Ilya 105
The Prince (Machiavelli) 14
process innovation: described 22–23;
   methods 22
product and cycle time excellence
   (PACE) 20–21
product innovation: described 20, 22–23;
   methods 20–21
Protestant Reformation of 1517 13
Purdy, J. M. 164

radical innovation 23
Ramaswamy, V. 94–95
Ranft, A. L. 147
rate of adoption theory 68, 69
R&D: described 31–32; and innovation
   31–32; and marketing 57, *57*
reductionism 102, 122
Reeves, M. 121–122
Reisman, F. 40
Ridgeway, C. 152, 155
Rifkin, J. 16
Rogers, Everett 27, 67–68
Rosen, Robert 106
Rosenberg, N. 57
Rosenthal, S. R. 45
Rothwell, R. 57, 58–59, 62
Rumelt, R. 144
Rumyantseva, Maria 147

Saatcioglu, A. 4, 43
Sannemann, E. 55–56
Santa Fe Institute 111
Sanz-Valle, R. 7, 85
Savioz, P. 55–56

220   *Index*

Schein, E. H. 28, 31, 167, 169
Schilling, J. 84
Schön, D. A. 124, 163
Schön, Donald 39, 77, 80
Schumpeter, Joseph 10, 16–17, 30–31
Schwab, K. 17–18
Science 109
Second Industrial Revolution 15–16, 90
Second Machine Age 18
self-actualisation 89, 96–97
Senge, Peter 31, 77, 82–83, 106, 123, 132
service innovation: described 20, 22–23;
    methods 21
"7S model" 98
"shared value" 94
Sheehan, M. 5
Shenton, A. K. 187
Sibbet, David 157
Simon, H. A. 38, 39, 51, 69–70, 106, 108
single-loop learning 80
6P model 138–141, *139*; partners 140;
    people 140; perspective 139; planning
    140; practice 140; purpose 139–140
Skyttner, L. 123
Smith, Roe 14
Snowden, David J. 128–130, 132,
    146, 157
SOAR model 146
social innovation 10, 95
Spotify 184
Srivastva, S. 146
Stacey, Ralph 125, 126, 128
Stata, R. 83
Stavros, J. 146
Sternberg, R. J. 42
strategy: crafting an innovation strategy
    145–146; innovation strategy 144–145;
    internal development 149–150;
    mergers and acquisitions 147–148;
    overview 143–144; partnerships
    148–149
Straub, Thomas 147
Strauss, A. 37, 47–48, 163
supply chain management 22
Sutton, R. 39, 48
systems 105–106
systems integration 58–62
systems thinking 106, 123–125, *124*, 183

Tabak, R. G. 67
Takeuchi, H. 16, 47, 62
Tamm, M. 37
Tanner, D. 40
Tarde, Gabriel 16

Tatikonda, M. V. 45
taxonomy of innovation 19, *20,* 23–24
technology and innovation 90–91
Telefónica Digital 189
Telefónica's Alpha 172
The Cox Review 174
*The Crisis of European Sciences and
    Transcendental Phenomenology*
    (Husserl) 181
theory of perceived attributes 68, 69
theory of reasoned action (TRA) 4,
    70–71
Third Industrial Revolution 16–17, 90
Thomke, S. 95–96
Thompson, T. A. 164
Tidd, J. 5, 136
Times Magazine 11
Torrance Test of Creative Thinking 42
total quality management (TQM) 22
Triarchic Theory of Human
    Intelligence 42
triple-loop learning 80
TRIZ 54
Trott, P. 58, 59
Tushman, M. L. 23–24, 99

Uber 18, 91, 184
Uhl-Bien, Mary 153
Ulwick, A. 96
United Kingdom Department of Trade
    and Industry 33
United Nations Development
    Programme (UNDP) 149–150
User Innovation model 59–60
Utterback, James 23, 91–92

Value Network Mapping 159
value realisation 63
Vandenbosch, 47
Van de Ven, A. H. 3, 31, 62–63, 64, 152, 170
Van Dijk, G. M. 153
Van Loon, R. 153
Vindeløv-Lidzélius, Christer
    114–117, 174
von Hippel, E. V. 95–96

Waldrop, M. Mitchell 106
Wallace, B. 152, 155
Wallas, George 40
Waterman, R. 98
Watkins, M. D. 167
Watzlawick, P. 81
Weaver, W. 108
Wheatley, Margaret J. 118–119, 121, 158

Whitehead, A. N. 4, 43
Wikipedia 135
Wisdom, 67
World Café 157–158
The World Café 158
World Economic Report on Global Competitiveness 26
Worley, C. G. 167, 168

Yin, R. K. 187
Yorke, James 105
Yukl, G. 168–169
Yunus, M. 95

Zahra, S. A. 73
Zhu, Z. 124
Zou, T. 74

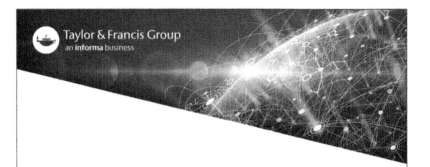

Taylor & Francis eBooks

www.taylorfrancis.com

A single destination for eBooks from Taylor & Francis with increased functionality and an improved user experience to meet the needs of our customers.

90,000+ eBooks of award-winning academic content in Humanities, Social Science, Science, Technology, Engineering, and Medical written by a global network of editors and authors.

TAYLOR & FRANCIS EBOOKS OFFERS:

- A streamlined experience for our library customers
- A single point of discovery for all of our eBook content
- Improved search and discovery of content at both book and chapter level

REQUEST A FREE TRIAL
support@taylorfrancis.com